Sustainable Tourism Practices in the Mediterranean

Sustainable Tourism Practices in the Mediterranean showcases and examines the current and future trends in sustainable tourism in this popular region where tourism is one of the leading determinants of economic development.

This volume examines the effects of specific recent events including terrorism, financial crises and various political changes in the Mediterranean region. Looking at a range of destinations, island and mainland, urban and rural, summer and winter and emergent and declining zones, it provides a comprehensive overview of this area. It also draws on a number of wide-ranging themes such as gastronomy (corporate), social responsibility, entrepreneurship, ethical issues, service quality, health and the slow city, offering an insightful study of the challenges the Mediterranean region faces and the sustainable practices that can be implemented in order to overcome them.

Written by leading academics in the field, this book will be of great interest to upper-level students, researchers and academics in Tourism, Development Studies and Geography.

Ipek Kalemci Tüzün is the director of the Institute of Social Sciences and the head of the Tourism and Hotel Management Department at the Faculty of Commercial Sciences of Baskent University, Ankara, Turkey. Her areas of research interest include developments in human resource management, social exchange practices tourism in organizations and HRM applications, employee attitudes and behavior, and social identification in hospitality operations. Her teaching portfolio includes Introduction to Hospitality Management, Human Resource Management in Hospitality Operations and Organizational Behavior.

Mehmet Ergül has been a faculty member at San Francisco State University, College of Business Department of Hospitality and Tourism Management since 2006. His teaching portfolio includes Restaurant and Catering Management, Introduction to Hospitality Management, Food and Culture, Tourism Management and International Tourism. He has a wide variety of research interests, including food tourism, children's and elderly populations' eating habits and their impact on the hospitality industry, new food products development/sensory evaluation, medical tourism and social entrepreneurship in the hospitality industry.

Colin Johnson has taught in seven colleges and Universities in the UK, Switzerland and the US. He has served as the department chair at San Jose and San Francisco State Universities, and also as deputy director at the International Travel and Tourism Institute, Neuchatel, dean of the Domino Carlton International Hotel Management Centre in Lucerne, and the dean and director of research at the Ecole hoteliere de Lausanne in Switzerland. Colin earned his doctorate in economic and social sciences from Fribourg University, Switzerland; an MBA from Manchester Business School and a BA from the Open University in the UK. His research interests include internationalization in the hospitality industry, sustainability and social entrepreneurship and gastronomy and gastronomic tourism. He has published widely in leading hospitality, tourism and management journals and has been a keynote speaker for the OECD and travel and tourism conferences in Korea and Europe. He has been a visiting scholar and professor at Macerata University in Italy and at Chemnitz University in Germany.

Contemporary Geographies of Leisure, Tourism and Mobility
Series Editor
C. Michael Hall
Professor at the Department of Management,
College of Business and Economics, University of Canterbury,
Christchurch, New Zealand

The aim of this series is to explore and communicate the intersections and relationships between leisure, tourism and human mobility within the social sciences.

It will incorporate both traditional and new perspectives on leisure and tourism from contemporary geography, e.g. notions of identity, representation and culture, while also providing for perspectives from cognate areas such as anthropology, cultural studies, gastronomy and food studies, marketing, policy studies and political economy, regional and urban planning, and sociology, within the development of an integrated field of leisure and tourism studies.

Also, increasingly, tourism and leisure are regarded as steps in a continuum of human mobility. Inclusion of mobility in the series offers the prospect to examine the relationship between tourism and migration, the sojourner, educational travel, and second home and retirement travel phenomena.

The series comprises two strands:

Contemporary Geographies of Leisure, Tourism and Mobility aims to address the needs of students and academics, and the titles will be published in hardback and paperback. Titles include:

Tourism and Hospitality in Conflict-Ridden Destinations
Edited by Rami Isaac, Erdinç Çakmak and Richard Butler

Positive Tourism in Africa
Edited by Mucha Mkono

Sustainable Tourism Practices in the Mediterranean
Edited by Ipek Kalemci Tüzün, Mehmet Ergül and Colin Johnson

Routledge Studies in Contemporary Geographies of Leisure, Tourism and Mobility is a forum for innovative new research intended for research students and academics, and the titles will be available in hardback only.

For more information about this series, please visit: www.routledge.com/Contemporary-Geographies-of-Leisure-Tourism-and-Mobility/book-series/SE0522

Sustainable Tourism Practices in the Mediterranean

**Edited by Ipek Kalemci Tüzün,
Mehmet Ergül and Colin Johnson**

Routledge
Taylor & Francis Group

LONDON AND NEW YORK

First published 2020 by Routledge

2 Park Square, Milton Park, Abingdon, Oxon OX14 4RN

605 Third Avenue, New York, NY 10017

Routledge is an imprint of the Taylor & Francis Group, an informa business

First issued in paperback 2022

Publisher's Note

The publisher has gone to great lengths to ensure the quality of this reprint but points out that some imperfections in the original copies may be apparent.

British Library Cataloguing-in-Publication Data
A catalogue record for this book is available from the British Library

Library of Congress Cataloging-in-Publication Data
A catalog record for this book has been requested

ISBN: 978-1-138-09737-7 (hbk)
ISBN: 978-1-03-233821-7 (pbk)
DOI: 10.4324/9781315104911

Typeset in Times New Roman
by Apex CoVantage, LLC

Contents

Figures

Tables

Contributors

Alessio Cavicchi, Associate Professor Department of Education, Cultural Heritage and Tourism, University of Macerata, Italy. a.cavicchi@unimc.it

Alessio Cavicchi's main fields of interest and research are consumer food choice, economics of food quality and safety, sustainable tourism and innovation in the agro-food sector.

Aysin Pasamehmetoğlu, Associate Professor, Hotel Management Program, School of Applied Sciences, Özyeğin University, Turkey. aysin.pmoglu@ozyegin.edu.tr

Aysin Pasamehmetoğlu's research interests include organizational behavior, organizational theories, organizational sociology, social capital and cultural studies, network organizations and industrial clusters.

Candide Çulhaoğlu Uludağ, Assistant Professor, Faculty of Economics and Administrative Sciences, Beykent University, Turkey. candideuludag@beykent.edu.tr

Candide Çulhaoğlu Uludağ's main research areas are organization and management, leadership, organizational behavior in the hospitality industry and sustainability in organizations.

Cristina Santini, Associate Professor, Università Telematica San Raffaele, Italy. santini.cristina@gmail.com

Cristina Santini's research interests include the food and wine business, entrepreneurship and ecopreneurship and strategic management. She is interested in research methodology and more specifically in case study, participatory approaches and action research.

Christopher Ziemnowicz, Professor, University of North Carolina at Pembroke, USA. christopher.ziemnowicz@uncp.edu

Christopher Ziemnowicz developed several entrepreneurial ventures while earning a PhD in Management and Marketing at the Warsaw University of Technology in Poland.

Dejan Krizaj, Assistant Professor, University of Primorska, Faculty of Tourism Studies – Turistica, Slovenia. dejan.krizaj@gmail.com

Dejan Krizaj's research and publications focus on R&D in tourism and the promotion and measurement of tourism innovation. He is the co-founder of

AIRTH – Alliance for Innovators and Researchers in Tourism and Hospitality. Since 2006, he is the chairman of the Slovenian National Tourism Innovation Awards Commission on behalf of Slovenian Tourist Board, and Ministry of Economic Development and Technology.

Gaye Acikdilli, Assistant Professor, University of North Carolina at Pembroke, USA gaye.acikdilli@uncp.edu
Gaye Acikdilli's research focuses on global marketing and business as well as entrepreneurship and sustainability.

Gonca Güzel Şahin, Associate Professor, Tourism and Hotel Management Department at Atılım University, Turkey. gonca.guzel@atilim.edu.tr
Gonca Güzel Şahin's main research areas are tourism marketing, destination marketing, urban tourism, cultural tourism and gastronomy.

Melanie Smith, Associate Professor and Researcher, Tourism, Budapest Metropolitan University in Hungary. msmith@metropolitan.hu
Melanie Smith's main research areas are urban tourism, cultural tourism, health tourism and well-being.

Mustafa Mehmet Gökoğlu, Ph.D, Lecturer, Dokuz Eylül University, Faculty of Business, Turkey.
mustafa.gokoglu@deu.edu.tr
Mustafa Mehmet Gökoğlu's primary areas of research are in institutional theory, organizational learning, sensemaking and sustainable development.

Nicolas Dubrocard, Director of Audit Diagnostic Solutions Tourism, France. nicolasdubrocard@gmail.com
Nicolas Dubrocard is an international sustainability specialist and director of Audit Diagnostic Solutions Tourism. He is a recognized auditor for various leading sustainability certifications in tourism and hospitality. He helped forge key documents pertaining to water use and management in the hospitality industry.

Özgür Özdemir, Assistant Professor, Department of Hospitality, University of Nevada, Las Vegas, USA. ozgur.ozdemir@unlv.edu
Özgür Ozdemir's research focuses on corporate governance, corporate social responsibility, financial management, the economic impact of tourism and operating performance in the hospitality industry.

Özlem Özbek, PhD, Lecturer, Department of Tourism and Hotel Management, Bandirma Onyedi Eylul University, Turkey. ozlemtekin10@gmail.com
Özlem Özbek's research interests include technology-based Marketing and augmented reality marketing in tourism destinations.

R. Arzu Kalemci, Professor, Faculty of Administrative and Economic Sciences, Department of Management, Cankaya University, Ankara, TURKEY.arzuk alemci@cankaya.edu.tr
R. Arzu Kalemci's research interests include historical institutionalism, transnational management and work ethic.

Roya Rahimi, Reader, Marketing and Leisure Management, University of Wolverhampton, Business School, United Kingdom. Roya.Rahimi@wlv.ac.uk

Roya Rahimi's research interests are innovation, big data, CRM, organizational culture, gender equality and tourism higher education.

Tevfik Demirçiftçi, PhD Student, The William F. Harrah College of Hospitality, University of Nevada Las Vegas, USA. tevfikd@gmail.com

Tevfik Demirçiftçi's research interests include revenue management, hotel branding, tourism technology and online distribution.

Vinod Sasidharan, Associate Professor, School of Hospitality and Tourism Management, San Diego State University, USA. vsasidha@mail.sdsu.edu

Vinod Sasidharan's research interests focus on the evaluation and implementation of grass-roots tourism initiatives, involving local community participation in planning and decision-making for sustainable tourism development at the destination level.

Willy Legrand, Professor, Hospitality Management, IUBH International University of Applied Sciences, Germany. w.legrand@iubh.de

Willy Legrand is the lead author of the textbook *Sustainability in the Hospitality Industry: Principles of Sustainable Operations* (3rd edition) and guest Editor-in-Chief of the "Hotel Yearbook Special Edition – Sustainable Hospitality 2020", a free-downloadable online publication gathering the thoughts of leaders in sustainable hospitality and tourism around the globe.

Preface

This text links the ancient region of the Mediterranean with the relatively new concept of sustainability. Sustainability is a multi-dimensional concept that focuses on the conservation of natural resources and preservation of quality of life through respect and regard for local people, protection of history and cultural heritage, and minimization of pollution. Tourism in the Mediterranean has been around for millennia. Sustainable tourism development has a vital role to ensure that future generations will still have a reason to visit the region, and will experience delight when they do so. Recent changes in global climate change, political and economic revolutions, urban migration and technology have fundamentally affected the balance of resources in the region. It is natural that these changes have influenced tourism flows to the area, and it is our view that sustainable tourism development will gain in importance.

The Mediterranean is a unique and fascinating geographical region, with more than a dozen countries spanning Europe, Africa and Asia. Historically, the most important factors linking Mediterranean countries have been economic, cultural and social relations that were bound together around a closed sea. The region is rich with natural beauty, along with an intriguing history and culture endowed with a mild climate and fruitful soils. Fourteen nations lie along the shores of the Mediterranean: Spain, France, Italy, Albania, Greece, Turkey, Syria, Lebanon, Israel, Egypt, Libya, Tunisia, Algeria and Morocco. Parts of the region were settled more than ten thousand years ago, and advanced civilizations gradually grew out of these early societies. Ironically, the region also saw some of the first sea-sand-sun-based mass tourism, with the resulting degradation of cultural and environmental heritage jeopardizing the future sustainability of tourism activities in the region. A number of recent initiatives have focused on sustainable development. On a general level, in 2015, the United Nations at the Sustainable Development Summit identified 17 Sustainable Development Goals. Agenda 2030 was put in place to accelerate the global progress in the three stakes of the sustainable development: (a) economic development, (b) social development and (c) environmental protection. Subsequently, the United Nations Environment Plan Blue (2017) emphasized five key dimensions of sustainable development: environmental integrity, social progress and equality, economic success and development, cultural heritage and assets and shared governance (more details of these may be found in Chapter 2). This was augmented by the General Council of the United Nations designating 2017 as "The International Year of Sustainable Tourism Development", giving a clear message by the Director General of UNESCO, Irina Bokova: "the importance of international tourism in fostering better understanding among peoples everywhere, in leading to a greater awareness of the rich heritage of various civilizations, thereby contributing to the strengthening of peace in the world".

In light of these changes, widespread interest in sustainable development has captured the attention of tourism industry representatives, researchers and an increasingly aware general public. The book attempts to bring together several diverse recent themes, looking through the lens of sustainability in such areas as: new technologies, including the role of social media, big data and CRM; social sustainability and tourism innovation and experiences; corporate social responsibility and ethical practices; the importance of the Mediterranean diet and gastronomic tourism.

Chapter 1 focuses on the consensual understanding of tourism scholars about sustainability and growth in the Mediterranean region. A content analysis study of the current sustainable tourism management literature was undertaken and 221 articles were analyzed in mainstream tourism journals. The chapter asserts that sustainable development includes economic, social, political and cultural elements. Chapter 2 looks at the link between regional economic development and sustainable tourism practices in the Mediterranean countries. The authors argue that sustainable tourism development may not be regarded as a distinct construct that is affected by the overall economic development, but rather should be seen as a component of the overall economic development. In Chapter 3, the socio-economic impacts of gastronomy in the Mediterranean are examined along with the relationship between gastronomy and sustainable tourism applications. Chapter 4 proposes a model for developing and accessing social sustainability innovations. A design framework is described for the holistic involvement of all stakeholders in tourism processes that considers social sustainability and its links to tourism innovation, tourism experiences and the ownership of certain parts of tourism systems. Chapter 5 presents a first analysis of social entrepreneurship and ethical practices in the Mediterranean basin. There is a related focus in Chapter 6 on corporate social responsibility practices of hotels in the Barcelona region. The methodology is a case study analysis regarding the progress in the implementation of corporate social responsibility practices leading to sustainable development. Chapter 7 deals with the vital role of information technology, social media and big data in the implementation of customer relationship marketing, thereby seeking to ensure sustainable relationships with customers in the Mediterranean region.

The vital importance of limited water resources in hotels and resorts are treated in Chapter 8. The chapter investigates the challenges of poorly managed water and wastewater resources in hotels and resorts and the consequences for the local communities around the Mediterranean basin, which are particularly prone to water security problems. Chapter 9 outlines some of the increasingly important issues associated with gastronomy and the Mediterranean diet. Italy has long been viewed as a "foodie" destination, but there have been changes in the consumption habits of the Mediterranean diet by native Italians that has major consequences for the agrifood sector. The issues and resultant initiatives and associations are discussed at length. A result of the "Slow Food" movement discussed in Chapter 9 was the "Slow City" movement. This is considered in Chapter 10, along with its history and organization. The case of "Seferihisar" is presented, evaluating how to use destination marketing, destination development and sustainable tourism. The final chapter concludes with the increasingly popular health tourism sector. Case studies are used to analyze the sustainability of the health tourism sector in Balkan countries, emphasizing the need for future product development and quality enhancement.

We hope that these diverse yet related chapters will stimulate new ideas, and will serve to foster additional research related to sustainable tourism development. We are also hopeful that the book will assist in developing new models and methodologies concerning Mediterranean sustainable development, thereby contributing to the body of literature. Finally, we hope you enjoy reading the chapters as much as we have enjoyed the process of editing the book.

İpek Kalemci Tüzün, Mehmet Ergül,
and Colin Johnson
2019

1 A content analysis of sustainable development in the tourism literature

R. Arzu Kalemci

Introduction

Sustainability is the creation of a community that respectfully utilizes natural resources to achieve high levels of economic security and to ensure that communities achieve democracy without compromising the ecological system and integrity of life (Gladwin, Krause and Kennelly, 1995). Thus, sustainability integrates social, environmental and economic responsibility for future generations to be able to live a normal life to use existing resources in a rational way (Gimenez, Sierra and Rodon, 2012; Kleindorfer, Singhal and Van Wassenhove, 2005). On the other hand, the concept of SD (sustainable development) is important in terms of understanding and explaining the concept of sustainability (Sharpley, 2000). SD is a concept that has emerged to reveal environmental problems, the effective use of natural resources and, in particular, their relationship to energy (Pjerotic, 2017). SD is usually associated with the growth phase of a country and the persistence of this growth over time. For this reason, SD can be associated with all activities related to public policy and sustainability promoted by the private sector (Martens and Carvalho, 2017, p. 1085).

Tourism is seen as one of the largest industrial enterprises worldwide. Because the tourism sector is a resource-based industry, it must be accountable in terms of sustainability both at the local and global scale (Lu and Nepal, 2009). Since the early 1980s, the possible negative consequences of tourism have begun to be noticed much more, and debates about the ecological and social costs of the tourism sector have begun to increase (Pforr, 2001). Thus, the undeniable relationship of natural resources with the tourism sector and increasing international tourism mobility in recent years has required that the concept of tourism be evaluated in the context of sustainability. This has also made the tourism sector, which has an important place in the development policies of many countries, one of the most discussed sectors in terms of sustainability. Lu and Nepal (2009, p. 5) stated that the concept of sustainability is often evaluated and implemented differently by individuals, stakeholders and social groups, and they highlighted the four basic principles of sustainability: (1) the idea of holistic planning and strategy-making; (2) the importance of preserving essential ecological processes; (3) the need to protect both human heritage and biodiversity and (4) development based on the idea that productivity can be sustained over the long term for future generations.

In addition, environmental factors are one of the important issues that the tourism industry should deal with. In fact, the environment–strategy–performance (ESP) relationship, which is the core concept of tourism management (TM), states that in order to maximize total tourism performance, the tourism industry should cope with environmental issues (Chang and Katrichis, 2016, p. 792). As a matter of fact, the concept of sustainable tourism development since the late 1980s has become one of the main research topics between tourism theorists and practitioners (Sharpley, 2000; Liu, 2003). The concept of sustainable tourism, as developed by the World Tourism Organization (WTO) in the context of the United Nations refers to tourist activities "leading to management of all resources in such a way that economic, social and aesthetic needs can be fulfilled while maintaining cultural integrity, essential ecological processes, biological diversity and life support systems" (see UNWTO, 1994). Definitions of sustainable development in tourism literature are mainly discussed under two categories. These are (a) focusing on sustaining tourism as an economic activity, and (b) those which consider tourism as an element of wider sustainable development policies (Cronin, 1990; Hunter, 1995; Sharpley, 2000). Previous studies have shown that there is a strong relationship between tourism and development, and it is emphasized that the concept of development is very important in terms of the creation of the tourism sector; in other words; "tourism is 'aligned' with "development" (Johnston, 2014). On the other hand, there are lots of definitions for sustainability and sustainable development in tourism literature. In fact, Garrod and Fyall (1998, p. 199) reflect this situation as "defining sustainable development in the context of tourism has become something of a cottage industry in the academic literature of late". A number of researchers shared this view and claim that despite the many attempts to identify sustainable development in the tourism literature, these definitions have ignored tourism's potential role in the development and the validity of the sustainable tourism development (Hunter and Green, 1995; Sharpley, 2000; Liu, 2003).

By adopting a descriptive approach, this study reveals what fundamental issues are addressed in the academic field for defining sustainable development which is a crucial concept for the tourism industry. In this direction, 221 articles with the keywords "sustainable development" in their titles were analyzed using content analysis.

Methodology

A text analysis technique was conducted in the study. Articles indexed in Scopus with the keywords "sustainable development and" and "tourism" in their titles were searched as of January 2018. Searching was limited with choosing business and management articles. Articles that do not have these terms in their titles but have them in their texts were not included in the scope of the searching process. Although this could constitute a limitation of this study, searching based only on the titles of articles was chosen to focus on articles considered exactly related to "sustainable development" and "tourism". It was observed that 221 articles with the keyword "sustainable development and" and "tourism" were published in 64 journals. The top five journals with the highest frequency are the *Journal of Sustainable Tourism* (52 articles), *Tourism Management* (18 articles), *Quality – Access to Success* (12 articles), *Tourism Recreation Research* (9 articles) and *Tourism Geographies* (7 articles) (see Table 1.1). In the literature, the *Journal of Sustainable Tourism*, which concentrated mainly on sustainable tourism, is a

Table 1.1 Journals and the number of articles with the keyword "sustainable development" and "tourism" in their titles.

Name of the Journal	Number of articles
Journal of Sustainable Tourism	52
Tourism Management	18
Quality – Access to Success	12
Tourism Recreation Research	9
Tourism Geographies	7
Current Issues in Tourism	6
Asia Pacific Journal of Tourism Research	5
Journal of Travel Research	
Tourism Economics	
Tourism Planning and Development	
Tourismos	
African Journal of Hospitality, Tourism and Leisure	4
International Journal of Contemporary Hospitality Management	
International Journal of Tourism Research	
Journal of Cleaner Production	
International Journal of Tourism Policy	3
Problems and Perspectives in Management	
Scandinavian Journal of Hospitality and Tourism	
Tourism Analysis	
Tourism and Hospitality Research	
Tourism and Hospitality, Planning and Development	
Tourism Management Perspectives	
Tourism	
Worldwide Hospitality and Tourism Themes	
Analele Stiintifice ale Universitatii Al I Cuza din Iasi – Sectiunea Stiinte Economice	2
Business Strategy and the Environment	
E a M: Ekonomie a Management	
Espacios	
European Journal of Tourism Research	
International Business Management	
Journal of Human Resources in Hospitality and Tourism	
Journal of Policy Research in Tourism, Leisure and Events	
Tourism in Marine Environments	
Academy of Strategic Management Journal	1
Annals of Tourism Research	
Communication and Management	

(*Continued*)

Table 1.1 (Continued)

Name of the Journal	Number of articles
Cuadernos de Turismo	
DETUROPE	
Developments in Corporate Governance and Responsibility	
European Research Studies Journal	
International Business Review	
International Journal of Action Research	
International Journal of Business Information Systems	
International Journal of Culture, Tourism, and Hospitality Research	
International Journal of Economic Research	
International Journal of Electronic Customer Relationship Management	
International Journal of Heritage Studies	
International Journal of Hospitality and Tourism Administration	
International Journal of Hospitality Management	
International Journal of Services and Operations Management	
Journal for Global Business Advancement	
Journal of China Tourism Research	
Journal of Hospitality and Tourism Technology	
Journal of Hospitality Marketing and Management	
Journal of Hospitality, Leisure, Sport and Tourism Education	
Journal of Promotion Management	
Journal of Quality Assurance in Hospitality and Tourism	
Journal of Retailing and Consumer Services	
Journal of Teaching in Travel and Tourism	
Leisure/Loisir	
South East European Journal of Economics and Business	
Tourism Review	
Tourist Studies	
Transformations in Business and Economics	
Total	221

major journal. The main objectives of the *Journal of Sustainable Tourism* are to promote research and application in the field of tourism and to assist in the development of reliable empirical evidence and to include interdisciplinary approaches (Lu and Nepal, 2009). In addition, the numbers of articles published in the journals by years are given in Table 1.2. As Table 1.2 clearly indicates, the number of articles about sustainable development for the tourism industry has increased from the 1990s to today.

Previous studies (e.g. Nag, Hambrick and Chen, 2007) have revealed that only an analysis of abstracts proves sufficient to deliver the desired quality of analysis. NVivo automated text analysis software was used, as it enables researchers to process large numbers of words analytically. As the NVivo software processed the abstracts given, thousands of root words emerged. As it would be impossible to analyze so many words analytically, some of the words were eliminated using the "Stop Words List" function of the software. This elimination was primarily used

Table 1.2 Number of articles by years

Year	Number of articles	Year	Number of articles
1990	1	2005	5
1991	1	2006	4
1992	5	2007	12
1993	2	2008	8
1994	3	2009	6
1995	6	2010	16
1996	1	2011	6
1997	2	2012	16
1999	7	2013	11
2000	6	2014	19
2001	7	2015	16
2002	9	2016	18
2003	6	2017	24
2004	3	2018	1
Total: 221			

for conjunctions and adjunctions, such as "a", "and", "at", "in", "so", "than" and "to". As the main purpose of this study is to explore fundamental issues of sustainable development in the tourism management literature, it was considered sufficient to focus on the top 100 words. Considering previous studies (e.g. Duman, Kalemci and Çakar, 2005; Kalemci and Tuzun, 2017) as a reference, it was observed that some of the words in the top 100 were related either to methodology or to the study itself. These words were excluded from the top 100 list. Words that were excluded from the top 100 words by frequency as follows: "abstract", "paper", "research", "study", "also", "analysis", "approach", "findings", "results", "within", "data", "using", "however", "model", "used", "may", "article", "one", "theory", "case" and "significant". In total, 19 words were excluded from the top 100 words. Finally, it was seen that some words have the same root. These words are combined (e.g. area and areas; communities and community, destination and destinations, develop and developed, environment and environmental, impact and impacts, importance and important, natural and nature, practice and practices, stakeholder and stakeholders). In total, 10 words are combined into one word, and 68 words are included.

Findings

A list of the most frequent words are shown in Table 1.3.

Discussion

First, it would be beneficial to assess the findings of the study in relation to the concept of SD and sustainability. The framework of Sharpley (2000) can provide

Table 1.3 List of most frequent words in the articles

Word	F (frequency)	Word	F (frequency)
tourism	1015	future	45
development	553	government	44
sustainable	465	concept	43
local	183	policy	43
community	152	context	42
environmental	137	key	42
sustainability	128	new	42
economic	126	residents	42
destination	122	sector	42
tourists	106	positive	39
developing	105	potential	38
area	99	principles	38
rural	99	many	36
cultural	92	reserved	36
management	83	political	35
social	79	growth	34
natural	78	use	34
stakeholders	75	knowledge	33
important	72	well	33
region	70	activities	32
industry	69	achieve	31
impacts	68	different	31
planning	67	implications	31
practices	67	indicators	31
based	60	limited	31
group	58	benefits	30
resources	56	perceptions	30
role	48	present	30
support	48	related	29
world	47	strategies	29
countries	46	effects	28
heritage	46	needs	28
issues	46	order	28
public	46	people	28

important information on this issue. Sharpley (2000, p. 3) defined SD by the following formula;

Sustainable development = development + sustainability

According to this definition, sustainable development is the sum of the concept of development theory and sustainability. When the findings of the study are evaluated, the words "tourism", "sustainable" and "development" have the highest frequency, which has expected results as for the sample of the current study; the articles that contain these three words were scanned. On the other hand, it is clear that the word "sustainability" ($F = 128$) among the concepts with the highest frequency when these three concepts are excluded. When evaluated the results in this way; the findings of the study confirmed the approach of Sharpley (2000).

According to this approach, the theory of development includes economic, social, political and cultural elements, whereas the concept of sustainability includes more environmental elements. Sharpley (2000, p. 8) has drawn a framework under the heading "A Model of Sustainable Development: Principles and Objectives", in which fundamental principles, development and sustainability objectives and the requirements for sustainable development were determined. When we evaluate the findings of the work in this framework, the words which can be considered to be related to the development objectives that includes economic, social, political and cultural elements are as follows: "local", "community", "economic", "destination", "tourists", "developing", "area", "rural", "cultural", "social", "region", "world", "countries", "public", "future", "government", "policy", "context", "residents", "political", "growth" and "indicator" (see frequency in Table 1.3). In addition, the words, which can be considered to be related to the sustainability objectives that include environmental elements, are as follows: "environmental", "natural", "resources" and "reserved" (see frequency in Table 1.3).

When the other findings of the study are evaluated, it can be seen that some words are highlighting the organizational issues. Words which can be considered to be related to the organizational objectives, are as follows; "stakeholders", "industry", "planning", "practices", "group", "role", "sector", "knowledge", "perceptions", "strategies", "people" (see frequency in Table 1.3). For this reason, it may be useful to draw attention to the organizational side of the concept of sustainability, especially for the companies involved in the tourism sector. Social, economic and environmental challenges that have become increasingly complex have necessitated organizations to renew themselves (Wilkins, 2003; Pope, Annandale and Morrison-Saunders, 2004; Martens and Carvalho, 2017). In this direction, organizations have begun to take steps to be innovative, to change management and to adopt new activities. Indeed, as tourism companies become part of the global economy, a number of collaborative activities have begun to gain importance. Among these collaborative activities, environmental protection and the development of environment-friendly tourism are on the forefront (Hassan, 2000). The organizational institutionalism approach draws attention to the social, cultural and historical aspects of the organizations. According to the organizational institutionalism approach, it is evident that the structural changes in the organizations are affected less by the degree of competition, efficiency and effectiveness; instead, the effects of the institutional processes reflect the organizations' structures more effectively. Factors such as professions, practices and technologies that affect the structure are institutionalized at a high rate, and they begin to see myth functioning. These myths are reflected in the process without questioning the contribution to effectiveness and efficiency. Organizations do not just make profit and activity calculations, but they also try to gain legitimacy, which is very important in terms of institutionalization (Meyer and Rowan, 1977). Scott (1991) described organizational legitimacy as the level of value given to the organizations. One of the main arguments of the new institutional theory is that the organizations maintain their lives by adopting the "institutions" (even if they decrease the productivity) imposed by the environment in order to ensure the legitimacy (DiMaggio and

Powell, 1983). Within institutional theory, there is a view that organizations will be legitimate with respect to harmony with the environment, will gain status and will make it easier to reach the resources in this sense. Institutional theory argues that organizations show isomorphism in order to gain value in society; in other words, to be legitimate. According to this approach, organizations provide their legitimacy by adopting structures and practices which have gained value in society or, in other words, institutionalized (Meyer and Rowan, 1977). These institutionalized structures and practices are spread among the organizations, thus creating isomorphism in organizational fields (DiMaggio and Powell, 1983). Sustainability gains importance in terms of legitimacy of organizations in this sense. A research conducted by the United Nations Global Compact has explored more than 1,000 CEOs' ideas about sustainability for organizations. According to this, 84% of CEOs expressed the opinion that organizations should set sustainability targets and set an example in this direction (Hayward et al., 2013). Sustainability is not just a management tool for organizations. Organizations need to contribute to the sustainable management of natural and human resources and take measures to contribute to the welfare of society and the economy as a whole (Mitchell et al., 2007). In addition, organizations can include the principles of sustainability in their activities in the following ways (Martens and Carvalho, 2017, p. 1086):

(a) by considering sustainability during the preparation and review of business strategies;
(b) by supporting new agreements and negotiations that promote sustainable practices;
(c) by developing new projects driven by sustainability principles;
(d) by broadening their vision of sustainability beyond the limits of the company.

Finally, Hunter's (1995) definition of sustainable tourism development can be evaluated with respect to the findings of the study. According to Hunter (1995, p. 157), "Sustainable tourism development meets the needs of present tourists and host regions while protecting and enhancing opportunity for the future". Findings of the study show that the words "present" and "future" are the most frequent words in the literature of tourism (see frequency in Table 1.3).

Conclusions

This study executed what fundamental issues are addressed in the tourism academic literature for defining sustainable development. In this direction, 221 articles with the keywords "sustainable development" in their titles are analyzed using content analysis. The concept of sustainable development is very important to understand because of the structural requirement of the tourism industry. In addition, the study supports the idea that the concept of sustainability is important to understand sustainable development for the tourism literature. Previous studies (e.g. Sharpley, 2000) have been more categorized sustainable development on the basis of developmental and environmental dynamics. However, this study argues that the organizational dynamics of sustainable development should also be emphasized. This study has attempted to explain the results from an institutional perspective. Organizations in the tourism industry often adopt sustainable development as a way to be legitimated. This shows that there is normative isomorphism among organizations. This study shows that sustainability for companies operating in the tourism sector has a legitimating effect both at the organizational level ("stakeholders", "industry", "planning", "practices", "sector", "knowledge", "strategies") and within the organization ("group", "role", "perceptions", "people") (see frequencies in Table 1.3).

References

Chang, W. and Katrichis, J.M. (2016). A literature review of tourism management (1990–2013): A content analysis perspective. *Current Issues in Tourism*, 19(8), pp. 791–823.

Cronin, L. (1990). A strategy for tourism and sustainable developments. *World Leisure and Recreation*, 32(3), pp. 12–18.

DiMaggio, P.J. and Powell, W.W. (1983). The iron cage revisited: Institutional isomorphism and collective rationality in organizational fields. *American Sociological Review*, 48(2), pp. 147–160.

Duman, Ş.A., Kalemci, R.A. and Çakar, M. (2005). Türkiye'de stratejik yönetim alanının kapsamını belirlemeye yönelik bir araştırma. *Yönetim Araştırmaları Dergisi*, 5(1), pp. 57–72.

Hassan, S. (2000). Determinants of market competitiveness in an environmentally sustainable tourism industry. *Journal of Travel Research*, 38, pp. 239–245.

Hayward, R., Lee, J., Keeble, J., McNamara, R., Hall, C., Cruse, S., Gupta, P. and Robinson, E. (2013). The UN Global Compact-Accenture CEO Study on sustainability: Architects of a better world. DOI: 10.5848/UNGC.5720.2014.0015.

Hunter, C. (1995). On the need to re-conceptualise sustainable tourism development. *Journal of Sustainable Tourism*, 3(3), pp. 155–165.

Hunter, C. and Green, H. (1995). *Tourism and the environment. A sustainable relationship?* London, New York: Routledge.

Garrod, B. and Fyall, A. (1998). Beyond the rhetoric of sustainable tourism? *Tourism Management*, 19(3), pp. 199–212.

Gimenez, C., Sierra, V. and Rodon, J. (2012). Sustainable operations: Their impact on triple bottom line. *International Journal of Production Economics*, 140(1), pp. 149–159.

Gladwin, T.N., Krause, T-S and Kennelly, J.J. (1995). Beyond eco-efficiency: Towards socially sustainable business. *Sustainable Development*, 3, pp. 35–43.

Kalemci, R.A. and Kalemci Tuzun, I. (2017). Understanding Protestant and Islamic work ethic studies: A content analysis of articles. *Journal of Business Ethics*, Available at: https://doi.org/10.1007/s10551-017-3716-y

Kleindorfer, P.R., Singhal, K. and Van Wassenhove, L.N. (2005). Sustainable Operations Management. *Production and Operations Management*, 14(4), pp. 482–492.

Liu, Z. (2003). Sustainable tourism development: A critique. *Journal of Sustainable Tourism*, 11(6), pp. 459–475.

Lu, J. and Nepal, S.K. (2009). Sustainable tourism research: An analysis of papers published in the Journal of Sustainable Tourism. *Journal of Sustainable Tourism*, 17(1), pp. 5–16.

Johnston, C.S. (2014). Towards a theory of sustainability, sustainable development and sustainable tourism: Beijing's Hutong neighbourhoods and sustainable tourism. *Journal of Sustainable Tourism*, 22(2), pp. 195–213.

Martens, M.L. and Carvalho, M.M. (2017). Key factors of sustainability in project management context: A survey exploring the project managers' perspective. *International Journal of Project Management*, 35, pp. 1084–1102.

Meyer, J.W. and Rowan, B. (1977). Institutionalized organizations: Formal structure as myth and ceremony. *American Journal of Sociology*, 83, pp. 340–363.

Mitchell, R.K., Busenitz, L.W., Bird, B., Gaglio, C.M., McMullen, J.S., Morse, E.A. and Smith, J.B. (2007). The central question in entrepreneurial cognition research 2007. *Entrepreneurship Theory and Practice*, 31(1), pp. 1–27.

Nag, R., Hambrick, D. and Chen, M. (2007). What is strategic management, really? Inductive derivation of a consensus definition of the field. *Strategic Management Journal*, 28, pp. 935–955.

Pforr, C. (2001). Concepts of sustainable development, sustainable tourism and ecotourism: Definitions, principles and linkages. *Scandinavian Journal of Hospitality and Tourism*, 1(1), pp. 68–71.

Pjerotic, L. (2017). Stakeholder cooperation in implementation of the sustainable development concept: Montenegrin tourist destinations. *Journal of International Studies*, 10(2), pp. 148–157.

Pope, J., Annandale, D. and Morrison-Saunders, A. (2004). Conceptualising sustainability assessment. *Environmental Impact Assessment Review*, 24(6), pp. 595–616.

Scott, W.R. (1991). *Unpacking institutional arguments, the new institutionalism in organizational analysis*. Chicago: University of Chicago Press.

Sharpley, R. (2000). Tourism and sustainable development: Exploring the theoretical divide. *Journal of Sustainable Tourism*, 8, pp. 1–19.

United Nations World Tourism Organization (UNWTO). (1994). *Agenda 21 for travel and tourism: Towards environmentally sustainable tourism*. London: WTO, WTTC and the Earth Council.

Wilkins, H. (2003). The need for subjectivity in EIA: Discourse as a tool for sustainable development. *Environmental Impact Assessment Review*, 23(4), pp. 401–414.

2 Sustainable tourism development

Issues and applications in the Mediterranean region

Özgür Özdemir and Tevfik Demirçiftçi

Introduction

Sustainability is one of the most widely debated and extensively admitted phenomena by academics, businesses and society in general. As the needs and wants of human populations have continually increased in time, resource scarcity and efficient use of these resources have become an explicit public issue for policy makers. The sustainability movement that started with a common awareness to protect the world's natural resources evolved in time to embrace social and economic considerations. Today, sustainability is perceived as a comprehensive framework with several dimensions that serve to protect societies' contemporaneous and future well-being.

This chapter reviews the application of sustainability ideas in the tourism industry and particularly focuses on the sustainability concerns, practices and developments in the Mediterranean region. The chapter starts with a review of the emergence of sustainability and sustainable development notions in the world, followed by a discussion of how the idea of sustainable development applies to the tourism domain. The next section discusses issues and concerns related to sustainable tourism development in the Mediterranean region. The last section illustrates cases and best practices regarding how Mediterranean tourism businesses comprehend the idea of sustainable development and implement exemplary business solutions.

Sustainability – a historical perspective

Over the last two decades, the term sustainability has become a great concern among the practitioners of numerous sectors as well as researchers in various disciplines. In particular, policy-oriented researchers took a normative approach in understanding what public policies should be in place for sustainability. The idea of sustainability emerged from the notion of sustainable development, which was the common language of the world's first Earth Summit in Rio in 1992. The United Nations World Commission on Environment and Development (WCED) report *Our Common Future*, better known as the Bruntland Report (WCED, 1987, p. 37), adopted the concept of sustainable development and made it a widely recognized concept across the world. The report defined the concept of sustainability as:

> Development that meets the needs of the present without compromising the ability of future generations to meet their own needs.

The Bruntland Report, named after the chairperson of the commission, Gro Harlem Bruntland, focused on the question "how can the aspirations of the world's nations for a better life be reconciled with limited natural resources and the dangers of environmental degradation?" (Kuhlman and Farrington, 2010). Later on, a more comprehensive definition of sustainability was further suggested by the WCED (1987, p. 3) as follows:

> A process of change in which the exploitation of resources, the direction of investments, the orientation of technological development and institutional change are all in harmony and enhance both current and future potential to meet human needs and aspirations.

As indicated by Kuhlman and Farrington (2010), the Bruntland Report zeroes in on two concerns that ought to be reconciled: development and environment, which can also be interpreted as needs versus resources. The notion of sustainability has evolved over time, and today it includes three major dimensions: social, economic and environment. As Kuhlman and Farrington (2010) argue, these three dimensions are reflected in the definition of sustainability embraced by the United Nations in its Agenda for Development (United Nations, 1997, p. 1):

> Development is a multidimensional undertaking to achieve a higher quality of life for all people. Economic development, social development and environmental protection are interdependent and mutually reinforcing components of sustainable development.

These definitions of sustainability indicate that resources on the earth are not limitless, and they are subject to certain unprecedented threats that are global in scale (Owen, Witt and Gammon, 1993). Owen, Witt and Gammon (1993) list these threats as population growth, global warming, destruction of the ozone layer, degradation of the environment, the loss of biological species and habitats, and all forms of pollutions. As noted in these definitions of sustainability, the idea of sustainability encompasses the growing concern for the environment and natural resources. However, it has also had increasing reverberation in social and economic issues (Mowforth and Munt, 2016). Therefore, sustainability today is interpreted in three dimensions, social, economic and environmental, and sustainable development requires a well-balanced integration of these dimensions.

Environmental sustainability is defined as all the environmental practices that are in place to save three basic functions of the environment. Namely, these functions are: (1) environment's capacity to provide resources, (2) the waste receiver function of the environment and (3) immediate usefulness to living habitats. As this definition implies, the goal with environmental sustainability is to increase the value of the environment and its peculiarities while preserving and renewing natural resources, and the environmental inheritance.

Economic sustainability can be defined as the capacity of an economic system to support a defined level of production, income and employment indefinitely to sustain the populations. This would require the most efficient mix of resources in order to generate the highest value for the society. From the perspective of a business, the economics element embraces creating economic value while sustaining adequate production capacity, employment and income for the welfare of the society. Investments in sustainable projects are generally cost-effective and the payback period is short (Bader, 2005). Thus, sustainability investments are financially sound investments that offer great financial outcomes, including cost savings through cost-reduction measures, additional revenue through lower costs, greater long-term financial stability, lower long-term risk, easier financing options, increased asset value and higher customer demand (Bader, 2005).

Social sustainability is the ability of a social system (e.g. country, family, organization, etc.) to assure welfare – health, education, security – to all participants of the society regardless of social classes and other distinguishing characteristics.

As the world experiences a shift from industrial to risk society, becoming sustainable emerges as a supreme necessity (Beck, 1992), and a true harmony among the three pillars of sustainable development is essential to acquire the greatest benefit as a society from the sustainability framework.

Sustainable tourism development

Tourism is a significant industry for many countries, and it has been considered as a prominent instrument of regional development particularly because of its ability to lead the way to the emergence of new economic activities. The regional development role of tourism has been particularly important in rural areas (Hall and Jenkins, 1998). Because tourism has positive impacts on the balance of payments, gross income and production and generates substantial employment opportunities, it has also garnered crucial attention from policy makers and has become a policy concern for many European countries (Williams and Shaw, 1998). At the national and regional levels, tourism development helps to balance regional inequalities, whilst at the local level the goal of tourism development is to control the structural changes of decreasing rural areas and industrial towns and to enrich the economic activities of these areas (Williams and Shaw, 1998). These positive economic impacts of tourism at the national and local levels are frequently at the highlights of the regional development perspective. However, unplanned and uncontrolled tourism development can entail major deterioration of ecosystems and compromise the growth in the tourism inflow. A strong consideration to prevent negative impacts and consequences of tourism development and to maximize benefits is tourism planning. Tourism planning can be explained in several ways depending on one's perspective and depth in perceiving the fundamental planning process. Inskeep (1991) defines tourism planning as a step-by-step process that is comprehensive, integrated and environmental, and that has a focus on attaining sustainable development and community involvement. Gunn and Var (2002) augment Inskeep's definition and argue that tourism planning is a process that has four main goals – sustainable use of resources, enhanced visitor satisfaction, community and area integration, and improved economy and business success. As the attempts in defining tourism planning point out, the idea of sustainability not only underlines the preservation of ecosystems but also pays attention to economic and sociocultural development (Hall, 2000). Kauppila, Saarinen and Leinonen (2009) discuss that sustainable tourism planning has two focal factors – a long-term viewpoint and comprehensiveness. The comprehensiveness factor refers to the three elements as argued by Hall (2000) – ecological, economic and sociocultural elements – and how these elements can be incorporated into a sound tourism planning process. A solid sustainable tourism planning process aims to support the local communities and economic goals in regional development while safeguarding the ecosystems (Kauppila, Saarinen and Leinonen, 2009). It is important to precisely define the phenomenon of sustainable tourism development so that sustainable tourism planning can achieve its development goal. In the simplest form, sustainable tourism development may be defined as the application of sustainable development ideas within tourism practices, which entails tourism development that meets the needs of the present while considering the ability of future generations to meet their own needs (Weaver, 2006). The World Tourism Organization (WTO, 2018) prefers the following integrated approach for the concept of sustainable tourism development:

> Tourism that takes full account of its current and future economic, social and environmental impacts, addressing the needs of visitors, the industry, the environment and host communities.

Prosser (1994) underlines four forces of social change that are driving the need for sustainability in tourism – dissatisfaction with current products, an increasing awareness towards environmental and cultural concerns, host destinations' realization of the value of their local resources and the vulnerability of these resources and changing attitudes of developers and tour operators.

Sustainable tourism essentially addresses the minimization of negative impacts and maximization of positive impacts of tourism development for the long-term viability of tourism assets. Bramwell and Lane (1993) emphasize this view as a positive approach to minimize the tension and the conflict between all groups (i.e. the tourism industry as a whole, tourists, the environment and the host communities) so that tourism resources can be maintained in the long term. In this perspective, Cater (1993) highlights three key goals of sustainable tourism development – responding to the needs of the host populations in terms of increasing their living standards, pleasing the demands of a growing number of tourists and protecting the natural environment to achieve the first two preceding goals. In line with these goals set forth for sustainable tourism development, we can practically infer that aggregate human effects impend the survival of human populations and the ecosystems on which humans depend (Pereira et al., 2010; Buckley, 2012). Buckley (2012) argues that the aggregate human impact depends on the size and distribution of the global human population; its social organization, including economy, governance and civil society; and the consumption, pollution and protection of nature as a product of such social organization. To minimize humans' negative effect on the environment, the notion of sustainability recommends modifications to human societies (Buckley, 2012).

Sustainable tourism development and environmental issues in the Mediterranean

The tourism industry is a major economic driver for most Mediterranean countries, offering consistent employment and economic growth. Tourism-related jobs comprised 11.5% of total employment in Mediterranean countries in 2014, and 11.3% of regional gross domestic product (GDP) was earned in the tourism industry (Fosse et al., 2017). The same study showed that tourism industry generated over 70% of total production and gross value added in the coastal areas of the Mediterranean region.

Mediterranean countries have developed a wide array of tourism products, including leisure, nature, cruise and culture (Patsouratis, Frangouli and Anastasopoulos, 2005). Due to its mild climate, rich history and culture and extraordinary natural resources, the Mediterranean region became the world's leading tourism destination in terms of both international and domestic tourism arrivals, with more than 300 million international visitors representing 30% of the total tourism activity in the world in 2014 (Fosse et al., 2017). Along with the mainland of Europe, Mediterranean islands gained significant momentum in tourism and became highly attractive tourism destinations; 2.2% of the total tourism product within the Euro zone was provided by the islands of the European Union (EU) countries. Beyond Europe, Mediterranean islands have also attracted 30% of the worldwide tourism activity (Dascalaki and Balaras, 2004; Michalena, 2008).

While tourism has expanded with great momentum and provided extensive economic benefits to the region, the uncontrolled growth in tourism products has been detrimental to both environmental integrity and social equity (Satta, 2004). Dependence on sea, sand and sun tourism, weak governance, environmental pollution, resource depletion, climate change, political insecurity and social instability, economic and human capital leakage, and degradation of cultural heritage are some of the fundamental problems that impend the long-term sustainability of the tourism development in the Mediterranean region (Fosse et al., 2017).

An inevitable consequence of the continuous tourism development is the increasing demand for usable water and energy in host destinations. An average tourist consumes three or four times more water than a local resident (Sabban, 2013). For example, 52% of the total water consumption is reported to be related to tourism activities in Alanya, Turkey, in 2009. Therefore, host destinations face a serious problem for water supply. Likewise, energy consumption of host destinations increases in parallel to the level of tourism activity. A striking example illustrates that 40% of the electricity is consumed by the tourism industry in Torremolinos, Spain (Sabban, 2013).

The increase in the level of greenhouse gas emissions in the atmosphere is closely related to the level of tourism activity, which accounts for 5.3% of total greenhouse gas emissions. Airport transportation services and private car owner-ship are the primary reasons for the greenhouse gas emissions in tourism desti-nations. The European Environment Agency's report shows that 25.8% of total EU gas emissions were generated by transportation activities (European Environ-ment Agency, 2017). Governments' role is momentous in preserving the air qual-ity, and therefore governments must be proactive in imposing environmentally friendly transportation modes (Schiller and Kenworthy, 2017). For example, in Barcelona, a public bicycle-sharing program was initiated to reduce use of motor vehicles. The city owned 400 bicycle stations spread around different locations, and 100,000 residents enrolled in this program (GBSB, 2017).

Climate change is also a critical issue for Mediterranean countries. Extreme heat caused by climate change is shown to be harmful for human health. A tragic example of the impact of extreme heat on human health was the death of 15,000 people due to an extreme heat wave in France in 2003. The life-threatening heat wave in Mediterranean coasts in 2003 diverted the tourism demand to North-ern and Western European beach destinations instead of to coastal cities in the Mediterranean region (UNWTO, 2008). Mediterranean islands are affected more negatively from the climate change than the mainland areas (Roper, 2005). The islands' social, cultural, political and economic characteristics, accompa-nied by their natural weaknesses (i.e. small surface area, geographic isolation and limited resources), intensify their vulnerabilities. For instance, water short-ages occur in Crete because of the climate change and severely low precipitation (Tsanis et al., 2011).

Cases of sustainable tourism practices in European countries

Efficient planning for destination management is vital for sustainable tourism practices. Hence, public and private organizations develop and implement vari-ous programs. The Turisme de Barcelona, a Destination Management Organiza-tion (DMO), promotes the city of Barcelona around the globe. This DMO sets a series of concrete objectives to improve sustainable tourism practices in Bar-celona. One of these objectives is to promote the regions that are yet unknown to tourists, thereby reducing traffic on famous tourist locations such as Ciutat Vella. DMO also evaluates and advertises environmental assets within Barcelona. While doing these practices, the organization aims to protect the life quality of residents and to preserve the cultural identity of Barcelona (Styles, Schönberger and Martos, 2013).

Protecting biodiversity is critical for sustainable tourism. Ile de France has an intense biodiversity axis that includes the forests of Yvelines, Rambouillet and Fontainebleau, and the wetlands of the Bassee. The biodiversity of the region is in danger because of urbanization, tourism activities, landscape fragmentation and diffuse pollution. Therefore, the region established NatureParif, an organization established to protect the nature and biodiversity. This organization prepared a master plan which includes protecting ecological communities, reducing pressure on natural habitats and forecasting the impact of climate change on the diversity of living systems. Furthermore, this organization aims to help farmers to apply agro-environmental measures and gain organic agricultural certification (Houdet, 2008).

Utilization of environmentally friendly transportation modes on a larger spectrum is essential for sustainable tourism. Energy-efficient transportation vehicles should be the preferred choice for transportation services, particularly in mass tourism activities. In such an effort, TUIfly Nordic replaced inefficient Boeing 747s in its fleet with super-efficient Boeing 787 Dreamliner aircrafts. Major tour operators contribute to the sustainable tourism practices by offering non-flight transportation alternatives. For example, Forum Anders Reisen Association in Germany imposed a restriction upon tour operators for not offering a flight option in the tour packages with destinations that are farther from the original destination up to 700 km. Furthermore, sustainable biofuels are being considered for commercial airplanes. KLM Royal Dutch Airlines tested a 50/50 blend of camelina-derived fuel and kerosene (Styles, Schönberger and Martos, 2013). Convenient public transportation is another key dimension for green tourism practices. Residents of many European cities are discouraged to use their own cars and are positively motivated to use bicycles and public transportation. A great example of this application is seen in Seville, a city located in Andalucía in Spain. The city provides a public bicycle program where you can take a bike from 250 points around the city and drop it at any designated station. Seville also has an extensive network of bicycle lanes all around the city which reduces carbon emission and helps the residents to have easier, quicker and safer transportation.

Sustainable tourism is used as a development tool for rural areas. The French government has successful initiatives for rural tourism. One of these initiatives is the Logis De France, a chain hotel group developed by the French government. The Logis brand is positioned as a decent quality, small, rural hotel group and reflects the cultural identity of the local area in 1949. More than 4,300 Logis properties operate in France, and they are promoted across the world for international inbound tourism (Swarbrooke, 1999).

Using Renewable Energy Technology (RET) is a valuable tool for achieving tourism sustainability in the Mediterranean islands. These islands have vast natural resources that motivate innovative energy projects. For instance, tourism establishments in Crete benefit from solar energy. One of the biggest solar thermal systems in Europe was founded at a 275-bed-capacity hotel in Crete. This system supplies 70% of the hotel's total demand in hot water (Michalena, 2008). Motivated on this success, other hotels in Europe started implementing solar collectors, which now produce 10% of their total energy needs (Bakos and Soursos, 2002; Michalena, 2008). In Cyprus, renewable energy sources are used for tourism activities. Some luxury resorts in Cyprus have solar vehicles which operate on golf courses. Cyprus also has a Waste and Energy Saving project under the

Cyprus Sustainable Tourism Initiative (CSTI) program. CSTI cooperated with the Cyprus hotels to save energy and water. At the beginning of the project, sustainability audits were made in three hotels located in Cyprus, Turkey and the Azores. The audits suggested the implementation of greener accommodation tools, which are purported to help European hoteliers improve their operations and control their expenses. As a result of this project, water consumption decreased by 10%, with savings of €160,000 over six months during the summer of 2008 and energy consumption decreased by 1% with a savings of €239,000 (Cyprus Sustainable Tourism Initiative, 2013).

Being at the forefront of the sustainability stage, the tourism industry motivated and encouraged all stakeholders to implement energy-efficient, cost-saving programs and practices. Governments and public organizations enforced precise environmental policies to garner a collective culture to protect communities from uncontrolled business growth. The fifth Environmental Action Plan of the EU, a collaborated effort of this kind, documents comprehensive environmental standards for the tourism industry (Erdogan and Baris, 2007; Mengi and Algan, 2003). In response to an ever-growing need for environmental protection, sustainability practices in hospitality industry zeroed in on designing energy-efficient properties equipped with smart energy technologies to minimize negative effects of hotel operations on environment (Hsieh, 2012). With this motivation, hotels started to implement Energy Management Systems (EMS), a systematic approach that enables hotel properties to organize their operations so that the negative environmental impacts of hotel operations can be minimized (Bader, 2005).

The hotel industry is known as a major consumer of energy. Globally, hotels use either fossil fuel-based energy or nuclear energy. A green hotel needs to find new ways to conserve energy and use renewable resources for their energy consumption. Wood or other biomass, wind energy, solar energy, fusion and hydropower are known as the renewable energy resources (Sloan, Legrand and Chen, 2009). Several hotel companies use biomass for their energy consumption. For instance, the Auchrannie House Hotel, located on the island of Arran off the west coast of Scotland, installed a biomass system for its spa. This new investment would help the hotel to save around 540 tons of CO_2 per year, and the government would pay around £60,000 each year as a part of the Renewable Heat Incentive Scheme (HW Energy, 2018). The winner of the 2015 Green Hotelier Awards, the Boutique Hotel Stadthalle in Vienna exemplifies how a small hotel can achieve big savings and position itself as a successful ecofriendly hotel company (O'Neill, 2018). The Stadthalle has put in place a cohesive sustainability plan tapping into the several dimensions of a going-green program, including good use of renewable energy, consideration of ways to reduce packaging, great staff policies and programs with the local schools. The hotel management estimates that the CO_2 emissions have decreased by 210,000 kg per year since the hotel switched to solar panels and photovoltaic panels for its primary source of energy. The Stadthalle is also conscious of water and waste management and does more than simple recycling. The hotel reduces the production of waste by not providing packaged portions in breakfasts, canned and bottled soft beverages in the hotel, and using refillable dispensers in bathrooms. Regarding water management, the hotel has conservative water consumption policies and uses biodegradable amenities to reduce pollutants. The Inspira Santa Marta Hotel in Lisbon offers an exemplary case for water preservation, running an extensive wastewater collection program and an on-site water bottling program for hotel guests.

Beyond the individual efforts of hotel companies, EU's tourism-related commissions develop and support various sustainability programs. Nearly Zero Energy Hotels (neZEH) was one of these initiatives, and the scope of the project was to support and accelerate the rate of large-scale renovations of existing hotels into Nearly Zero Energy Building (NZEB) (Intelligent Energy Europe, 2018). The project was initiated through a pilot study that included 16 hotels from seven European countries (Croatia, France, Greece, Italy, Romania, Spain and Sweden) that went through major renovations. Results of the pilot study were promising in regards to savings in primary energy (1.134 toe/year) and reduction in greenhouse gas emissions (2.556 tCO_2e/year). Hotel buildings use a significant amount of energy, and they are responsible for 2% of the world's CO_2 emissions (Tsoutsos et al., 2013). Therefore, implementation of neZEH-like projects is paramount for sustainability of resources and company efficiency.

One of the most important globally accepted environmental certifications is ISO 14001. This certification indicates a set of EMSs and applications, including determining environmental objectives and policies, providing training documentation, designation of responsibilities and internal performance reviews (King, Lenox and Terlaak, 2005). ISO 14001 is a global environment management standard which is one of the most respected standards for service companies (Chan and Hawkins, 2010; Segarra Oña, Signes and Verma, 2011). Mediterranean countries strongly emphasize the importance of this certification for tourism organizations. Spain and Italy are the top two countries with the highest number of ISO 14001 certifications in the services sector (Bonilla Priego and Avilés Palacios, 2008; Segarra Oña et al., 2011). These certifications allow hospitality companies to decrease their costs and improve their quality and reputation (Segarra Oña et al., 2011).

Hospitality management associations highlight the importance of sustainability practices in the hospitality industry. They provide best practice examples and procedures related to sustainability practices. For instance, the International Tourism partnership designed a set of sustainable hotel setting, design and construction principles, and the International Hotel and Restaurant Association (IH&RA) determined a set of ecological, business-smart solutions related with the natural resources conversation, using more recycled products and alternative energy resources (Sloan, Legrand and Chen, 2009).

Consumers also consider environmental issues while booking a hotel. For instance, a survey conducted by Devon County Council in England reveals that 54% of 400 respondents see environmental issues as a key factor while booking a hotel, and that 82% of them are ready to pay a premium for green products (Bader, 2005). Mensah (2004) indicated that 90% of the consumers would like to book a hotel which has a green management policy. Moreover, Butler (2008) pointed out that 16% of the Kimpton (a US hotel group) guests prefer to stay in Kimpton Hotels since it has ecofriendly practices.

Conclusion

Given the economic significance of the tourism industry to the region, there is no doubt that sustainable tourism development has been of utmost priority for the Mediterranean countries. The Mediterranean region receives approximately one third of the world tourism income, with Spain, France, Italy and Greece keeping the lead positions in total tourism receipts (European Union, 2012). The region has been exceptionally successful in achieving a continued growth rate in tourism income despite the security risks, natural disasters, oil price hikes and economic uncertainties of the region (European Union, 2012). The economic contribution of the tourism industry for the region is undebatable. Tourism is an effective way of distributing wealth over the entire region by bringing income into a community that may not be otherwise generated (European Union, 2012). Sustainability programs developed by the Mediterranean countries indicate that there is great awareness about the impact of the tourism industry on the region's long-term economic viability. Both local and state governments and private businesses engage in these sustainability programs. While the governments develop and implement well-defined sustainability policies and support the industry in many ways, businesses are involved in the sustainability practices to a varying degree depending on the size and scope of their operations.

Since the early efforts that gave emergence to the idea of sustainability, tourism has been one of the leading industries that welcomed and adopted the idea, and subsequently formulated best practices that are in accord with the core premises of sustainability and sustainable development. The preceding discussion underlines the fact that sustainability emerged as a concept to increase awareness about the unplanned and uncontrolled consumption of natural resources, and the protection of the environment. More recently, two important dimensions have been introduced – social and economics. Environmental and social elements are critical for companies to ensure that they observe the best interests of all the stakeholders in their community. From the business point of view, the economic element signifies that businesses should sustain adequate production capacity, employment and income for the welfare of the society while observing the financial performance of their investment. Companies in the tourism industry, particularly hotels, operate with so many difficulties that long-term viability is always a major consideration. Their financial performance is highly dependent on continuous customer demand and minimizing costs (Bader, 2005). As evident in the Mediterranean cases illustrated previously, tourism firms yield high returns from their sustainability investments. The positive financial outcomes of sustainability investments along with the social and environmental impacts explain why tourism firms invest heavily in these practices. Mediterranean countries have significantly benefited from their geographic location and attracted a large share from the world's tourism business. Hence, in order to retain their fair share in this business, they need to adhere to the very principles of sustainability not only to be environmentally and socially responsible, but also to retain the economic benefits both at the macro- and micro-levels.

References

Bader, E.E. (2005). Sustainable hotel business practices. *Journal of Retail & Leisure Property*, 5(1), pp. 70–77.

Bakos, G.C., and Soursos, M. (2002). Technical feasibility and economic viability of a grid-connected PV installation for low cost electricity production. *Energy and Buildings*, 34(7), pp. 753–758.

Beck, U. (1992). *Risk society: Towards a new modernity*. London: Sage.

Bonilla Priego, M.J. and Avilés Palacios, C. (2008). Analysis of environmental statements issued by EMAS-certified Spanish hotels. *Cornell Hospitality Quarterly*, 49(4), pp. 381–394.

Bramwell, B. and Lane, B. (1993). Sustainable tourism: An evolving global approach? *Journal of Sustainable Tourism*, 1(1), pp. 1–5.

Buckley, R. (2012). Sustainable tourism: Research and reality. *Annals of Tourism Research*, 39(2), pp. 528–546.

Butler, J. (2008). The compelling "hard case" for "green" hotel development. *Cornell Hospitality Quarterly*, 49(3), pp. 234–244.

Cater, E. (1993). Ecotourism in the third world: Problems for sustainable tourism development. *Tourism Management*, 14(2), pp. 85–90.

Chan, E.S.W. and Hawkins, R. (2010). Attitude towards EMSs in an international hotel: An exploratory case study. *International Journal of Hospitality Management*, 29(4), pp. 641–651.

Cyprus Sustainable Tourism Initiative (CSTI) (2013). *Water and energy saving in the Cyprus hotel industry*. Available at: http://csti-cyprus.org/?page_id=71

Dascalaki, E. and Balaras, C.A. (2004). XENIOS – A methodology for assessing refurbishment scenarios and the potential of application of RES and RUE in hotels. *Energy and Buildings*, 36(11), pp. 1091–1105.

Erdogan, N. and Baris, E. (2007). Environmental protection programs and conservation practices of hotels in Ankara, Turkey. *Tourism Management*, 28(2), pp. 604–614.

European Environment Agency (2017). *Greenhouse gas emissions from transport*. Available at: www.eea.europa.eu/downloads/28da20e34ff54fb7ae05a2eca8a9aad8/1508758152/transport-emissions-of-greenhouse-gases-10.pdf

European Union (2012). *Sustainable tourism in the Mediterranean*. Available at: https://cor.europa.eu/en/documentation/studies/Documents/sustainable-tourism-mediterranean/sustainable-tourism-mediterranean.pdf

Fosse, J., Tellier Julien, L., Manca, E., Santarossa, L. and Tambaktis, T. (2017). *Sustainable tourism in the Mediterranean: State of play and strategic directions*. Available at: http://planbleu.org/en/publications/sustainable-tourism-mediterranean-state-play-and-strategic-directions

GBSB (2017). *Sustainable transportation in Madrid & Barcelona: How will you get to school?* Available at: https://doi.org/www.global-business-school.org/announcements/sustainable-transportation-madrid-barcelona-how-will-get-school

Gunn, C.A. and Var, T. (2002). *Tourism planning*. New York: Taylor & Francis.

Hall, C.M. (2000). *Tourism planning. Policies, processes and relationships*. Harlow: Pearson.

Hall, C.M. and Jenkins, J.M. (1998). The policy dimensions of rural tourism and recreation. In: R.W. Butler, C.M. Hall and J. Jenkins, eds., *Tourism and recreation in rural areas*. Chichester: John Wiley & Sons, pp. 16–42.

Houdet, J. (2008). Integrating biodiversity into business strategies. In: *The biodiversity accountability framework*. Paris: FRB – Orée.

Hsieh, Y.C. (2012). Hotel companies' environmental policies and practices: A content analysis of their web pages. *International Journal of Contemporary Hospitality Management*, 24(1), pp. 97–121.

HW Energy (2018). *Biomass helps the hotel industry attract new visitors*. Available at: www.hwenergy.co.uk/biomass-helps-the-hotel-industry/

Inskeep, E. (1991). *Tourism planning: An integrated and sustainable development approach*. New York: Van Nostrand Reinhold.

Intelligent Energy Europe (2018). *Nearly zero energy hotels (neZEH)*. Available at: https://ec.europa.eu/energy/intelligent/projects/en/projects/nezeh

Kauppila, P., Saarinen, J. and Leinonen, R. (2009). Sustainable tourism planning and regional development in peripheries: A Nordic view. *Scandinavian Journal of Hospitality and Tourism*, 9(4), pp. 424–435.

King, A.A., Lenox, M.J. and Terlaak, A. (2005). The strategic use of decentralized institutions: Exploring certification with the ISO 14001 management standard. *Academy of Management Journal*, 48(6), pp. 1091–1106.

Kuhlman, T. and Farrington, J. (2010). What is sustainability? *Sustainability*, 2, pp. 3436–3448.

Mengi, A. and Algan, N. (2003). *Küresellesme ve yerellesme çaginda bölgesel sürdürülebilir gelişme AB ve Türkiye örneği*. Ankara: Siyasal Kitabevi, Çevre Dizisi.

Mensah, I. (2004). *Environmental management practices in US hotels*. Available at: www.hotel-online.com/News/PR2004_2nd/May04_EnvironmentalPractices.html

Michalena, E. (2008). Using renewable energy as a tool to achieve tourism sustainability in Mediterranean islands. *Études Caribéennes*, 11.

Mowforth, M. and Munt, I. (2016). *Tourism and sustainability. Development, globalisation and new tourism in the third world*. Oxon: Routledge.

O'Neill, S (2018). *How European hotels raise the sustainability bar*. Available at: www.greenhotelier.org/destinations/europe/how-european-hotels-raise-the-sustainability-bar/

Owen, E.R., Witt, S.F. and Gammon, S. (1993). Sustainable tourism development in Wales: From theory to practice. *Tourism Management*, pp. 463–474.

Patsouratis, V., Frangouli, Z. and Anastasopoulos, G. (2005). Competition in tourism among the Mediterranean countries. *Applied Economics*, 37(16), pp. 1865–1870.

Pereira, H.M., Leadley, P.W., Proenca, V., Alkemade, R. and Scharlemann, J.P.W. (2010). Scenarios for global biodiversity in the 21st century. *Science*, 330, pp. 1496–1501.

Prosser, R. (1994). Societal change and growth in alternative tourism. In: E. Carter and G. Lowman, eds., *Ecotourism, a sustainable option?* Chichester: John Wiley, pp. 89–107.

Roper, T. (2005). Small island states and the clean development mechanism (CDM). *Les Énergies Renouvelables Pour Un Tourisme Durable*, 287.

Sabban, M. (2013). *Report on sustainable tourism in the Mediterranean*. Available at: https://cor.europa.eu/en/activities/arlem/activities/meetings/Documents/sudev-report2012-tourism-en.pdf

Segarra Oña, M.D.V., Peiró Signes, A., and Verma, R. (2011). Environmental management certification and performance in the hospitality industry: A comparative analysis of ISO 14001 hotels in Spain. *Cornell Hospitality Quarterly*, 11(22), pp. 4–14.

Satta, A. (2004). Tourism in the Mediterranean: Processes and impacts on the coastal environment. In *Forum on integrated coastal management in the Mediterranean: Towards regional protocol. United Nations environment programme, Mediterranean action plan.* Cagliari: Priority Actions Programme Regional Activity Centre, pp. 59–73.

Schiller, P.L. and Kenworthy, J.R. (2017). *An introduction to sustainable transportation: Policy, planning and implementation.* New York: Routledge.

Sloan, P., Legrand, W. and Chen, J.S. (2009). *Sustainability in the hospitality industry.* Boston: Butterworth-Heinemann. Available at: www.sciencedirect.com/science/book/9780750679688

Styles, D., Schönberger, H. and Martos, J.L.G. (2013). Best environmental management practice in the tourism sector. In: *JRC scientific and policy report on best environmental management practice in the tourism sector.* Luxembourg: Publications Office of the European Union.

Swarbrooke, J. (1999). *Sustainable tourism management.* Oxon: Cabi.

Tsanis, I.K., Koutroulis, A.G., Daliakopoulos, I.N. and Jacob, D. (2011). Severe climate-induced water shortage and extremes in crete. *Climatic Change,* 106(4), pp. 667–677.

Tsoutsos, T., Tournaki, S., de Santaos, C.A. and Vercellotti, R. (2013). Nearly zero energy buildings application in Mediterranean hotels. *Enery Procedia,* 42, pp. 230–238.

United Nations (1997). *Agenda for development.* New York: United Nations.

UNWTO (2008). *Climate change and tourism. Responding to global challenges.* Available at: http://sdt.unwto.org/sites/all/files/docpdf/climate2008.pdf

Weaver, D. (2006). *Sustainable tourism.* Oxford: Elsevier Butterworth-Heinemann.

Williams, A.M. and Shaw, G. (1998). Introduction: Tourism and uneven economic development. In: A.M. Williams and G. Shaw, eds., *Tourism and economic development. European experiences,* 3rd ed. Chichester: John Wiley & Sons, pp. 1–16.

World Commission on Environment and Development (WCED) (1987). *Our common future.* Available at: www.un-documents.net/our-common-future.pdf

World Tourism Organization (2018). *Sustainable development of tourism.* Available at: http://sdt.unwto.org/content/about-us-5

3 Sustainability in gastronomy tourism

The Mediterranean region

Candide Çulhaoğlu Uludağ

Introduction

Gastronomy is the science-looking part of human culture and heritage. It teaches us to view food as a product of thousands of years of evolution and civilization and as a manifestation of a society's cultural, historical, ecological and economic conditions. As such, it is a quintessential part of tourism. While gastronomy tourism is a new field of study, it is a fundamental component of any touristic travel, be it inside one's region or beyond it. With thousands of years of food and cultural trade within the region and beyond, the Mediterranean is ideally placed for gastronomical tourism. Routes have been formed to accommodate these attractions and particularities and to help tourists experience different but interconnected cultures and traditions. While environmental sensitivities shall be taken under consideration and cannot be overlooked, gastronomical tourism can help promote – and thus preserve – old traditions and cultures and help bring about sustainable growth for industries and localities of the region.

The origins of gastronomy

Gastronomic tourism is the cultural heritage of the Mediterranean region. Gastronomy's etymology is Greek: *gastro* relating to the stomach and the whole digestive system beginning with the mouth, and *nomos* meaning laws that govern (Santich, 2004; Kivela and Crotts, 2006). It was first found in use by the Sicilian Greek Archestratus in his book titled "γαστρονομία" (gastronomy). Modern-day researcher Santich writes that in the fourth century BC, the enigmatic Archestratus traveled throughout the "Mediterranean area – thus establishing an early link between gastronomy and tourism – in order to discover what was best to eat and drink and where to find it. By recording his findings he offered guidance to everyone who came after him" (Santich, 2004). Perhaps his was the first travel guide for gastronomy tourists. After vanishing for some 15 centuries, the word gastronomy was revived in another part of the Mediterranean – France – by a lesser-known French poet, Joseph Berchoux, as the title of his poem, "*La Gastronomie*".

The notion and term "gastronomy" became a more clearly defined and established concept in the 19th century, and "Like any new social practice, gastronomy drew on a nexus of social, economic and cultural conditions. . . . All of these elements – the food, the people and places, the attitudes and ideas – came together in early 19th-century Paris" (Ferguson, 2000). The definitive publication *La Physiologie du Goût – The Physiology of Taste*, published in 1826 by the French lawyer and judge Brillat-Savarin, augmented this emerging concept of gastronomy in terms of both theory and practice with the goal to define it as a "science". Buford (2009) states that: "There is, manifestly, a science at work in cooking – chemistry rather than physiology; botany, maybe; physics, occasionally; and a kitchen is a laboratory where elements are tested, combined, subjected to extreme temperatures, and studied". In the same publication, Brillat-Savarin (2009) defines gastronomy:

> Gastronomy is the intelligent knowledge of whatever concerns man's nourishment. Gastronomy is part of:
>
> *Natural history*, by its classification of alimentary substances;
>
> *Physics*, because of the examination of the composition and quality of these substances;
>
> *Chemistry*, by the various analyses and catalyses to which it subjects them;
>
> *Cookery*, because of the art of adapting dishes and making them pleasant to the taste;
>
> *Business*, by the seeking out of methods of buying as cheaply as possible what is needed, and of selling most advantageously what can be produced for sale;
>
> Finally, *political economy*, because of the sources of revenue which gastronomy creates and the means of exchange which it establishes between nations.

Thus, Brillat-Savarin attempted to consolidate gastronomy with an interdisciplinary approach (Andrews, 2008). However, this type of approach proved too advanced for Brillat-Savarin's era only to re-emerge and be revisited by advocates, researchers and academics a century later and into the current millennium. As Scarpato (2000) points out, gastronomy remains "a field still without boundaries"; however, he then stresses that "research within an emerging gastronomy study's methodology should contain at least two commitments: (a) re-positioning gastronomy activities in the community, and (b) giving 'a cultural voice' to identities and discourses (gastronomy and sustainability, gastronomy and tourism) oppressed by dominant narratives". In the Mediterranean region, interest in a proactive, interdisciplinary and sustainable approach to gastronomy galvanized the "Slow Food" movement founded by Carlo Petrini in Italy in 1986. In 2004, Slow Food established the University of Gastronomic Sciences, where gastronomy is studied as a distinct science with "courses on food history, gastronomic tourism, sensory evaluation, the sociology of consumption and the geography of wine, amongst others" (Andrews, 2008).

Gastronomy tourism and the cultural heritage of the Mediterranean

Over the past 50 years, the Mediterranean diet has evolved from a healthy diet to the model of a diet that is sustainable (Dernini et al., 2016). When declaring the Mediterranean diet an Intangible Cultural Heritage of Humanity in 2010, UNESCO not only recognized the health and environmental benefits of the diet but also placed it at the center of the region's cultural heritage:

> The Mediterranean diet constitutes a set of skills, knowledge, practices and traditions ranging from the landscape to the table, including the crops, harvesting, fishing, conservation, processing, preparation and, particularly, consumption of food. The Mediterranean diet is characterized by a nutritional model that has remained constant over time and space, consisting mainly of olive oil, cereals, fresh or dried fruit and vegetables, a moderate amount of fish, dairy and meat, and many condiments and spices, all accompanied by wine or infusions, always respecting beliefs of each community. However, the Mediterranean diet (from the Greek *diaita*, or way of life) encompasses more than just food. It promotes social interaction, since communal meals are the cornerstone of social customs and festive events.
>
> (UNESCO, 2010)

The Mediterranean food culture is the gastronomic expression of the region: the vital connection between geography, tradition and culture. The vernacular is continuously defined, built-up and recreated by communities as generations adapt to changing geographical and ecological environments and to the events of history (conquering and being conquered) (Gamboni, Carimi and Migliorini, 2012). "Food plays a central role in social and cultural life in the Mediterranean area. It is deeply influenced by the evolution of traditional values towards post-modern values as well as by the globalized production system" (CIHEAM/FAO, 2015).

The Mediterranean diet is at the intersection of the numerous cuisines and customs of the distinct countries of the Mediterranean area. As food historian Massimo Montanari has written:

> Every culture, every tradition, every identity is a dynamic, unstable product of history, one born of complex phenomena of exchange, interaction, and contamination. Food models and practices are meeting points amongst diverse cultures, the fruit of man's travels, of commercial markets, techniques, and tastes from one part of the world to another.
>
> (Montanari, 2004)

The 2008 Food and Agriculture Organization Regional Conference for Europe report states:

> Many delegations highlighted the Mediterranean diet as rich in biodiversity and nutritionally healthy. The promotion of the Mediterranean diet could play

a beneficial role in the sustainable development of agriculture in the Mediterranean region. . . . [They also] remarked that the goal of increased global food production, including biofuels, should be balanced against the need to protect biodiversity, ecosystems, traditional foods and traditional agricultural practices.

(FAO, 2008)

The Mediterranean diet has the advantage of being incredibly healthy and sustainable. It is aptly suited to provide ample opportunities for gastronomy tourism. Research is ongoing and further needed, but studies such as Burlingame and Dernini's have concluded:

The Mediterranean diet provides opportunities for conserving diversity in the cultural knowledge of foods and diets, understanding indigenous or local food systems using a multicultural approach to sustainable diets.

(Burlingame and Dernini, 2011)

The Mediterranean diet has lower environmental impacts than the global-average diet. Tilman and Clark (2014) calculated that the Mediterranean diet "could reduce emissions from food production below those of the projected 2050 income-dependent diet, with per capita reductions being 30% as compared to the typical 2009 global-average diet".

In 2013, a team of six food science and human nutrition researchers in Rome compared contemporary food consumption patterns within Italy with the Mediterranean dietary model in terms of their respective sustainability. The results indicated that the Mediterranean diet has a 29% lower carbon footprint, a 17% lower water footprint and a 24% lower ecological footprint compared to the actual average diet of the Italian population (Germani et al., 2014).

Gastronomy tourism: socio-economic impact in the Mediterranean

The tourism industry has one of the highest growth rates of all the sectors in the global economy. In 2015, the Mediterranean region alone received more than 320 million tourists, a 100% increase in the number of visitors compared to 1995. The statistics relating to numbers of visitors and growth rates differ from country to country. While France, Spain, Italy and Greece have consistently hosted the most visitors, the growth rates in Greece and Spain growth have doubled in these countries since 1995. The most notable countries to gain popularity among tourists during this time period are Turkey, Albania and Croatia. As the numbers of international visitors to Turkey nearly quadrupled, Turkey has surpassed Greece for fourth place in the rankings of the most visited countries in the Mediterranean (MGI, 2017).

Since 1990, the southeastern Mediterranean region (consisting of Algeria, Egypt, Israel, Jordan, Lebanon, Libya, Morocco, Occupied Palestinian Territory, Syria, Tunisia and Turkey) has achieved the highest growth rate in international visitors for touristic purposes globally. Simultaneously, domestic tourism also rose considerably in the 11 countries despite significant destabilizing forces affecting personal and national security, energy costs and economic stability, among others (Lanquar, 2013).

The growth in tourism despite these setbacks is indicative of the importance of this sector for this region, and it has been predicted that tourism will continue growing (Lanquar, 2013; WTTC, 2015). However, Lanquar notes significant threats to this growth that need to be attended to, such as "the negative consequences of climate change, including more frequent natural disasters . . . local revolts due to food insecurity or local governance problems . . . budget cuts in education and tourism training as well as in tourism marketing".

Gastronomy tourism, with its potential to both support and enhance existing sustainable development, biodiversity, local economies, traditional agricultural practices and local identity, provides viable solutions to the aforementioned threats. As Richards (2002) highlights, tourism and food consumption are interdependent. Tourists and locals need to eat. "If their demands can be met from local resources this can provide an important boost to the local economy." Gastronomy tourism has the added advantage of reaching areas that are in need of economic improvement, as "local food networks may contribute to protecting existing jobs and creating employment by stimulating agrarian economies and favoring local farming communities and small-scale businesses, ultimately representing a tool for rural development area" (Rinaldi, 2017).

Rising food prices combined with food shortages, population growth and climate change over the past two decades have placed agriculture and agricultural production at the forefront of the international agenda. Sustainable solutions have been recognized as a priority to meet these challenges. Agricultural diversity is an extremely viable solution. As the conservation and agricultural biodiversity expert Frison and his colleagues state:

> There is a new recognition of the profound challenges faced in increasing production to meet the needs of a growing population under changing climates and the need to do so in a sustainable manner. From this perspective, agricultural biodiversity clearly has an increasingly important role to play.
>
> (Frison, Cherfas and Hodgkin, 2011)

Research-based evidence is mounting in support of the positive impact that current developments in gastronomy have on local economies. Benefits cited include rising revenues, increasing levels of employment opportunities, economic diversity, innovation and feasibility (Feagan, 2007; Rose and Larsen 2013; WTTC, 2015).

Therefore, gastronomy tourism, through its support of sustainable local food production and retailers, can be seen as something of a silver bullet. It holds the key to reducing the threats of food shortages exacerbated by climate change, economic instability in rural areas through providing new markets to drive economic growth while minimizing the ecological footprint. In contrast, tourism planning that does not have a focus on gastronomy can lead to an increase in the threats to the region by relying on imported foods, weakening local agriculture and diminishing the economic advantage of tourism (Richards, 2002).

Gastronomy and sustainability: environmental and sociocultural perspectives

Hall and Sharples (2003) state that "food tourism is quite literally the consumption of the local and the consumption and production of place", and that gastronomy tourism can be seen as one of the cornerstones of sustainable development. Gastronomy tourism has the capability to strengthen seasonality, biodiversity, ecofriendliness, traditional and local food products, culture and identities. It interacts with all components of sustainable development.

Owing to the widespread international appeal of the Mediterranean diet, the Mediterranean region is uniquely placed to excel in the gastronomy tourism sector, reaping both economic and environmental benefits in the process. As mentioned above, in 2010 the local and global significance of the Mediterranean diet was recognized by UNESCO through its inclusion in the Representative List of Intangible Cultural Heritage of Humanity "to raise awareness at the local, national and international levels of the importance of the intangible cultural heritage". The recognition and preservation of intangible cultural heritage is considered by UNESCO as a key factor in guaranteeing sustainable development within a region.

However, the Mediterranean diet has become endangered throughout the region (Wasserman, 2009). Current data demonstrate a decrease in adherence to the Mediterranean diet in Northern, Southern and Eastern Mediterranean countries despite the evidenced health and ecological advantages of the Mediterranean diet (CIHEAM/FAO, 2015). "Paradoxically, just as the Mediterranean diet is becoming more popular in the world and increasingly recognized by the international scientific community, the Mediterranean populations are moving further and further away from this dietary model" (Lacirignola and Capone, 2009). Urbanization and "McDonaldization" (Ritzer, 1993) have heavily influenced the decline.

Globalization had a significant impact on the agricultural practices and lifestyle of the region. Food production has changed, leading to the promulgation of monocultural farming methods as opposed to traditional practices such as rotation farming, resulting in a reduction of biodiversity. The past knowledge and agricultural techniques that the Mediterranean diet is founded upon are becoming less widespread (González-Turmo, 2012). This has taken its toll on the natural environment and the livelihood of smallholder farmers who have suffered redundancy, are unable to survive economically and have been displaced (Padilla, Capone and Palma, 2012). The intercultural shifts caused by tourism and migration (particularly as a result of urbanization) have brought about changes in lifestyles, including a tendency for a more Western diet with higher proportions of meat and calorie-dense foods (Alexandratos, 2006, Padilla, 2008; Berry and DeGeest, 2012, Germani et al., 2014).

Referring to the decline of the Mediterranean diet and the environmental issues mentioned previously, Wasserman (2009) points out:

> The food and agriculture sector is central to efforts to improve public health today and protect and restore natural systems necessary to support good health in the future. The sector has a greater direct impact on land and water resources, employment, and economic activity than any other.

Furthermore, Mirela (2016) states that gastronomy tourism "can contribute to regional attractiveness; sustain the local environment and cultural heritage; and strengthen local identities and sense of community".

Geographical indications that signify agricultural products' place of origin and the qualities, characteristics or reputation of the product that are directly related to the geographic location in which they are produced support the sustainable development of location-specific agriculture, and therefore gastronomy tourism. The *Strengthening Sustainable Food Systems Through Geographical Indications* study published in 2018, conducted by the Food and Agriculture Organization of the United Nations and the European Bank for Reconstruction and Development (FAO/EBRD, 2018), has demonstrated that food products linked to their place of origin benefit rural areas economically and socially and promote sustainable development. The report found that geographical indications help consumers identify and value the special characteristic of local product, such as taste, color, texture and quality, for which they are prepared and willing to pay. Thus, geographical indications can provide essential economic support and incentive for sustainable local production. As Emmanuel Hidier, the Senior Economist in FAO's Investment Centre, emphasizes in the report, "They can be a pathway to sustainable development for rural communities by promoting quality products, strengthening value chains, and improving access to more remunerative markets."

The appeal of gastronomy to the tourist

At a surface level, gastronomy tourism fulfills the "need to educate tourists about what ingredients are available, what they are called in the local language and how they can be turned into tasty local dishes" (Swarbrooke, 1999). Furthermore, alongside offering "the pursuit and enjoyment of unique and memorable food and drink experiences, both far and near" (World Food Travel Association), gastronomy tourism also encompasses "visitation to primary and secondary food producers, food festivals, restaurants and specific locations for which food tasting and/or experiencing the attributes of specialist food production regions are the primary motivating factor for travel" (Hall and Mitchell, 2001).

Gastronomy tourism is the synergy of food and beverage with art, culture, and science while traveling/experiencing a different culture. It is a combination of cultural heritage and practices, agriculture and local history. However, only during the past 20 years has gastronomy tourism developed from its embryonic state into a significant and disciplined academic field (Scarpato, 2002; Hall and Sharples, 2003; Rinaldi, 2017). As such, gastronomy tourism offers fresh opportunities for important areas of research and policy-making in sustainability and economic research such as food production and consumption habits that have up until very recently been largely ignored (Guyomard et al., 2011).

Recommendations

For gastronomy tourism to play an active and effective role in supporting sustainable development in the Mediterranean (which, as we have shown, it in fact relies upon), gastronomy tourism as a sector itself needs to be sustainable. Three main areas for research and action to achieve this have been identified: (1) gastronomy studies academics, researchers and professionals need an active role in community policy-making, training of tourism management and business planning; (2) tourism and gastronomy researchers need to work in close collaboration, and "gastronomic tourism research should become a ground of active trans-disciplinary approaches involving other disciplines"; and (3) gastronomic tourist resort managers, marketeers and community planners need to be trained in the key ingredients, perspectives and approaches of gastronomy tourism (Scarpato, 2002).

Johns and Sthapit (2004) call for action at an even more grassroots level, recommending an organized approach that supports the cross-pollination of food production knowledge systems of traditional and contemporary agricultural practitioners. "Farmer-based research demonstrates the wealth of traditional knowledge and beliefs concerning the health, sensory, and culinary properties of local crop varieties." Similarly, Plieninger et al. (2018) call for the "strengthening of efforts to raise societal awareness of existing models and to enhance the capacity for fostering biocultural diversity in landscapes". It is well worth remembering that traditional farmers and rural communities are in fact already the experts in this field, holding a bank of knowledge that is the most valuable resource from which sustainable contemporary models of food production can evolve. The presentation and distribution of this knowledge, backed by scientific research, into the health, environmental, sociocultural and economic advantages of preserving traditional food biodiversity are of paramount importance.

Agricultural policies that support tried-and-tested initiatives with a landscape approach that foster the cooperation of multiple stakeholders and sectors to achieve sustainable futures such as those outlined by García-Martín et al. (2016) are recommended.

As discussed, food standards, labelling and certification such as geographic indications have been proven to reinforce links between quality products, localized production, biodiversity, consumer satisfaction and economic feasibility (Plieninger et al., 2018).

The inclusion of a focus on food produce and production in school curriculums highlighting the importance of food diversification and sustainability is also advised. A practical and engaging approach in which students grow their own crops to be used in their school meals can instill an appreciation and knowledge of local produce and farming techniques (Harmayani et al., 2017). For gastronomy tourism itself to be sustainable, it is imperative that we begin to nurture and inspire the next generation of practitioners.

Conclusion

The 21st century has finally caught up with Brillat-Savarin's vision for the recognition and establishment of gastronomy as an interdisciplinary science, and it could not be more timely. The need for viable solutions to the global ecology in crisis has never before been felt so urgently. The science of sustainable gastronomy is as integral to the field of ecology as it is to life itself. We eat in order to live, and throughout history, the ways in which we find and produce food have determined how we organize ourselves in communities, families and the relationships between people and their natural environment. It was also the main incentive for early migrations, explorations and travel, such as Archestratus in Ancient Greece, and remains a major reason for modern-day tourism. Gastronomy tourism is ideally placed, then, to leverage the fundamental appeal of good eating and to support the preservation and advancement of sustainable development.

References

Alexandratos, N. (2006). The Mediterranean diet in a world context. *Public Health Nutrition*, 9(1A), pp. 111–117.

Andrews, G. (2008). *The slow food story: Politics and pleasure*. London: Pluto Press.

Berry, E.M. and DeGeest, S. (2012). Tell me what you eat and I will tell you your sociotype: Coping with diabesity. *RMMJ*, 3(2), e0010.

Brillat-Savarin, J.A. (2009). *The physiology of taste. Or meditations on transcendental gastronomy*, transl. Kennedy Fisher, M.F. New York: Alfred A. Knopf, Inc.

Burlingame, B. and Dernini, S. (2011). Sustainable diets: The Mediterranean diet as an example. *Public Health Nutrition*, 14(12A), pp. 2285–2287. Available at: https://doi.org/10.1017/S1368980011002527

CIHEAM/FAO (2015). *Mediterranean food consumption patterns: Diet, environment, society, economy and health*. A White Paper Priority 5 of Feeding Knowledge Programme, Expo Milan 2015. CIHEAM-IAMB. Rome: Bari/FAO.

Dernini, S., Lairon, D., Berry, E., Brunori, G., Capone, R., Donini, L., et al. (2016). The Med Diet 4.0 framework: A multidimensional driver for revitalizing the Mediterranean diet as a sustainable diet model. DOI: 10.1079/9781786392848.0187.

FAO/EBRD (2018). *Strengthening sustainable food systems through geographical indications: An analysis of economic impacts*. Rome: FAO. Available at: www.fao.org/3/I8737EN/i8737en.pdf

Food and Agriculture Organization (2008). *Twenty-sixth FAO regional conference for Europe*. Rome: FAO.

Feagan, R. (2007). The place of food: Mapping out the 'local' in local food systems. *Progress in Human Geography*, 31(1), pp. 23–42.

Ferguson, P.P. (2000). Is Paris France? *The French Review*, 73(6), pp. 1052–1064.

Frison, E., Cherfas, J. and Hodgkin, T. (2011). Agricultural biodiversity is essential for a sustainable improvement in food and nutrition security. *Sustainability*, 3, pp. 238–253.

Gamboni, M., Carimi, F. and Migliorini, P. (2012). Mediterranean diet: An integrated view. In: B. Burlingame and S. Dernini, eds., *Sustainable diets and biodiversity: Directions and solutions for policy, research and action*. Rome: FAO, pp. 262–273.

García-Martín, M., Bieling, C., Hart, A. and Plieninger, T. (2016). Integrated landscape initiatives in Europe: Multi-sector collaboration in multi-functional landscapes. *Land Use Policy*, 58, pp. 43–53. Available at: http://dx.doi.org/10.1016/j.landusepol.2016.07.001.

Germani, A., Vitiello, V., Giusti, A.M., Pinto, A., Donini, L.M. and del Balzo, V. (2014). Environmental and economic sustainability of the Mediterranean diet. *International Journal of Food Sciences and Nutrition*, 65, pp. 1–5.

González, Turmo, I. (2012). The Mediterranean diet: Consumption, cuisine and food habits. *Mediterra*, pp. 115–132. Paris: CIHEAM – Sciences Po Les Presses.

Guyomard, H., Darcy-Vrillon, B., Esnouf, C., Marin, M., Momot, A., Russel, M. and Guillou, M. (2011). Eating patterns and food systems: critical knowledge requirements for policy design and implementation, INRA. Document prepared for the Commission on Sustainable Agriculture and Climate Change.

Hall, C.M. and Mitchell, R. (2001). Wine and food tourism in Douglas. In: N. Douglas, N. Douglas and R. Derrett, eds., *Special interest tourism: Context and cases*. John Wiley and Sons, Brisbane, pp. 307–329.

Hall, C.M. and Sharples, L. (2003). The consumption of experiences or the experience of consumption? An introduction to the tourism of taste. In: C.M. Hall, L. Sharples, R. Mitchell, N. Macionis and B. Cambourne, eds., *Food tourism around the world: Development, management and markets*. London: Butterworth-Heinemann, pp. 1–24.

Harmayani, E., Lestari, L.A., Sari, P.M. and Gardjito, M. (2017). Local food diversification and its (sustainability) challenges. In: R. Bhat, ed., *Sustainability challenges in the agrofood sector*. DOI: 10.1002/9781119072737.ch6.

Johns, T. and Sthapit, B.R. (2004). Biocultural diversity in the sustainability of developing-country food systems. *Food and Nutrition Bulletin*, 25(2), pp. 143–155. Available at: https://doi.org/10.1177/156482650402500207 [Accessed 14 Mar. 2019].

Kivela, J. and Crotts, J.C. (2006). Tourism and gastronomy: Gastronomy's influence on how tourists experience a destination. *Journal of Hospitality and Tourism Research*, 30, pp. 354–377.

Lacirignola, C. and Capone, R. (2009). Mediterranean diet: Territorial identity and food safety. *New Medit*, 4, pp. 2–3.

Lanquar, R. (2013). Tourism in the Mediterranean: Scenarios up to 2030, MEDPRO Report No. 1, Brussels: CEPS, July 2011 (revised and updated May 2013).

Mediterranean Growth Initiative (2017). *Tourism in the Mediterranean*. Available at: www.mgi.online/content/2017/8/4/tourism-in-the-mediterranean [Accessed 17 Mar. 2019].

Mirela, C.S. (2016). Agrotourism and gastronomic tourism, parts of sustainable tourism. *Journal of Horticulture, Forestry and Biotechnology*, 20(3), pp. 106–109.

Montanari, M. (2004). *Food is culture*, transl. Sonnenfeld, A. New York: Columbia University Press.

Padilla, M. (2008). Dietary patterns and trends in consumption. In: B. Hervieu, ed., *Mediterra 2008: The future of agriculture and food in Mediterranean countries*. Paris: CIHEAM – Presses de Sciences Po, pp. 149–170.

Padilla, M., Capone, R. and Palma, G. (2012). Sustainability of the food chain from field to plate: Case of the Mediterranean diet. In: *Sustainable diets and biodiversity: United against hunger*. Rome: FAO/Biodiversity International, pp. 230–241.

Plieninger, T., Kohsaka, R., Bieling, C., Hashimoto, S., Kamiyama, C., Kizos, T., et al. (2018). Fostering biocultural diversity in landscapes through place-based food networks: a "solution scan" of European and Japanese models. *Sustain Sci*, 13, pp. 219–233.

Richards, G. (2002). Gastronomy: An essential ingredient in tourism production and consumption? In: A. Hjalager and G. Richards, eds., *Tourism and gastronomy*. London: Routledge, pp. 3–20.

Rinaldi, C. (2017). Food and gastronomy for sustainable place development: A multidisciplinary analysis of different theoretical approaches. *Sustainability*, 9, 1748.

Ritzer, G. (1993). *The McDonaldization of society*. Thousand Oaks: Pine Forge Press.

Rose, N. and Larsen, K. (2013). *Economic benefits of 'creative food economies: Evidence, case studies and actions for Southern Melbourne*. Brisbane: Victorian EcoInnovation Laboratory, University of Melbourne, and Food Connect Foundation.

Santich, B. (2004). The study of gastronomy and its relevance to hospitality education and training. *International Journal of Hospitality Management*, 23(1), pp. 15–24.

Scarpato, R. (2000). New global cuisine: The perspective of postmodern gastronomy studies, unpublished MA thesis. Melbourne: RMIT University.

Scarpato, R. (2002). Gastronomy as a tourist product: The perspective of gastronomy studies. In: A. Hjalager and G. Richards, eds., *Tourism and gastronomy*. London: Routledge, pp. 51–70.

Swarbrooke, J. (1999). *Sustainable tourism management*. Wallingford: CAB International.

Tilman, D. and Clark, M. (2014). Global diets link environmental sustainability and human health. *Nature*, 515, pp. 518–522.

UNESCO (2010). *Representative list of the intangible cultural heritage of humanity*. Paris: UNESCO.

Wasserman, A. (2009). Recipe for a better tomorrow: A food industry perspective on sustainability and our food system. *Journal of Hunger & Environmental Nutrition*, 4, pp. 446–453. DOI: 10.1080/19320240903329063.

World Travel and Tourism Council (2015). *Travel & tourism economic impact 2015*. Available at: https://zh.wttc.org/-/media/files/reports/economic-impact-research/regional-2015/mediterranean2015.pdf [Accessed 13 Mar. 2019].

4   Social sustainability and innovations in tourism

Cases from Slovenia

Dejan Krizaj and Vinod Sasidharan

Introduction

This chapter addresses social sustainability and its links to tourism innovation, tourism experience and the ownership of certain parts of tourism systems and processes. The EDIT model (Experiences through Design, Innovation and Touchpoints), developed initially as a tourism and hospitality development framework (Zach and Krizaj, 2017), was utilized to propose a new model, S-EDIT – Sustainable Experiences through Design, Innovation and Touchpoints – incorporating the specifics of social sustainability perspectives pertaining to tourism dynamics and gains. Previous EDIT research insights were used and revisited based on the study by Sasidharan and Krizaj (2018), focusing on several nationally recognized best sustainable and innovative tourism cases in Slovenia, followed by the identification of tourism-related social sustainability gaps in Slovenia, the most northern country touching the Mediterranean region. In addition, other cases were used to identify social sustainability-related tourism innovations emerging globally and to formulate suggestions on how to start bridging the gap with the help of the revised S-EDIT design framework.

Theory

The theoretical and methodological starting point of this chapter is the EDIT model (Figure 4.1), developed by Zach and Krizaj (2017). Their aim was a holistic approach to introducing tourism innovations by focusing on the characteristics of the tourist perception of new offered experiences. The first of the axes of the proposed model strolls through touchpoints. The touchpoints present steps that tourists make on their customer journeys that tourist providers should be aware and take care of. In the second axis, all possible categories of innovations, which can be introduced by tourism providers to develop further and increase the attractiveness of their offerings, are arranged. The third axis focuses on design elements in the form of approaches that providers can try to make the tourist experience (of each of the innovations in each of the touchpoints) to ensure the comfort and engagement of tourists to the best possible extent.

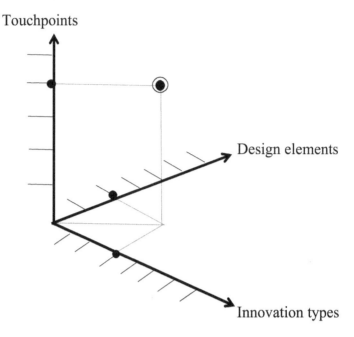

Touchpoints

Design elements

Innovation types

Figure 4.1 EDIT model

The EDIT model was later utilized in general manufacturing development processes (Brehm, Krizaj and Pohjola, 2017) and tested for experience analysis and redesign of awarded tourism innovations (Stare and Krizaj, 2018). In this chapter, the EDIT model is adapted for the study of social sustainability and innovations in tourism. Firstly, experiences and related touchpoints are analyzed beyond the sole perspective of a tourism provider. This is followed by an overview of innovations and how they affect the entire social system in which a tourist experience is offered. Instead of the third design axis, which represents a focus on designing only the tourist's comfort, the last part of the theoretical section focuses on the foundations and examples of social sustainability and thus the well-being of the whole business and local communities that are part of human society and tourism systems at large. In the methodological section, the upgrade of all three S-EDIT axes is summed up with the help of theoretical starting points and reflections on how to integrate more of the social sustainability dimensions into the development of tourism innovations.

Customer *experience*, one of the driving forces (Kandampully, Zhang and Jaakkola, 2017; Mahrous and Hassan, 2017; Rajaobelina, 2018) in tourism, has become the mantra of most economic sectors (Jain, Aagja and Bagdare, 2017; Jaiswal, 2017). With the increasing digitization of our lives and the simultaneous rise of the service industry, Service-Dominant Logic (SDL) is entering the many spheres of the economy (Vargo and Lusch, 2017). SDL has intensively sparked the awareness of customer experience and thus has helped in making the customer-focus an everyday and ubiquitous business orientation (Wu et al., 2014; Pires, Dean and Rehman, 2015). Lemon and Verhoef (2016) have validated the significance of customer focus but also emphasize that the history of customer experience and its importance is, imaginably, more complex.

Firstly, one of the researchers who focused primarily on customer experience, almost 20 years ago, is Schmitt (1999) with the book *Experiential Marketing: How to Get Customers to Sense, Feel, Think, Act, and Relate to Your Company and Brands*. This area was also significantly influenced by the popular experience economy authors Pine and Gilmore (1999). Secondly, in their work, Lemon and Verhoef (2016) mention a long-lasting, 50-year process which has enabled today's in-depth understanding of customer experience. For each decade from 1960 until 2010, they had marked the main areas that, today, can serve as a theoretical foundation of customer experience: customer buying behavior, customer satisfaction and loyalty, service quality, relationship marketing, customer relationship management, customer centricity and customer focus; and customer engagement. And thirdly, based on the review of diverse and plentiful customer-related studies over the past five decades, it became apparent that the focus of global business and its metrics was primarily on customer's value creation for firms, and not on value creation for customers (Kumar and Reinartz, 2016; Lemon and Verhoef, 2016).

At this point, a causality dilemma could continue regarding what triggered a contextual and not just a marketing-motivated shift towards the customer. Lemon and Verhoef (2016) recap the general belief that technological development waves are the source of the complex development of the global business environment and its layers in which we live; surrounded by media, tools and services that a few decades ago existed only in theory and science-fiction movies. All of this led to an explosion of opportunities for the creation and consumption of new types of experiences (Mahrous and Hassan, 2017) and new connections between providers and consumers of products and services (Melián-González and Bulchand-Gidumal, 2017). From the consumer or customer perspective, Lemon and Verhoef (2016, p. 74) called the customer experience a "multidimensional construct focusing on customer's cognitive, emotional, behavioral, sensorial and social responses to the company's offerings during the customer's entire purchase journey". A single actual or possible connection between the provider and the customer in this multidimensional construct is called a *touchpoint* (Schmitt, 2003). Lemon and Verhoef (2016) suggest the grouping of diverse touchpoints into the four main categories, based on their owner: firm,[1] partner, customer or social/external/independent:

The *"firm"* ownership category includes all marketing elements, carriers and activities that are owned by a firm offering a product or service. In addition to marketing, firm-owned touchpoints include the following (selling-chain-related) activities and attributes: the article itself, its price, delivery method, sales, customer service, etc. The *"partner"* type of touchpoints covers those points that, besides the firm, are owned by the firm's partners and subcontractors in the fields of production, marketing, sales, distribution, etc. The *"customer"* is the owner of touchpoints, on which the firm or its partners do not have direct influence. These are, for example, the customer's wishes, which he/she compares with the characteristics of a firm's product or service. Particularly important are the contact points in which the customer decides what he/she will do with the purchased goods. For instance, one can find a plethora of online images and videos, in which customers interpret to other customers how they consume, enhance, maintain or repair purchased goods.

Apart from the firm, partner and customer categories, the fourth, a very important category for this chapter's topic, represents "*social/external/independent*" touchpoints. Suggesting its complex nature with the category's triple designation, Lemon and Verhoef (2016) use this term to include the role of *others* in the customer experience system. The usual three players in this system (firm, partners, customer) are covered in the previous three categories of touchpoints, but each system is also part of its outer environment in which it is located. From a marketing point of view, the term "earned media" could be used for this outer category (Lemon and Verhoef, 2016; Chang, Chou and Wu, 2017). From the touchpoints point of view, the fourth category includes environmental impacts beyond the first three touchpoint categories that can positively or negatively affect: (a) the purchasing decision, (b) the experience itself and (c) the customer's post-interpretation of the consumed experience. Case (a) includes trend setters, opinion makers and others who have a potential pre-purchasing impact on the observed customer and are not controlled by the firm and its partners. These persons may be physically or virtually present during the client's purchasing decision, or their independent opinions are available in different media. Case (b) relates to fellow customers who might be present during the consumption of the purchased goods (fellow travelers, or restaurant guests and similar), and the environment in which the experience takes place (for instance, natural and cultural artifacts, and local community at the tourist destination). In case (c), the actual decision of the client, whether the experience was satisfactory, is again post-influenced by the opinions of other people in their physical or virtual surroundings. If the opinion of the rest of the people is predominantly negative or positive, this presents an additional factor influencing the reflection on the actual quality of the experienced, depending on the individual's susceptibility to external influences.

This chapter and the social sustainability S-EDIT model proposal are based on the same structure of innovation categories as used by Zach and Krizaj (2017) in their first introduction of the model. For the suggested categories, Zach and Krizaj combined the categories' definitions from two well-established sources (Jacob et al., 2003; Hjalager, 2010). They are explained in the Zach and Krizaj (2017) paper and summarized in Table 4.1. The categories are used in the following paragraphs, identifying the innovations' potential to appear in the previously presented touchpoint categories: firm, partner, customer, and social/external/independent.

Product innovations are the most visible and tangible innovation touchpoints of the customer experience and are owned by the firm and eventual partners if the product is co-developed. Customers become more or less justified (depending on the firm's disclaimers) owners of the product with the purchasing act and have control over the interaction with it. The customer is in similarly intensive contact

Table 4.1 Tourism innovation categories

Category	Definition
Product innovation	Tangible artifacts consumers can immediately observe and identify as new.
Service innovation	Intangible artifacts consumers can immediately observe and identify as new.
Process innovation	Internal operational procedures (mostly) aimed at efficiency and effectiveness.
Management innovation	Mechanisms to recruit, manage and retain human resources (paid and volunteer).
Marketing innovation	Ways to communicate and build relationships with customers.
Market innovation	Entering new markets (geography and segments) and at the destination level entrance of new business types.
Institutional innovation	Changes to organizational structure, habits and traditions in the marketplace.

Source: Zach and Krizaj (2017)

with *service* innovations, as he/she is with product innovations. The difference is that the service is intangible and perishable, which means that only memories, emotions and possible recordings remain with the customer after the experience.

Process innovations are usually not exposed to the user, as they focus on the firm's internal efficiency and effectiveness. The fact stays, though, that through process innovations, the firm still directly or indirectly influences its surroundings. The customer may not directly see this impact (unless it is too obvious or extreme, as for instance in the case of a spillage of hazardous chemicals), but process innovations are very likely to affect the environment in which the company operates. While the first three innovation categories are mostly related to firm-, partner- and customer-owned touchpoints, process innovations might positively or negatively affect the fourth "social/external/independent" category of touchpoints.

Management innovations affect employees. People can commute to work from other, distant places, but in most cases, the company also employs the local workforce. Both groups of employees can be affected by management changes, thereby simultaneously affecting the way employees might (in)directly show their agreement or disagreement with the changes towards the staff, and how the local community, linked with the local employees, responds to such changes in the firm.

Usually, *marketing* innovations are the most recognizable changes in the existing set of touchpoints, related to the firm's global and local communication with potential buyers, customers, partners and the local community. Those are the innovations one usually thinks of when talking about improving business-to-customer communication. Although, as presented, other innovation categories indicate many other situations where the firm can be in (in)direct contact with the subjects and objects outside the firm's walls.

Market innovations relate to changing the customer segments with which the firm communicates and who its goods may attract. During this process, the firm's touchpoints are likely to proliferate among the new customer segments. At the same time, a firm might induce the arrival of new types of customers to a local environment, in the cases of a brick-and-mortar type of firm, a tourist tour to a specific area, etc. This could again influence the relationship between the firm and the community, the latter responding positively or negatively to the change.

Institutional innovations – the seventh, and last, innovation category studied in this chapter – have a very important impact on broader systems, part of which is the firm that introduces such innovations. These can include novel partnership approaches, new business models and new habits and traditions within existing institutions and their networks. Accordingly, these changes relate to introduction, diffusion and establishment of new or revamped institutions into local and global communities being affected by the change, bringing the debate to the chapter's primary focus: social sustainability innovations.

Social sustainability represents one of the three pillars of the ubiquitous sustainable "Triple Bottom Line" concept by which societies try to maintain an appropriate level of human development that fosters economic growth while simultaneously ensuring social inclusion of all segments of human society and minimal impact on the environment in which the development takes place. Colantonio and Dixon (2011) define critical social sustainability themes based on analysis of different definitions, which they claim to be changing with new upcoming generations. In their view, traditional social sustainability themes were related to basic needs such as housing, environmental health, education, equity, human rights, gender issues, poverty and social justice. With an ever-changing society, Colantoni and Dixon (2011) summarize the following contemporary topic replacements to this list: demographic change, social mixing, identity, sense of place and culture, empowerment, health, safety, social capital, well-being and happiness.

According to the authors, out of the identified themes, the fundamental principles are hidden in equity, inclusion, adaptability and security. The principal activities through which we can then evaluate social sustainability achievements are related to essential human needs: living, working, sense of place, playing, engaging, learning and moving (ibid.). Several listed needs are closely related to tourist activities, in which the social sustainability concept enters primarily through social entrepreneurship, where the latter is still yet emerging in tourism and is not, however, part of the established offerings (Lange and Dodds, 2017). For tourism, taking place in a specific geographical framework, as well as for a general social cause (Hervani, Sarkis and Helms, 2017), the primary development interest should lay in the communities that would like to remain sustainable on their own, and ought to be soberly influenced by external development endeavors in a similar sustainable manner. According to the EU Ministerial Informal on Sustainable Communities Policy definition, sustainable communities are areas that satisfy the diverse needs of current and future residents and contribute to a high quality of life. Such communities are active, inclusive, safe, well run, environmentally sensitive, well designed and built, well connected, thriving, well served and fair for everyone (ODPM, 2006).

In 2015, the United Nations Foundation defined *17 global goals* presented at https://sustainabledevelopment.un.org/sdgs. Through the 17 goals, the UN announced steps by 2030, with which they want to end poverty, promote prosperity and well-being for all, and protect the planet. In a straightforward way, objectives drive the key activities needed to achieve sustainable development at all levels. The UN's sustainable development goals (UN SDGs) are:

GOAL 1: No Poverty
GOAL 2: Zero Hunger
GOAL 3: Good Health and Well-being
GOAL 4: Quality Education
GOAL 5: Gender Equality
GOAL 6: Clean Water and Sanitation
GOAL 7: Affordable and Clean Energy
GOAL 8: Decent Work and Economic Growth
GOAL 9: Industry, Innovation and Infrastructure
GOAL 10: Reduced Inequality
GOAL 11: Sustainable Cities and Communities
GOAL 12: Responsible Consumption and Production
GOAL 13: Climate Action
GOAL 14: Life Below Water
GOAL 15: Life on Land
GOAL 16: Peace and Justice Strong Institutions
GOAL 17: Partnerships to Achieve the Goals

If the objectives of the UN SDGs are to be met, they could bring significant global benefits to tourism and vice versa, where social sustainability (Lange and Dodds, 2017) provides early measurable results (Wang, Xu and Chen, 2018) and tourism innovation implications (Horng et al., 2017). For this purpose, the previous section presented the opportunities that the S-EDIT model's combination of the proposed perspectives can bring in the area of social sustainability and innovation in tourism. In the later research section, examples of how tourism providers in Slovenia can look for opportunities for the next social sustainability development steps will be presented. Before looking at concrete tourism examples, we examine examples of *global good practices* related to tourism and social sustainability.

In the first case, an established US meat producer, Greenfield Natural Meat Co., has introduced an initiative that seems counterproductive at first sight. Through the Meatless Monday[2] initiative, the company warns that meat production has a negative impact on the environment and that everyone can help with this issue by an appropriate change of habits. It suggests that customers do not buy meat on one day of the week, and instead purchase high-quality meat that has been cultivated sustainably on the other days. Every Monday, all pictures of items this meat producer sells online are hidden, and the Meatless Monday initiative logo and messages are shown instead. Another meat-related case also comes from the USA. The owner of the smaller chain of Federal Donuts restaurants, for whom one of the best sellers is fried chicken, decided to use all chicken trimmings in a unique social-oriented project. Chicken residues are the main ingredient of soups sold by the newly established Rooster Soup restaurant.[3] In the next step of an elaborate business model, 100% of the profit generated by Rooster Soup is donated to a local community that takes care of the welfare of the poor in Philadelphia (health, quality dining, social events).

The following two examples come from Spain and Japan. The Spanish project "Robin Hood restaurant"[4] offers breakfasts and lunches at regular rates in Madrid. In the evening, the restaurant closes its doors to paying customers and serves dinner for free to homeless people. The food is of the same quality as it was during the day, with the same dining utensils and crystalline glasses, in the same atmosphere. Japanese Mirai Shokudo[5] from Tokyo has a slightly different social approach. Customers can help with work at the restaurant and get a free meal for 50 minutes of their help; or get a free meal ticket instead that can be left in the restaurant for anyone else who needs it.

The last example is global and was initiated in the Netherlands. When the Good Hotel Group[6] opens new hotels, they invite long-term unemployed locals, regardless of their past experience, to attend free courses, with the objective of helping them build a new career in the Good Hotel or with other local accommodation providers. In addition to the aforementioned vocational education, the profits generated by Good Hotels at different locations are invested in other local initiatives that promote education of children and the involvement of local entrepreneurs and artisans in the tourist offering associated with Good Hotels and the surrounding area.

Methodology

The method presented in this section relies on the current insights into the introduction of tourism innovations through the prism of the EDIT model, which was originally focused on tourists' touchpoints, possible new innovations and design aspects for enhancing the tourist experience during tourists' journeys. In the theoretical part of this chapter, additional views on touchpoints were presented, which are still designated according to the steps taken by the customer during the journey. Since this chapter deals with social sustainability innovations, these new views refer to a broader design paradigm. In the original EDIT model, the design aspect focuses on the tourist's experience and comfort. From the social sustainability point of view, the focus of comfort now extends to the entire human ecosystem. This S-EDIT upgrade thus sends a message that both employees and the local community (and their experience with existing and new tourism solutions) should be more sincerely involved in finding suitable, fair and more authentic design solutions.

Therefore, in the previous section, touchpoints were also analyzed from the ownership perspective, which, whether one wants it or not, exceeds far further from the sole tourism provider's domain. It is true that through the tourism provider's delegated touchpoints, the tourist is the one who moves, decides, enjoys, experiences, evaluates and shares. However, as it was shown, the tourism provider cannot solely own or be responsible for the whole set. The offered tourist experience is placed in a certain living and non-living environment, the process is carried out by employees and external partners and it is co-created by the tourists themselves, as well as by the local population.

In this first step of the social sustainability upgrade of the EDIT model, the design axis is simply replaced with the ownership category. So, when we are thinking about a customer journey through the touchpoints, we need to ask ourselves what and who is or might be influencing (or is influenced by) touchpoints at a particular stage in the journey. By designing touchpoints, the tourism provider affects the experiences of the tourist *and* the experiences of all others that are part of the social system in which the tourist process is carried out (and in which all the elements affect one another as in any live situation). Simply put, the sustainability behavior we are after is related to fair play, considering all others that are part of the destination, the region, the state, the continent and the world we are part of.

Therefore, an updated perception of the innovations that are included in one of the EDIT axes is also essential. We should be thinking not just about which types of innovation can be added to individual points of the customer journey, but also about how they will affect the tourist and its living and non-living surroundings; how all parts of the ecosystem will react to innovation, and whether or not they will additionally alter the touchpoints of the tourist experience. The UN's sustainability goals are the cornerstone of reflection on relevant social innovations and such impacts on tourism systems. The goals represent a straightforward record of the fundamental guidelines for the fair-play coexistence of the human species, and they are globally (relatively well) accepted as the general common language in the diverse range of cultures and specific personal, social, political and economic interests.

The adapted S-EDIT model for social sustainability innovations is presented in Figure 4.2. In this form, it is set as the basis for further reflections on the appropriate

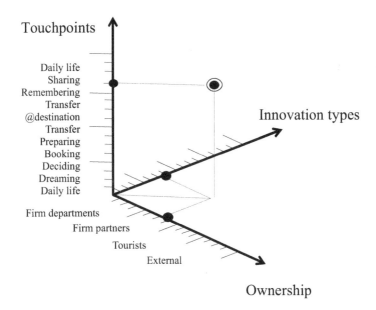

Figure 4.2 S-EDIT model, adapted for social sustainability innovations

systemic involvement of all stakeholders in the tourism process, and it emphasizes the key development areas that need to be taken into account. It represents the design framework, which can be used as an inspirational outline for the comprehensive design of new, and the improvement of existing, tourist experiences; or as the basis of a research model, in which one can analyze the relationships between the critical variables of social sustainability innovations in tourism.

In this chapter, the use of the S-EDIT model will be presented through the process of generating ideas for upgrading an existing sustainable tourism offering. The selected cases represent tourism providers and their products, which were previously discussed in a pilot study conducted in Slovenia in 2017 (Sasidharan and Krizaj, 2018), focusing on several nationally acknowledged, innovative and/ or sustainable tourism practices and their identified social sustainability gaps. In the next step, this chapter suggests how the owners of the analyzed tourism products could fill the identified gap with the help of suggested innovation examples following the basic social sustainability guidelines.

In their 2017 study, Sasidharan and Krizaj (2018) found that tourism providers were aware that in their sustainable efforts, they are primarily addressing the natural environment while missing more ideas, guidelines and opportunities for the sustainable inclusion of their social environment. The providers also agreed that the right approach towards integration of their microsocial environment could also help to increase the authenticity of their tourism offerings. Moreover, they were aware that if this integration was carried out at an elaborate level, their products could become even more boutique, even more differentiated and of even higher quality – and thus also suitable for more demanding guests, and generating higher financial and other returns for the interviewed providers and their surroundings.

For each of the visited and interviewed tourist providers in 2017, the next section contains a brief description and a proposal in which direction they could think about the social sustainability advancement of their products. None of the proposals guarantees actual success (which is not the added value of this chapter), but they try to illustrate how to use the suggested, advanced S-EDIT model. In the next step, tourism providers are encouraged to build their mental mockups themselves, so that they can – through advancement in the explained S-EDIT directions – find the best formulas for local collaborative improvement of the tourist offer and the well-being of all involved in their environments and processes.

Results and discussion

The analyzed providers in this study and in Sasidharan and Krizaj (2018) are briefly described before presenting each of the sample ideas for further development, generated through the S-EDIT design framework and supported by the relevant UN sustainable development goals.

The Green Gold beer fountain[7] was built in the Žalec city center in Slovenia by the municipality. The city is located in the center of the Slovenian hops region and was not a vital tourist center until the beer fountain was introduced in 2016, receiving many accolades, including the national tourism innovation award. The visitor flow and tourism offer have been intensively increasing since then, attaching to the beer fountain story, the brewing industry's heritage and sustainability efforts, acknowledged with the national Slovenia Green Destination certificate. In the case of Žalec, the applicable UN goal could be "Responsible consumption and production". Following the idea of the Meatless Monday concept, they could use or upgrade the #drinklessdrinkcraftbeer campaign, which has already made an appearance on social media. It is an initiative of lower consumption and an incline towards the higher quality of consumed foods or beverages. The action could first focus on beer (alcohol) and later diffuse to surrounding restaurants, which could, in the same way, promote the whole philosophy of smaller and better consumption of culinary ingredients and care for health. The approach is suitable for introducing marketing innovations throughout the entire customer journey, until the tourists' return and possible transformative effects on their daily routines (Anderson et al., 2013), while raising the brand reputation of the entire Žalec destination. Additional touchpoints, owned by the Municipality of Žalec and its partners, could thus be all forms of thoughtful consumption invitations and reminders, and even different forms of souvenir-style low consumption certificates for tourists. The customers would have the opportunity to share all this in their circles. And finally, the local population had their fears allayed that the beer fountain would encourage drunkenness.

Matjaž Pavlin is the owner of Matjaž Homestead in the village of Paha.[8] In the past, he has been the longtime owner and director of a popular travel agency in the nearby Novo mesto city, the urban center of the mostly rural Dolenjska region. The homestead benefits from a sizeable nearby spa center and is located in the hilly landscape along the Krka River. The tourism activities benefit also from the many vineyards and their historical, geographical and culinary character. Matjaž developed several new tourism products, four of which have received national tourism innovation awards. The relevant suggested example focuses on an already realized activity that could be even more intensively adopted in their tourist offer: For the needs of his tourist homestead and hobbies, Matjaž is heavily involved in restoring historical rural buildings and objects in them. Since this is his great passion, he also actively participated in the community's complete renovation of the local village church. Matjaž suggests to the guests who stay at his homestead to include a visit to the church in their free time, and he even occasionally takes them there as part of his guided tours. The idea for a new tourist product and segment is obvious: a whole day tour where his tourists would visit similar religious and farm buildings, which were renovated and maintained by other local communities in the same way. The applicable UN's goal is "Sustainable cities and communities". Other partnering communities would most likely be interested in taking co-ownership of such touchpoints and thus help Matjaž to promote these kind of tours to related niche segments. The two most important new potentials segments are religious tourists and cultural tourists who would like to see more of these projects, which they may also take part in their domestic environments.

Matjaž comes from a rural environment in which he is intensively involved, as shown previously, and in which he tries to preserve local heritage in his own way. He is also among the authors of a 10-year-old initiative to create a network of local wine cottages by using a scattered hotel model to stimulate the regional economy, which is used here as the second Matjaž example. We are not adding it again as an entirely new proposal – i.e. an unrealized idea – but it is an example of how Matjaž and his partners introduced the local sharing tourism ecosystem before the current sharing economy wave, and of its innovation and social sustainability characteristic. Firstly, this innovation has not yet reached a substantial expansion; i.e. it is maturing only now that sharing platforms have been widely accepted and global tourists are more intensively looking at such accommodation and experiences offered by the local communities. In addition to UN goal 11, sustainable cities and communities, this project also addresses UN goals 8 (decent work and economic growth) and 9 (infrastructure). Owners of wine cottages have different backgrounds. Some are wealthy owners of recently renovated luxury cottages. Others are the owners of basic, tool storage houses with a bed or two, which stood beside a small vineyard and which then-Yugoslav citizens were still able to afford during the socialist regime, despite a generally lower standard.[9] The reason for the low property prices thus comes from the fact that this rural region was traditionally not very developed; several cottages still preserve the spirit of the socialist times. In addition to financial issues, many cottages could not promptly join the wine cottage network initiative because they were not wholly (or at all) legalized during the time of socialism, which was one of the important supply-side reasons why the scattered hotel model innovation did not progress faster. So the network initiative also contributed (and still does) to urban benefits, i.e. systematic bottom-up development and promotion of the region. It thus represents an essential local institutional innovation that changes the customer journey and touchpoints for many visitors to the area: both those who actually sleep in such cottages, and those who, through global or local marketing activities, gain additional insight into the supply connection of the entire local community with a specific type of tourist experience and local cultural peculiarities.

The remaining three examples will be processed in a common category of proposals that, in the spirit of social sustainability, also address the UN's community goal no. 11, but each of the ideas involves another segment of the local community. Along with this, diverse external touchpoints segments are appropriated by the respective participating locals. Since all the remaining cases would also deal with new relationships between local business activities and local communities, all three projects could be the starting point for new institutional innovations and, eventually, new sustainable community business models, like the already-presented Matjaž's network.

The Spa Snovik[10] lies in the rural region between Kamnik and Vransko, close to the Kamnik-Savinja Alps. Indoor and outdoor thermal pools, saunas, massages, and a restaurant are offered, together with a four-star apartment complex with 370 beds. The surroundings offer hiking, biking, golf, organic farms and baroque churches. Spa Snovik is one of the country's sustainable tourism pioneers and the recipient of the EU Ecolabel and Slovenia Green Accommodation Certificate. In their offer, they have introduced the nationally well-known philosophy of German priest Sebastian Kneipp from the 19th century, including water therapy, recreation, healthy nutrition, and herbs. According to owners, Spa Snovik connects with the local community as much as possible through various projects and events. Combining Kneipp's legacy and local community activities, a new, potentially important segment of Spa Snovik could become seniors visiting the spa because of thermal water, traditional therapies and a special local context. Namely, the company could invite local seniors to group therapies with senior foreign guests, giving residents reduced or free treatment if they join others with a similar issue and developing "local-treatment-peers". This creates a new, possibly highly interactive set of touchpoints between tourists and locals, and possible new benefits for the owners and introducers of the new service and market innovation.

The Ortenia Apartments[11] are located in Podčetrtek, targeting guests from the nearby famous spa resort. Marketed as one of the first ecofriendly apartments in Slovenia, the complex relies mostly on elaborately designed apartments in the higher price/quality range, following sustainable construction principles. Kozjansko, Podčetrtek, is a primarily rural region and offers historical attractions and opportunities for recreation in the hilly surroundings. The apartments have received a Green Globe sustainability certificate and national Slovene Green Accommodation certificate. One of the main Ortenia Apartments customer segments are families with children. According to a similar principle, instead of seniors as in the case of Spa Snovik, in this case local community ambassadors could be children. Ortenia Apartments could organize workshops with local and guest youngsters oriented towards hospitality role-playing (guests' children would be playing guests, and local children would be playing hosts in their mentored workshops). Such workshops could help local children develop a hospitality mindset and culture. Although Ortenia Apartments are located in a rural, yet relatively more developed tourism environment (compared to other parts of the country), one of the Slovene features is that, due to the past socialist history, there is no strong private tourist tradition and culture. This comes in complete opposition, for example, with the Slovenian neighbor of Austria, where entrepreneurial hospitality culture has a long tradition (Kallmuenzer and Peters, 2018). The experience of both groups of children provides an important potential for opportunities for new touchpoints, not only between children during and after the visit, but also through the parents of both parties. Such service innovation could thus have a significant impact on the sense of association with the local community for tourists and further development of the region (UN goal 4, education) for the local community.

The Eco Camp Koren[12] lies at the Soča River, one of the five best-preserved natural waterways in the European Alps. The camp offers tent, camper and caravan sites, energy-efficient infrastructure and eco chalets, all built from natural materials. Usual tourists' activities include adrenaline activities in the sky, on the rapids of the river and natural climbing walls. Pristine and picturesque surroundings offer hiking and biking tours and fly fishing. The location is close to the restored front line from World War I and the renowned Kobarid World War I Museum. The camp has received EU Ecolabel and Slovenia Green Accommodation certificates. The last proposal for a social sustainability innovation lies at the intersection of Eco Camp Koren activities and local traditions which are in diverse forms globally renowned: voluntary firefighting brigades. In addition to relaxing in unspoiled nature, Eco Camp Koren promotes its own and its partners' offer of adrenaline experiences in nature. The combination of the adrenaline offer and social cause would be local firefighting exercises and workshops organized by the local fire brigade in the camp. Local firefighting associations in Slovenia still have exceptional social and historical significance; they organize summer parties annually and collect funds for their operation in various interactive ways. A mingling of a local community's segment with foreigners would, as in the Ortenia Apartments children's case, encourage the creation and ownership of new authentic external touchpoints; and, in addition to UN objective 11, also target the UN nature conservation objectives (13, 14 and 15) and the related firefighters' efforts at home and abroad.

Conclusion

The chapter introduced an adapted S-EDIT model for developing and accessing social sustainability innovations, suggested as a design framework for the holistic involvement of all tourism process stakeholders. Proposing the most crucial development areas that need to be considered, it can be used as an initial sketch for new and redesigned tourist experiences; in the case of this chapter, for generating ideas on how to upgrade an existing tourism offer. Several cases from Slovenian proposals were given as examples for tourism providers to consider, especially in relation to the social sustainability advancement of their products. Tourism providers are challenged to use the tool for finding feasible and fulfilling local collaborative endeavors focusing on the well-being of tourists and all others involved in their environments and tourism processes.

Researchers, on the other hand, have an additional approach when building a research model for analyzing the relationships between the critical variables of social sustainability and tourism innovations. As shown, many local peculiarities exist in this field, but also many global inspirations, encouraging thought from this perspective. Such perspectives might enrich the well-being of all involved, thus affecting the level of quality and context of the given tourism experiences.

Notes

1 Originally, "brand" was the term used. Here, it was changed to "firm" in order to align it with concepts used in other sections of the chapter.
2 Greenfield Natural Meat Co. (n.d.). Meatless Monday. Retrieved from http://green fieldmeat.com/us/meatless/
3 Krader, K. (2017, April 28). What If a Restaurant Gave Away All Its Money? Retrieved from www.bloomberg.com/news/articles/2017-04-28/michael-solomonv-s-rooster-soup-gives-its-money-away
4 Frayer, L. (2017, January 24). Spain's 'Robin Hood Restaurant' Charges the Rich and Feeds the Poor. Retrieved from www.npr.org/sections/thesalt/2017/01/24/511267616/spains-robin-hood-restaurant-charges-the-rich-and-feeds-the-poor

5 Mullin, J. (2018, March 10). Retrieved from Tokyo Restaurant Mirai Shokudo Lets Customers Eat for Free – But Diners Have to Do the Washing up in Return. www. thesun.co.uk/travel/5772016/tokyo-restaurant-mirai-shokudo-free-meal/
6 Karels, J. (2018, April 12). Doing-Good Hotel Brand. Retrieved from www.airth. global/depositview.aspx?dpid=8670&lng=en
7 ZKŠT Žalec (n.d.). Beer Fountain. Retrieved from www.beerfountain.eu
8 Marta Pavlin (n.d.). Matjaževa domačija. Retrieved from www.matjazeva-domacija.si
9 Until 1992, Slovenia was one of the six republics of the Socialist Federal Republic of Yugoslavia.
10 Terme Snovik (n.d.). Terme Snovik. Retrieved from http://terme-snovik.si
11 Ortenia (n.d.). Ortenia Apartments in Nature. Retrieved from http www.ortenia.com
12 Koren Lidija (n.d.). Kamp Koren. Retrieved from http www.kamp-koren.si

References

Anderson, L., Ostrom, A.L., Corus, C., Fisk, R.P., Gallan, A.S., Giraldo, M., . . . Williams, J.D. (2013). Transformative service research: An agenda for the future. *Journal of Business Research*, 66(8), pp. 1203–1210. Available at: https://doi.org/10.1016/j. jbusres.2012.08.013

Brehm, L., Krizaj, D. and Pohjola, P. (2017). Generalizing of the EDIT model for non-tourism domains. *Academica Turistica-Tourism and Innovation Journal*, 10(2), pp. 205–211.

Chang, H.L., Chou, Y.C., Wu, D.Y. and Wu, S.C. (2017). Will firm's marketing efforts on owned social media payoff? A quasi-experimental analysis of tourism products. *Decision Support Systems*. Available at: https://doi.org/10.1016/j.dss.2017.12.011

Colantonio, A. and Dixon, T. (2011). *Urban regeneration and social sustainability: Best practice from European cities*. Chichester: John Wiley & Sons.

de Lange, D. and Dodds, R. (2017). Increasing sustainable tourism through social entrepreneurship. *International Journal of Contemporary Hospitality Management*, 29(7), pp. 1977–2002. Available at: https://doi.org/10.1108/IJCHM-02-2016-0096

Hervani, A.A., Sarkis, J. and Helms, M.M. (2017). Environmental goods valuations for social sustainability: A conceptual framework. *Technological Forecasting and Social Change*, 125, pp. 137–153. Available at: https://doi.org/10.1016/j.techfore.2017.07.015

Hjalager, A.M. (2010). A review of innovation research in tourism. *Tourism Management*, 31(1), pp. 1–12. Available at: https://doi.org/10.1016/j.tourman.2009.08.012

Horng, J.S., Liu, C.H.S., Chou, S.F., Tsai, C.Y. and Hu, D.C. (2017). Developing a sustainable service innovation framework for the hospitality industry. *International Journal of Contemporary Hospitality Management*, 30(1), pp. 455–474. Available at: https://doi. org/10.1108/IJCHM-12-2015-0727

Jacob, M., Tintoré, J., Aguiló, E., Bravo, A. and Mulet, J. (2003). Innovation in the tourism sector: Results from a pilot study in the Balearic Islands. *Tourism Economics*, 9(3), pp. 279–295. Available at: https://doi.org/10.5367/000000003101298394

Jain, R., Aagja, J. and Bagdare, S. (2017). Customer experience – A review and research agenda. *Journal of Service Theory and Practice*, 27(3), pp. 642–662. Available at: https://doi.org/10.1108/JSTP-03-2015-0064

Jaiswal, V. (2017). Startup success mantra: Stay insanely focused on customer experience from day ONE | CustomerThink. Available at: http://customerthink.com/startup-success-mantra-stay-insanely-focused-on-customer-experience-from-day-one/ [Accessed 24 Jan. 2018].

Kallmuenzer, A. and Peters, M. (2018). Innovativeness and control mechanisms in tourism and hospitality family firms: A comparative study. *International Journal of Hospitality Management*, 70, pp. 66–74. Available at: https://doi.org/10.1016/j.ijhm.2017.10.022

Kandampully, J., Zhang, T. and Jaakkola, E. (2017). Customer experience management in hospitality: A literature synthesis, new understanding and research agenda. *International Journal of Contemporary Hospitality Management*, 30(1), pp. 21–56. Available at: https://doi.org/10.1108/IJCHM-10-2015-0549

Kumar, V. and Reinartz, W. (2016). Creating enduring customer value. *Journal of Marketing*, 80(6), pp. 36–68. Available at: https://doi.org/10.1509/jm.15.0414

Lemon, K.N. and Verhoef, P.C. (2016). Understanding customer experience throughout the customer journey. *Journal of Marketing*, 80(6), pp. 69–96. Available at: https://doi.org/10.1509/jm.15.0420

Mahrous, A.A. and Hassan, S.S. (2017). Achieving superior customer experience: An investigation of multichannel choices in the travel and tourism industry of an emerging market. *Journal of Travel Research*, 56(8), pp. 1049–1064. Available at: https://doi.org/10.1177/0047287516677166

Melián-González, S. and Bulchand-Gidumal, J. (2017). Information technology and front office employees' performance. *International Journal of Contemporary Hospitality Management*, 29(8), pp. 2159–2177. Available at: https://doi.org/10.1108/IJCHM-10-2015-0585

ODPM (2006). *UK presidency: EU ministerial informal on sustainable communities policy papers.* London: Office of the Deputy Prime Minister (OPDM).

Pine, B.J. and Gilmore, J.H. (1999). *The experience economy: Work is theater & every business a stage*, 1st ed. Boston, MA: Harvard Business Press.

Pires, G.D., Dean, A. and Rehman, M. (2015). Using service logic to redefine exchange in terms of customer and supplier participation. *Journal of Business Research*, 68(5), pp. 925–932. Available at: https://doi.org/10.1016/j.jbusres.2014.09.019

Rajaobelina, L. (2018). The impact of customer experience on relationship quality with travel agencies in a multichannel environment. *Journal of Travel Research*, 57(2), pp. 206–217. Available at: https://doi.org/10.1177/0047287516688565

Sasidharan, V. and Krizaj, D. (2018, in press). Tourism ecolabels and social sustainability: Challenges and innovations from a Slovene perspective. *Academica Turistica-Tourism and Innovation Journal*, 11(1), pp. 19–29. Available at: https://doi.org/10.26493/2335-4194.11.

Schmitt, B.H. (1999). *Experiential marketing: How to get customers to sense, feel, think, act, and relate to your company and brands.* New York: Free Press.

Schmitt, B.H. (2003). *Customer experience management: A revolutionary approach to connecting with your customers*, 1st ed. New York: Wiley.

Stare, M. and Krizaj, D. (2018, in press). Crossing the frontiers between touch points, innovation and experience design in tourism. In: A. Scupola and L. Fuglsang, eds., *Integrating service, innovation and experience research.* Cheltenham, UK: Edward Elgar Publishing, pp. 81–106.

Vargo, S.L. and Lusch, R.F. (2017). Service-dominant logic 2025. *International Journal of Research in Marketing*, 34(1), pp. 46–67. Available at: https://doi.org/10.1016/j.ijresmar.2016.11.001

Wang, C., Xu, H., Li, G. and Chen, J.L. (2018, in press). Community social responsibility and the performance of small tourism enterprises: Moderating effects of entrepreneurs' demographics. *International Journal of Tourism Research*, 0(0). Available at: https://doi.org/10.1002/jtr.2216

Wu, P.L., Yeh, S.S., Huan, T.C. and Woodside, A.G. (2014). Applying complexity theory to deepen service dominant logic: Configural analysis of customer experience-and-outcome assessments of professional services for personal transformations. *Journal of Business Research*, 67(8), pp. 1647–1670. Available at: https://doi.org/10.1016/j.jbusres.2014.03.012

Zach, F.J. and Krizaj, D. (2017). Experiences through design and innovation along touch points. In: D.R. Fesenmaier and F. Zhen, eds., *Design science in tourism*. Basel, Switzerland: Springer, pp. 215–232.

5 Social entrepreneurship and ethical issues

Examples from the Mediterranean

Gaye Acikdilli and Christopher Ziemnowicz

This chapter focuses on social entrepreneurship (SE) and their ethical functioning within the tourism and hospitality sector around the Mediterranean Basin. It begins with conceptual frameworks to identify similarities and differences that underpin SE and traditional profit-driven firms. There are distinct stances among the nations along the Mediterranean. This includes differing definitions of SEs, their origin, and suitable fields of operation. There are special considerations in the types of business models depending if the home nation of the SE is part of the European Union or not a member country. This chapter reviews some of the ethical issues that may be problematic due to the unique goals of SE endeavors. Mini-cases are provided as examples of actual SE roles. These include endeavors to moderate difficulties caused by youth unemployment, water scarcity, nonrenewable energy, land degradation, waste and emissions, as well as providing employment for refugees. An area of increasing emphasis is sustainable practices and developing "green" based projects as a means to build better local communities and boost business potential. Tourism-related SE undertakings thus include efforts to mitigate social, cultural, or environmental issues. These illustrate success in the face of adversity such as limited funding, organizational and legal constraints, as well as lack of public or governmental support. An area of opportunity within the hospitality and tourism sector is the ethically inspired entrepreneurship. The chapter attempts to emphasize innovation in SE practices. The analysis of the examples that are provided should contribute actionable ideas. Further enhancements for SE organizations ought to advance prospects and their undertakings within the Mediterranean Basin.

Introduction

There is increasing attention to the social entrepreneurship (SE) movement, even though the concept has existed for a long time. SE is broadly interpreted as activities that aim for social change (Martí, 2006). This movement refers to a wide range of flexible enterprises that are engaged in various innovative social and economic pursuits combining "profit with purpose" that are now found in many industries and nations (Besley and Ghatak, 2017). The growing importance of SEs includes government publications (e.g. OECD, 2010), media reports (e.g. McGill and Sachs, 2013) and academic research (e.g. André and Pache, 2016). The majority of published SE research is qualitative and typically focuses on a region or has a particular national perspective. Examples include research articles concerning SE in developing nations (Foryt, 2002; Jamali, 2007), in areas such as North Africa (Halabi, Kheir and Cochrane, 2017) and Western Balkans (Varga, 2017) or are conducted in specific nations such as the United Kingdom (Nicholls, 2007) or Turkey (Türker, Özerim and Yıldız, 2014). Despite the large number of studies, it seems that the theoretical foundation has not been fully explored, and further research is needed into the SE movement (Austin, Stevenson and Wei-Skillern, 2006; Hlady-Rispal and Servantie, 2018). Moreover, numerous considerations appear to have imprecise analysis with problems that include the degree of focus on profit, the sector of the actual enterprise (government, non-government organizations or private firms), blended social-purpose commercial ventures as well as the issues with the size and scope of these activities (Mair and Marti, 2006; Martin and Osberg, 2007; Besley and Ghatak, 2017; Panwar et al., 2017).

The basic objectives of SE originate from traditional entrepreneurship. These objectives include the discovery, development and exploitation of new ideas, products and services; seeking opportunities in different or underserved markets; innovations such as using existing technologies to new fields or sectors; as well as the creation of business ventures, industries, infrastructures or ways of doing business (Ziemnowicz, 2013; Lubberink et al., 2018). Mainstream entrepreneurship literature is still dominated by the assumption that entrepreneurs are almost exclusively motivated by self-interest (Bacq, Hartog and Hoogendoorn, 2016). This characteristic is often described as "the spirit of entrepreneurship", an attitude that some individuals exhibit as part of their nature (Buchholz and Rosenthal, 2005). Entrepreneurship is also implicitly associated with the pursuit of commercial objectives that are sometimes in conflict with ethical behavior (Haugh and Talwar, 2016).

According to André and Pache (2016), social entrepreneurs have additional objectives and aspirations with a higher goal of fulfilling a social mission. Waddock and Steckler (2016) declared that social entrepreneurs seek to make a difference in society through the actualization of a social-focused enterprise. They aspire to creating "pattern-breaking social change" (Mitchell, 2013; Newey, 2018). Their ideas are often experimental, that may succeed or fail not only for them as individual entrepreneurs, but also their endeavors may or may not deliver the expected results for society (Buchholz and Rosenthal, 2005). Waddock and Steckler (2016) empirically found that the visions of social entrepreneurs unfold in an iterative process from a baseline aspiration to make some kind of a positive difference in the world.

The inherent quality of SE focuses on "the innovative use of resources to explore and exploit opportunities that meet a social need in a sustainable manner" presents a more ethical variant of the spirit of entrepreneurship (Sud, VanSandt and Baugous, 2009). SE offers solutions to a range of social problems and is acknowledged to be an effective mechanism for generating economic, social and environmental value (Zahra et al., 2009; Haugh and Talwar, 2016). Social entrepreneurs are assumed to draw on the guiding principle of beneficence or "actively doing good", instead of resorting to the traditional entrepreneurial objectives of non-maleficence or "doing no harm" (Fisscher et al., 2005). However, balancing social wealth with the desire to make profits and maintain economic efficiency is very difficult (Zahra et al., 2009).

Buchholz and Rosenthal (2005) raised concerns about the accountability and actual contributions of social entrepreneurs because of their use of new and untested organizational concepts and operating environments. This is a similar problem with innovations that entrepreneurs introduce, but the actual impacts of these changes on people and their environments may be unknown (Buchholz and Rosenthal, 2005). According to Dey and Steyaert (2016), ethics, rather than being within the purview of an individual, encompass a wide domain through which social entrepreneurs engage in a critical and creative manner, such as with existing relations of power. Ethics in social enterprises should be examined from the perspective of how they are actually performed (Dey and Steyaert, 2016). A close examination of ethical issues is necessary to understand the "rights" or "wrongs" in all endeavors including the applications, behaviors and activities of social entrepreneurship (Chell et al., 2016).

Tourism is experiencing continued growth and deepening diversification, making it one of the largest and fastest-growing economic sectors of the world. These dynamics, plus an increasing number of new destinations, have turned tourism into an important force as well as an economic and social phenomenon (Cohen and Kennedy, 2012; UNWTO, 2017). Mark Twain concluded in his 1869 book *Innocents Abroad* that "travel is fatal to prejudice bigotry and narrow-mindedness, and many of our people need it sorely on these accounts" (Stitsworth, 1988). Twain was promoting tourism as a means to broaden people's minds and reduce prejudgments (Cao et al., 2014; Francis, 2016). An increasing number of tourism businesses have expanded beyond offering the traditional "home away from home" holiday into delivering a broader experience with mutually advantageous opportunities as well as exposure to local culture and people (Richards and Wilson, 2006; Kim and Brown, 2012). This more "immersive" travel may also integrate direct benefits to the local communities and the natural environments (Scheyvens, 1999; Stem et al., 2003). There are examples of ethically and socially inspired business endeavors in tourism and hospitality sectors at the destination level (Jamal and Camargo, 2014). This industry has numerous facets and activities that offer not only unique opportunities for serving the traveling public, but also positive benefits for local people and their locales beyond a focus on environmental sustainability. These social endeavors include efforts to bring fairness, equity and justice through tourism, especially for disadvantaged and poor people (Lea, 1993).

This chapter aims to examine social entrepreneurship to facilitate opportunities and provide alternatives within tourism and hospitality services. The chapter discusses a range of opinions, presents some ethical dilemmas and offers selected examples of SE in the Mediterranean region. The Mediterranean coastal areas arguably represent one of the most popular destinations for visitors and vacationers from around the globe (Amelung and Viner, 2006). The nations around the Mediterranean Sea also offer an opportunity for SE endeavors in that the area contains some of the most developed, wealthy and thriving regions as well as zones of conflict, poverty and underdeveloped areas (Petmesidou and Papatheodorou, 2006; Coleman and Essid, 2012; Berenger and Bresson, 2013). This chapter contributes to the literature by exploring SE in all the nations in the Mediterranean Basin, along with providing operating examples in each country.

Social entrepreneurship begins with "Entrepreneurship"

Jean-Baptiste Say, an economist and businessman, described the entrepreneur in the early 19th century as an individual who "shifts economic resources out of an area of lower and into an area of higher productivity and greater yield" (Butler-Bowdon, 2010). Say expanded the literal translation from the French, "one who undertakes", to encompass the concept of value creation.

Schumpeter (1934) examined entrepreneurship as a key process through which the economy as a whole is advanced. He identified the entrepreneur as the force required to drive economic progress, absent which economies would become static, structurally immobilized and subject to decay. Schumpeter's entrepreneurial spirit includes the identification of a commercial opportunity – whether a material, product, service or business – and the people to organize a venture to implement it. Successful entrepreneurship sets off a chain reaction, encouraging other entrepreneurs to iterate upon and ultimately propagate the innovation to the point of "creative destruction", a state at which the new venture and all its related ventures effectively render existing products, services and business models obsolete (Ziemnowicz, 2013).

Peter Drucker (1985), on the other hand, thought entrepreneurs not necessarily as agents of change, but rather as being canny and taking advantage of change. According to Drucker (1985), "the entrepreneur always searches for change, responds to it, and exploits it as an opportunity". This premise is expanded by Kirzner (2009), who identifies "alertness" as the entrepreneur's most critical ability.

In general, traditional entrepreneurs focus on economic value and sustainability with a strategy that is measured by profit growth. On the other hand, social entrepreneurs strive to work for social value that is focused on achieving both social objectives and self-sufficiency with a strategic goal of expanding their mission. Numerous types of organizations are established for profit or non-profit, but they can all be placed on continuums depending on their principal characteristics. For example, an enterprise's primary focus can be on emphasizing either social or financial returns. According to Bibb et al. (2004), a social enterprise is generally a non-profit organization that uses business tools to accomplish social goals. Some enterprises may also be considered to offer blended characteristics. This may depend, for example, on their desired degree on meeting their social mission needs or the drive to satisfy commercial market demands. These relationships are shown in Figure 5.1.

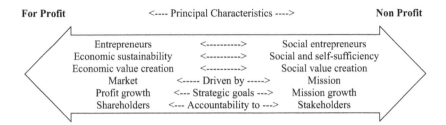

Figure 5.1 The For Profit–Non Profit continuum

Social entrepreneurship: associated meanings

The roots of "social entrepreneurship" go back to the 18th century, when industrialists like Robert Owen started to protect employees by seeking to improve their working conditions, provide adequate education for them and their families and involve them in various cultural activities (Shaw and Carter, 2007, p. 419). Banks published the term "social entrepreneurship" for the first time in 1972 in relation to social movements (Banks, 1972).

Drucker (1979) introduced the concept of "social enterprise" while advocating ethical responsibilities of corporations. The term "social entrepreneur" is attributed to William "Bill" Drayton, who established Ashoka in 1980, an organization that functions as a social venture capital fund in developing nations (Sen, 2007). Drayton (2006) recognized social entrepreneurship as a potential method by which individuals may address social problems within their communities. Social entrepreneurship is an important tool for economic and social development not just for underdeveloped countries, but also for the developing and industrialized nations (Perić and Delić, 2014).

One of the most frequently cited definitions is by Dees (2001), who defines social entrepreneurs as people who function as managers of change in the social sector

> by: a) adopting a mission to create and sustain social value (not just private value), b) recognizing and relentlessly pursuing new opportunities to serve that mission, c) engaging in a process of continuous innovation, adaptation and learning, d) acting boldly without being limited by resources currently in hand, and e) exhibiting heightened accountability to the constituencies served and for the outcomes created.

Thus, the "social entrepreneurship" concept seems to refer to the same area of activity as "social enterprise".

The OECD (2013) describes social enterprises as "a new innovative business model that meets both social and economic objectives contributing to labor market integration, social inclusion and economic development". However, Galera and Borzaga (2009) identified differences in what is a social enterprise among nations, and they suggest two main approaches. Their first finding was a "rediscovery" of the role of non-profit organizations in providing social services and employment assimilation along with increased interest by cooperatives for their communities. The result of this has been in increasing differentiation in the functioning of these enterprises that diverges from the traditional ways of doing business in the public sector as well as in the for-profit marketplace. Galera and Borzaga's (2009) second approach is based on the typical US context that focuses on revenue maximization. This approach also reflects the reality that many social enterprises face when their sources of funding are reduced or even eliminated. Unfortunately, this is a common problem in the United States that requires social enterprises to adjust and to find ways to generate income through commercial endeavors. However, these additional profit-generating activities may or may not be related to their social mission (OECD, 2013).

In short, "social enterprise" has no worldwide definition and has been, and continues to be, a source of much confusion. The CECOP CICOPA-Europe provided a definition based strictly on national legislation regulating social cooperatives or social enterprises (or equivalent term) in 11 European Union (EU) countries. This definition is very similar to the one formulated by the European Commission in its Communication on a Social Business Initiative (SBI) released in 2011. Broadly speaking, this refers to the area of activity in which social cooperatives are involved (namely social services of general interest, including work integration), but extended to other enterprise forms (CICOPA, 2013). Similarly, there is a lack of agreement even among the member EU countries as to the definition of "social entrepreneurship" because of different traditions and meanings that are attached to these words among the nations.

Problems that emerge from definitions according to Cho (2006) include that they are tautological and from a singular voice prescriptive. Most definitions clarify the components of "entrepreneurship" and simply leave the "social" undefined, a major problem given that the social dimension is significant and responsible for the concept's inherent complexity (Cho, 2006). The definitions tend to be in a form of a monologue (as opposed to a dialogical) approach seeking to expound the supposedly "social" objectives (Cho, 2006). The lack of semantic clarity regarding the common usage of terms such as "social enterprise", "social entrepreneurship", "social cooperative", and "social economy" creates problems, even though "cooperative" and "social cooperative" are standardized in international usage (CICOPA, 2013). In the United States, many associate social entrepreneurship exclusively with not-for-profit organizations, while others use it to describe only the people who establish a not-for-profit organization (Dees, 2001). Nevertheless, there are numerous social enterprises that have a for-profit strategy – or more precisely, "profit with purpose" (Besley and Ghatak 2017). Although the concept of "social entrepreneurship" is still poorly defined and is treated differently depending on the nation, it is gaining in popularity. For purposes of this chapter, the term "social entrepreneurship" will encompass all the social-related enterprises under discussion.

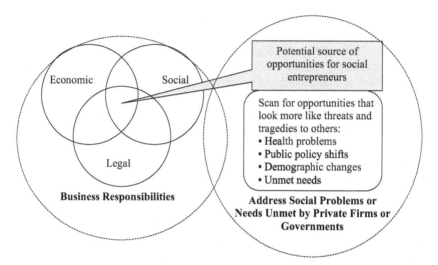

Figure 5.2 Challenges and opportunities from business responsibilities in the SE environment

Social entrepreneurship and ethical issues

Ethics are generally accepted as a set of principles prescribing a behavioral system. These are rules provided by an external source, such as codes of conduct, of what is expected in business or the ground rules of religions (Gilman, 2005). These explain what is bad and wrong or good and right. They provide the guidelines or rules for what is "acceptable" and most often outline obligations and moral duties. According to Fisscher et al. (2005), the relationship between entrepreneurship and ethics can be characterized as an intense love–hate relationship. The reasons for these conflicts are challenges and changes among mores, values and societal norms. Moreover, there is a distinction between ethics and morality, which is an individual's own principles regarding what is right and wrong. Business environments are dynamic, such as with ongoing technological innovations and changing societal expectations. This requires a continuing process of re-defining the goals and rules of business activity; for example, even seeking a common societal good will involve significantly different goals and methods based on differences in people, accountability to constituents and even client relationships (Henderson, 1984).

Figure 5.2 illustrates that all entrepreneurs must balance economic, legal and social responsibilities. The most fruitful sources of activities for social enterprises are where these three responsibilities intersect. Here are difficult-to-solve areas that are often perceived as difficult, risky or even catastrophic by the general public. Some of these problems may receive government support or assistance from other private initiatives, but these efforts may be lacking or sometimes non-existent in certain countries. In the case of the EU, there are guidelines in many of these issues, but they may not receive as much attention in some nations and cultures. These issues include gender inequality, employment for the disadvantaged, education for all, employment for youth, water scarcity, non-renewable energy sources, land degradation, waste and emissions as well as the burdens caused by the refugee crisis. The areas happen to be examples for potential business opportunities that are undertaken by social entrepreneurs (Figure 5.2).

The multiple challenges within all enterprises require a balance among the economic, legal and social responsibilities. Successful entrepreneurs find ways to meet and to develop strategies to enable each of these. Nevertheless, their decisions involve ethics, and this area is ill defined with arguments on what is good or bad, as well as what actions account for being morally right or wrong. Ethics are easily described, but actual decision-making by individuals is much more involved, and attempting to describe the task is like "nailing gelatin to a wall" (Lewis, 1985). Definitions of what is ethical will vary and will be spread on a broad spectrum. Ethical conflicts are common because there are so many interests that confront an enterprise at all levels, and there is constant change in modes, values and societal norms. In contemporary global and dynamic environments, what is good and right or bad and wrong is by necessity "situational", so all decision-makers must have an ethical process, not just fixed ethical principles.

According to Henderson (1984), even the basic definitions of what is ethical will vary across people, cultures and nations. What is considered good or bad, proper or wrong in a dynamic business environment is by necessity very situational. Moreover, entrepreneurs can support anything by using their own morals that simply define what they believe to be right or wrong. For these reasons, a systemic and reasoned basis with proper justification is required to be ethically grounded. The trends indicate that every organization has to move beyond a simple and occasional "check-the-box" exercise into fully embracing a culture with a long-term focus on ethics, values and compliance. Some organizations continue to make unsubstantiated ethical claims, and their so-called "green washing" behavior has resulted in increasing consumer cynicism and distrust (Jahdi and Acikdilli, 2009). Nevertheless, issues of corporate responsibility and ethics require recognition that organizational strategy, incentives and culture mandate new approaches and thinking among all participants. The costs to organizations and to society of getting something wrong – as well as the benefits of making the correct decisions – are progressively more and more obvious regardless of the particular people, culture or country.

An ethical premise that helps to determine right from wrong is by examining the outcomes of a decision. As a form of consequentialism, utilitarianism weighs that desirable ethical decisions are those that produce the greatest good for the greatest number (Hunt and Vitell, 1986). In measuring outcomes, Mahoney (1990) calls upon two main principles from medical ethics: nonmaleficence and beneficence. The first is basically "do no harm", or the responsibility to mitigate human pain, social inequality and environmental pollution. The second is actively doing good, or the responsibility to contribute to positive social change within given capacities. Thus, entrepreneurs have a positive relationship with ethics in that entrepreneurship should evolve from being part of the problem to being part of the solution with regard to social and environmental issues (Mahoney, 1990). Social entrepreneurs focus more on the guiding principle of beneficence rather than on nonmaleficence.

According to Sethi (1979), the challenge to the enterprise is first to their social obligation (by obeying existing laws), then raising their social responsibility (by actively responding to needs), and finally reaching social responsiveness (by being proactive and open to public inquiry in their activities). There is an inherent conflict, and according to Zahra et al. (2009), social entrepreneurship represents a harmful marriage between opposing values where the increased emphasis on efficient and profitable market models clashes with many of the founding ideals, not only among social enterprises but also in the public sector and in non-government organizations (NGO) dedicated to fostering the public good. However, the problem remains of defining the "social" in social entrepreneurship, because "the act of defining the domain of the social inevitably requires exclusionary and ultimately political choices about which concerns can claim to be in society's 'true' interest" (Cho, 2006). For example, the contingency nature of social entrepreneurship will be subject to debate because it is difficult for social entrepreneurs to forecast how various stakeholders will react to the changes the enterprise seeks to accomplish and even the potential broader implications they might have, as Bloom and Dees (2008) noted, "creating systemic change is often an experimental and learning process".

Spreckley (1981) proposed three measures of benefits needed to assess the value of a corporation: economic, social and environmental. This form of "social accounting" was described by Elkington (1994) as a triple bottom line framework: of making money, serving a constituency and doing no harm to the planet. The objective is to measure an organization's degree of social responsibility, its economic value and its environmental impact. The concept was made popular with the motto "People, Planet, Profit" (Elkington, 1997), promoting a new, responsible approach within businesses by taking into consideration the concept of "sustainable development". Establishing values-based management systems and evaluating performance in a broader perspective, all managers can create greater business value. Nevertheless, ethical leaders who display empathy are already aware of the additional "bottom lines" beyond basic financial statements that report their organization's responsibilities in many areas.

Kidder (1995) stated that "if a situation is not a clear cut case of right vs. wrong, then there are four ethical dilemma paradigms, a) truth vs. loyalty, b) short term vs. long term, c) justice vs. mercy, and c) self vs. community". Pomerantz (2004) provided an example of leadership issues that presented ethical dilemmas in a SE whose objective was training and employing disabled workers, but the employees were not capable of operating the machinery in an efficient way to generate profits. The short-term advantages of employing more disabled workers were overridden by the long-term prospect of the enterprise accumulating ever-higher losses. Pomerantz (2004) argues that this was not a "right vs. wrong" situation, because the only way the enterprise could function was to have more machinery and additional capable workers, but a "right vs. right" situation, because the organizational mission was to serve developmentally disabled workers. The solution was to find other jobs for the more disabled workers (Pomerantz, 2004). The need to generate profits by the organization thus made it possible to continue operations and to help all the workers in its community. According to Pomerantz (2004), this solution was seen within the organization as a case of difficult, but ethical, decision-making.

According to Nicholls (2007), social enterprises have facilitated the development of ethical markets. This follows from their beginnings, and their strategic focus can be classified under three types: (a) addressing existing institutional voids and market failures through new products or services, the "institutional social enterprise", (b) reconfiguring markets to create new or greater social value, the "normative social enterprise", and (c) challenging institutional arrangements through advocacy and political action, the "transformative social enterprise" (Nicholls, 2007). Each functions in rather different ways to address social and environmental issues, and thus each type requires different bundles of resources and strategic skill sets.

Social entrepreneurs face unique ethical challenges because of their motivation to achieve social activities, the resources needed to execute their mission and various influences that may control their behaviors. They also take entrepreneurial risks to create social change and have to function with limited funding and financial insecurity. These constraints, along with competition, sometimes force individuals to make difficult decisions. They may encounter many situations, such as during mission development, resource mobilization and performance management that can enhance or obstruct their ethical principles. The enterprise's social mission itself provides challenges beyond what is encountered by typical businesses. Zahra et al. (2009) portrayed the normal routine of social entrepreneurs as "replete with ethical dilemmas and therefore pre-existence of ethics in social entrepreneurship is contradictory". Even though they have an "ethical obligation" as well as the "noble desire" to make a difference and to assist society, "egoism can make them to follow unethical practices", according to Zahra et al. (2009). Moreover, Dey and Steyaert (2016) wrote, "ethical virtuousness is required to deal with the problems of society through social entrepreneurship".

Mass tourism originated with a social entrepreneur

Thomas Cook originated the concept of modern mass tourism in 1841 when he organized the first excursion for about 500 passengers by a special train, and this idea was based on social entrepreneurship (Brendon, 1991). As a religious person, Cook reasoned that "most Victorian social problems were related to alcohol and that the lives of working people would be greatly improved if they drank less and better educated"; thus he came up with the idea of "the practicability of employing the great powers of railways and locomotion for the furtherance of this social reform" (thomascook.com, 2018). The innovative railroad technologies allowed him to organize inexpensive journeys for the new working class that itself was created by the industrialization process in the United Kingdom.

According to Higgins-Desbiolles (2006), Cook was motivated by philanthropic aims rather than business goals; thus, his enterprise did not generate profits for many years. Cook offered short train journeys within England, developed all-inclusive tours to the Great Exhibition in Paris in 1855 that further promoted industrial organization, and then expanded his services to destinations around the world such as India, Egypt and the Holy Lands. A broad social agenda underpinned his efforts. Turner and Ash (1975) claim that Cook viewed the railway as "a great and beneficial social force", and they quote Cook describing travel as "appertaining to the great class of agencies for the advancement of human progress" (Higgins-Desbiolles, 2006). His social entrepreneurship view was that education and travel were the only real tools to uplift the lower classes and thus improve the entire society. Whereas travel was previously limited to the elite and privileged sectors of society for "polite" visits, Cook's vision was that culture and travel could make all people better (Justraveling.com, 2016).

The economic opportunities and transportation innovations have caused numerous problems in conditions within the tourism and hospitality sectors. In 1975, Turner and Ash described the modern tourist industry and the masses of international vacationers as "barbarian invaders because of the cultural disintegration that follows in their wake". These visitors may learn to appreciate the customs and ways of life in foreign countries as well as being a source for economic development and prosperity for developing nations (Jafari, 1974). However, according to Crick (1989), tourism increasingly "seems to generate consistently ambivalent or contradictory representations".

This is a not a new phenomenon. Mark Twain described the 19th-century images of travel and the shift to its 20th-century "contemporary degenerate offspring – mass tourism" (Crick, 1989). MacCannell (1976) examined the worldwide proliferation of tourist attractions and noted that "tourist" to an increasing extent is being "used as a derisive label for someone who seems content with his obviously inauthentic experiences". Mass tourism also creates pressures in popular destinations that have negative impacts on the environment, culture, biodiversity and social issues. The consequences of mass tourism include many problems that include crowds and noise, waste disposal, loss of cultural identities, destruction of natural habitats, unethical business practices and a lack of qualified staff (Kettle, 2017).

Social entrepreneurship in tourism

Social entrepreneurship is expanding and establishing new enterprises in many sectors for social progress while also attracting attention by the media and studies by scholars. Tourism is an especially potent social force. Higgins-Desbiolles (2006) described the opportunities that could be realized from tourism when "its capacities are unfettered from the market fundamentalism of neoliberalism and instead are harnessed to meet human development imperatives and the wider public good". Higgins-Desbiolles (2006) also analyzed the human rights in a vision of tourism's role in societies and the global community. Further enriching experiences include "social tourism" that involves participation in travel by economically weak or otherwise disadvantaged elements in society (Minnaert, Diekmann and McCabe, 2012).

There is also an apparent lack of knowledge within the traditional tourism industry of the opportunities possible from combining tourism with the preservation of the environment. In particular, social entrepreneurship can transform the industry for the better by effectively making changes to the economic and social systems that are no longer serving the best interests of the tourists and in the destinations. The contemporary concept of mass tourism for social entrepreneurs is related more to function as a "force for good" not only for the participants, but also from the perspective of various communities and stakeholders that are impacted by the travel activities. The massive numbers of people traveling has both positive and negative impacts. Most obvious is the harm caused, but there is a significant, and often unmet, potential for good.

Sheldon, Pollock and Daniele (2017) describe the traditional model of tourism as characterized by success through economic growth and monetary returns. They suggest a shifting paradigm in tourism where social entrepreneurs measure success in richer qualitative terms associated with development and well-being as experienced by all shareholders, including individuals, enterprises and communities. The new model requires a rethinking of how to sustain visitor economies that benefits the planet, and not only to satisfy the enormous increases in tourist wants.

Benefits of the new model include cultural competence, education, and environmental sustainability. Due to its rapid international market growth, tourism represents one of the economic sectors where a great contribution is needed from the entrepreneurial sector (Neto, 2003). Sigala (2016) argues that factors that incorporate the need for tourism sustainability, as well as the role of social entrepreneurship in achieving sustainable development in the tourism sector with more inclusive opportunities, has "the ability to lead to social change". Increased demand for new types of tourism also enables the diversification of tourism products and services, thus creating a great degree of involvement by the entrepreneurial sector (Lordkipanidze, Brezet and Backman, 2005). As was with mass tourism becoming mainstream, new tourism trends have now emerged, such as "alternative", "green", "sustainable" and "natural" (Holden, 2000).

Social entrepreneurship can provide many alternatives to traditional mass tourism, according to Theng, Qiong and Tatar (2015). These approaches are now described as ecotourism, responsible tourism and sustainable tourism (Swarbrooke, 1999). There are different meanings for these terms because of the many activities they can involve and an even wider range of diverse tourists that interpret their marketing. Nevertheless, activities such as ecotourism feature:

> all forms of nature tourism aimed at the appreciation of both the natural world and the traditional cultures existent in natural areas, deliberate efforts to minimize the harmful human impact on the natural and socio-cultural

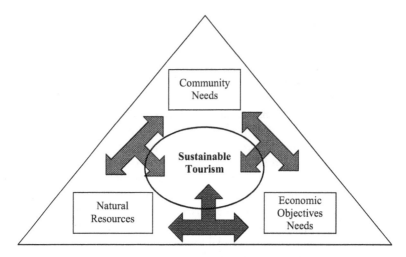

Figure 5.3 Balancing the forces by social entrepreneurs to achieve sustainable tourism

environment and support for the protection of natural and cultural assets and the well-being of host communities.

(Neto, 2003)

Not only can reformulating the travel experience expand opportunities for visitors, but this also can add value to the local economy, natural areas and culture as well as provide spin-off effects of educating and enriching that integrates the tourist at the local level. Examples of other forms of tourism include activities focused on wildlife, culture, religion and agriculture as well as indigenous festivals and foods.

Figure 5.3 illustrates the overall environment within which social entrepreneurs operate. They need to achieve symmetry among the three main dimensions to achieve sustainable tourism endeavors. This requires them to perform a three-way equilibrium among the conflicting dimensions: natural environment, community needs and traditional economic objectives. One requirement is achieving appropriate use of the scarce natural resources in their locale in conjunction with the economic benefits or profits that are gained from having the tourists visit their locale. Another balancing task is the economic growth and development that results from the visitors in relationship with tourism's impacts on indigenous social values and community needs. A third duty is appropriately utilizing the local environmental and natural resources with the changes within the social or community values regarding those resources. Achieving stability within these three elements (as shown in Figure 5.3) to effectively operate sustainable tourism activities is difficult. Complicating matters is what Liu (2003) described as the considerable debate regarding sustainable tourism that is sometimes incomplete, unconnected and often flawed with false assumptions and arguments.

By seeing an opportunity that others omit, by seizing uncertain methods and by creating sustainable solutions to better improve the community they live in, social entrepreneurs are often seen as agents of change (Peredo and Wurzelmann, 2015). One of the primary goals for social entrepreneurs has been poverty alleviation, and social entrepreneurs believe that this change can happen through education, training and empowerment, and by giving the local community the possibility of getting more involved in their work (Bornstein, 2004). Daniele and Quezada (2017) studied social entrepreneurship tourism enterprises by evaluating their value proposition, key resources and networks, as well as by examining operational elements that included their capital foundation, revenue streams, cost structures and legal structures as well as their marketing and distribution channels.

Daniele and Quezada (2017) argue that tourism social entrepreneurs use the traditional for-profit business model to help them become more successful and sustainable. A clear vision and strategy is needed because there are cases of tourism SEs that did not reach full potential due to problems that included competing aims between their profit and non-profit endeavors (Laeis and Lemke, 2016). Nevertheless, the importance of tourism as an engine for economic, sustainable and inclusive growth in general means moving towards coherent and comprehensive national policy approaches to help reframe tourism growth to better spread the benefits, address inequalities and improve the resilience of their economies (OECD, 2017). In short, social entrepreneurship and small business development are essential to building a strong and sustainable tourism sector (Goodwin, 1998). Dey and Steyaert (2016) noted apprehension regarding whether social entrepreneurs are more virtuous and ethical than ordinary people and if they are always ethical. Dey and Steyaert (2016) claim that assumptions about social entrepreneurs' magnanimous abilities are misleading. Thus, this subject is a rather sensitive problem that may affect individual decisions and organizational actions in both positive or negative ways depending on not only the ethics of individuals, but also the standards and controls within each organization.

Ethics, social entrepreneurship and tourism in the Mediterranean

Ethics knowledge is emerging more in the tourism literature, and Fennell (2015) noted a disconnect between theory and practice when it comes to behavior. The area of ethical tourism is fraught with different perspectives. There are disagreements on what does or does not make up ethical or responsible tourism. It can bring major benefits to destinations as well as harm to the environment and to people living there (McKercher, 1993). Another problem is that the definition of what is "good" in tourism often reflects personal travel preferences, as if in self-justification (Swarbrooke, 1999), and may not be based on a pragmatic analysis of what is "good" for the communities and the people on which the tourists impact (Butler, 1990; Swarbrooke, 1999).

According to Lovelock and Lovelock (2013), there is also an increasing need for tourism businesses to reduce some of the excesses in the industry. They need a more ethical approach not only with customer interactions, but also with the natural resources as well as in the relationships with local citizens, especially in tourist destinations that are experiencing poverty or human rights abuses (Lovelock and Lovelock, 2013). According to Donyadide (2010), other industries have realized the uncertain rewards and drawbacks of doing business, and now tourism needs to adopt the triple bottom line of social, environmental and economic responsibility. For example, ethical tourism attempts to highlight and promote appropriate practices within the industry. This movement emerged from tourists who realized that their spending did not provide positive benefits to the communities they visited, as it would be expected.

A study of residents in lower-income destinations in the Mediterranean region has a range of responses to tourism because of concerns about adverse sociocultural and environmental effects (Bramwell, 2004). Bramwell (2004) found that local sensitivities to waves of visitors and operations by travel providers have not developed to the level typically found in affluent countries. The traditional problems of increasing tourism activities in these destinations has focused on the unbalanced economic outcomes to the detriment of local people as well as to contributing to sociocultural problems and damage to their often fragile coastal environments. However, there are also other potential threats facing these destinations, including an aging infrastructure that is not able to support further development, shifting consumer expectations and external events as well as increased competition from ever more destination options (Bramwell, 2004).

Csapo (2012) predicts that classic mass tourism is unlikely to experience a major drop in market share, but new tourists will have diversified expectations such as to appreciate/experience the different cultures and customs of more remote places. In general, enterprises within the tourism industry as well as all tourists should be cognizant of social and cultural traditions and practices. For example, Article 1 of the Global Code of Ethics for Tourism states, "the understanding and promotion of the ethical values common to humanity, with an attitude of tolerance and respect for the diversity of religious, philosophical and moral beliefs, are both the foundation and the consequence of responsible tourism" (UNWTO, 2001).

The challenges with tourism also include detrimental acts because of the problems caused by some of the deeds and pursuits by the tourists themselves. These go beyond the traditional search for wholesome fun, cultural engagement or relaxation when they are on a holiday. For example, some tourists engage in criminal acts or activities that may be prohibited by the laws of the country they visit. Because they are away from their home constraints, they may participate in conduct perceived to be offensive or injurious by the local people and authorities. Obvious forbidden acts include trafficking in illicit drugs, arms, antiques and protected species as well as products and substances that are dangerous or prohibited by national regulations. An example of a low-level offense is certain required fishing licenses in Italy where violators can be fined, but there are few fishing regulations in Lebanon (Cacaud, 2005). Tourists should become familiar with and abide by unique customs, laws and characteristics of the countries they are preparing to visit.

Another major area of ethical problems related to undesirable tourism includes sex tourism and abuse of children (Lovelock and Lovelock, 2013). Strictly viewed from a pragmatic point of view, the income from these activities supports some regional economies, especially in low-income areas (Cabezas, 1999). According to Cooper and Hanson (1998), the moral repugnancy of these activities has also meant a willingness to ignore undesirable facts. The consequences of this include inadequate health protection, few consequences for unscrupulous intermediaries and many opportunities for criminal entrepreneurs (Cooper and Hanson, 1998).

On the other hand, there can be positive effects of mass tourism. Lever (1987) described the development of the Spanish hotel industry on the Costa Brava attracting migrant females as housemaids and receptionists from far away. Rather than continuing traditional agrarian roles such as staying home or setting work in the local fabric trade, they were able to make good wages by their standards, and they mixed with people from other cultures (Lever, 1987). These female workers provided financial support to their families, thus changing their status within their tradition-bound family structure. Moreover, these females were able to establish new careers as managers within an industry that is not bound by orthodox Spanish practices. Both foreign and domestic hotel and tourism operators look for the best staff and thus became catalysts for the improving role of females in this part of Spanish society (Ryan, 2002).

The tourism industry in many locations is subject to seasonal business variability, and this characteristic impacts the stability of employment. There are also issues with work integration for vulnerable or excluded individuals as well as with job quality and employment conditions. The tourism industry employs many low-skilled employees (Cooney, 2013). A study of 12 European nations by Bidet and Spear (2003) noted that social enterprises offer temporary training or employment as well as permanent employment. Nevertheless, Amin (2009) cautions that people who have been exposed to social exclusion may find it difficult to become effective economic agents simply by employment within a social enterprise. Proving work is not enough because people from marginalized populations may still need long-term professional assistance from a variety of sources, including the government (Amin, 2009). In other words, social enterprises with a strictly commercially oriented focus may be overlooking and even compromising their principal social benefit objectives (OECD, 2013).

The International Organization for Migration calls Europe the most dangerous destination for irregular migration in the world, with the Mediterranean ranked as the world's most dangerous border crossing (Park, 2015). The European immigrant and refugee crisis beginning in 2015 continues to impact the Mediterranean countries and to affect the tourism sector. EU member states such as Greece and Italy have served as the main points of entry for migrants and refugees due to their proximity to the Mediterranean Basin (Park, 2015). Members of the EU have struggled to cope with the influx of people and how to deal with their resettlement, and this has also ignited ideological divides, creating divisions among and within the nations. Nevertheless, many social enterprises have assisted these people. Examples include organizing courses to obtain necessary skills and knowledge to work in a new country. The first acquisition goal is learning the language necessary to find employment. Social enterprises also create workplaces for the refugees and other immigrants, and many of these organizations are focused on providing social services, healthcare and environmental protection (IED, 2016). Not only can the new arrivals contribute to their new country, but their work also brings them income and further assimilation within a new society (IED, 2016). The immigrants will become conscious citizens of the country, and the rate of crime and difficult families will decrease (IED, 2016).

Social entrepreneurship in the Mediterranean nations

The nations around the Mediterranean Sea have different traditions and aspirations. For example, they have distinctive social welfare regimes, particularly in the degree of backing as well as the distribution of support for children, elderly, minorities or other vulnerable people (Tillmar, 2012). There is a diversity of definitions, regulations, policies, programs and initiatives in the field of SE among them (ESELA, 2015). The meaning of SE may differ not only between nations, but even between separate regions of one country (Groot and Dankbaar, 2014). There are also differences in the levels of development, in the primary areas of activity and in the relative sizes of the SE ecosystem among these countries. Many governments face financial and budgetary constraints that force public officials to innovate and seek enhancing cooperation or harnessing opportunities between the public and private sectors. Because of this, SEs have increasingly important roles in producing goods and providing services that were either not available or were previously considered to be of a general public character and the full responsibility of governments (Rondinelli, 2003). There are also inconsistencies not only because of the subjective nature of social values that may differ greatly depending on the context, but also from the broad spectrum of development and implementation of the legal infrastructure for SEs, as well as the level and quality of financial and capacity support for SE among the nations (Zahra et al., 2009). Not only are there differences within EU member countries, but also noticeable gaps in the variability of data. There are differences in SE recognition among nations outside the EU, and this is particularly problematic in areas of continued conflict and strife. Policy makers are considering ways to promote SE outside the EU area (Euclid Network, 2017).

Table 5.1 presents the summary of conditions in all the Mediterranean countries along with selected examples of SEs in each. While the phenomenon may be not well bounded in theory, it is already having a practical impact. The current state of SE reception and relative activity in each nation is followed by selected brief samples of socially focused endeavors within tourism and related activity. These sketches of SE activities provide a glimpse of the wide variety of these activities in the Mediterranean Basin, even among the divergent cultures that serve as a major conditioning factor for entrepreneurial initiatives (Jaén et al., 2017).

Table 5.1 Mediterranean social entrepreneurship examples, main focus, and social impact

Mediterranean countries	SE name and activity	Main focus	Social impact
Albania (*EU Member*) SEs in Albania have been driven by non-profit organizations, a variety of early stage businesses, as well as special social and work integration opportunities for vulnerable groups. Most are in agricultural production, education, social services, as well as vocational training and consultancy. Average employment is less than ten and they are dependent on grants and charitable donations for start-up and operations (Varga, 2017).	Pana http://www.pana.com.al/ Reclaimed wood furniture, office accessories, jewelry, etc.	Preserving the environment by using reclaimed wood as well as employing people from marginalized communities (e.g. Roma, immigrants, people with disabilities, retired people, and orphans) that also make up 75% of their staff. This SE provides products below market price for new SEs to help in their start-up phase. Their marketing objective is on uniqueness of its products to attract customers, not on the social purpose of the enterprise.	Promote inclusive and sustainable economic growth. Changing people's lives through an opportunity to conduct professional work.
	Yaps http://www.yaps.al/shp/?lang=en Delivery and janitorial services	Two separate enterprises: a) since 2001 it offers postal mail delivery services in Albania and b) provides professional cleaning services for offices, public places, hotels, and residencies. Employees are orphans, Roma, Egyptians, individuals with financial problems, and people with disabilities. The organization has also added minors who are in conflict with the law.	Promote sustained and inclusive growth through productive employment. Integrate vulnerable groups, in particular youth through work and provide them with appropriate professional support.
Algeria Algeria remains in the evolving stages of SE awareness. There are opportunities, among the youth where unemployment is high, but social and security problems (criminality, drug usage, suicides, illegal immigration, terrorism, etc.) exist, as well as significant cultural barriers, such not	Collectif Torba http://agroecologie-algerie.org Agriculture	Roughly translated as "the collective of soil" the focus is on permaculture, agro-ecology, and organic farming practices. Operating a farm located within the Chrea National Park and other agricultural land. Members of this agricultural cooperative have a food-sharing program. To expand awareness, they have workshops for adults as well as children from primary and secondary schools.	Ensure sustainable consumption and production patterns. Protect, restore, and promote sustainable use of land ecosystems. Grow organic produce, land cultivation by planting trees, and encouraging urban Algerians to reconnect with nature, the land, and farming.

(*Continued*)

Table 5.1 (Continued)

Mediterranean countries	SE name and activity	Main focus	Social impact
accepting females as entrepreneurs (Ghiat, 2014; Aliouche and Fernandez, 2017).	Res'Art http://resart.over-blog.fr Local Artisans	Network of women artisans to establish independent businesses. The SE trains women to become economically independent by using their crafts expertise. Helps young females to preserve cultural traditions by learning the art of crafting using local materials and recycling. Assists in marketing, e-commerce, and entrepreneurial skills. Improves the economic status of women, increases their self-esteem, and independence in a culture that limits opportunities for females.	Helping women in Algeria to confront the nation's discriminatory laws, customs, and policies that prevent them from achieving economic independence.
Bosnia and Herzegovina The private sector is young and the number of SEs in Bosnia & Herzegovina is unknown. Public sector support of SMEs focuses on entrepreneurship in general, but includes programs for women and youth as special vulnerable categories. The Employment Service and Fund is dedicated to the employment of persons with disabilities (Varga, 2017).	Fenix http://centar-fenix.com Mental health services and lobbying for rights	A non-profit dedicated to improving and humanizing the lives of mental patients. It promotes mental health policies in accordance with international standards. Offers opportunities for those individuals who need to use mental health services and helps to break the stigma about such use. Works to increase the human and technical capacities of its clients and to enable their re-socialization because they are often shunned or socially excluded.	Promote sustained, inclusive, and sustainable economic growth through full-time and productive employment for vulnerable individuals. Providing employment to women who were returning refugees, serving preparing food to vulnerable citizens, and delivering various types of care for the elderly.

	Youth Bank of the Mozaik Foundation https://mozaik.ba Financing, consulting, and business incubation	Started as a "Youth Bank" to support young people through community projects offering education and training in self-employment. Goal is increasing participation of young people in local development of rural communities and for them to serve as a role model for others. Strategy is to build a generation of entrepreneurial and innovative youth. For long-term sustainability of SEs, it has shifted its activities to providing mentoring as well as financial support.	Opportunities for youth-led groups according to the needs in their communities. This includes working on cultural and sports projects. Youth participate as active citizens in their communities as well as developing their professional governance and management skills. Ensure inclusive and equitable quality education and promote lifelong learning opportunities.
Croatia (*EU Member*) Croatia lags behind in recognizing SEs as a concept. Non-profit organizations are turning to SEs as a self-financing technique using fees for services (Perić and Delić, 2014). Croatian SEs are in environmental study, social services, education and research, culture as well as community development. Problems remain with lack of clarity about responsibilities for SE implementation by institutions dealing with social issues (Varga, 2017).	Impact Hub https://zagreb.impacthub. net Consulting, and business incubation	A community for entrepreneurs and social innovators offering business space, inspiration laboratory, and a business incubator. Members, connect, collaborate, co-create, and evolve. Also conducts a yearlong educational program on SE targeting students in Croatia.	Build an infrastructure for entrepreneurs and foster innovation. Ensure inclusive and equitable quality education as well as promote lifelong learning opportunities. Offer collaborative space for networking, working, and as an inspirational place for events.
	Roda http://www.roda.hr/en/ Education and lobbying for parental and children's rights	Mission is to foster a society that promotes and handles issues involving children, parents, prospective parents, and families. Informs, educates, and campaigns for policy improvements by focusing on maternity and parental leave, and medically assisted pregnancy. Works to improve birthing conditions, breastfeeding promotion, education and counseling. Provides support for parents and future parents as well as child traffic safety.	Ensure inclusive and equitable quality education and promote lifelong learning opportunities. Implement appropriate health and safety policies as well as promote plans and suitable measures to prevent health problems. Creation of infrastructure and legal frameworks for parents and children. Promotes well-being at all ages.

(Continued)

Table 5.1 (Continued)

Mediterranean countries	SE name and activity	Main focus	Social impact
Cyprus (*EU Member*) SEs in Cyprus must engage in economic activity and have market orientation and thus be considered an "enterprise" and thus be differentiated from voluntary or public sector organizations. Legally formed SE may be as either as a private firm with shareholders or they can register as a charity or a cooperative. Government is supportive of SEs, but problems include lack of understanding or awareness of SEs, hostility from private enterprises, as well as legal and financial voids. (European Commission, 2014b).	Alion Beach Hotel http://alion.com Tourism and hospitality	Alion was one of the nation's first hotels to join a recycling initiative. Paper, glass, plastic, metal, and drink cartons (PMD) as well as cooking oil, chemical containers, batteries, printer toners, and electrical equipment waste is collected by licensed recyclers. This waste management system has reduced landfill requirements.	Ensure sustainable consumption and production patterns. Take action to combat pollution and its impacts.
	Agia Skepi Therapeutic Community http://agiaskepi.com Addiction treatment and organic food production	Provides services for adults who are long-term substance abusers and also assists their families. Vocational therapy and integration into society is through meaningful employment is a part of the therapy program. Members of the community farm land and produce organic products that include fruit, vegetables, dairy, eggs, and bread. Their products are then sold through a local supermarket chain.	Ensure healthy lives and promote well-being for all at all ages Ensure sustainable consumption and production patterns.
Egypt Social and community problems are drivers for SE development. Some SEs began out of necessity or chance coincidences by people with little to no training in entrepreneurship.	Sekem http://www.sekem.com/en/index/ Education, Agriculture and Health	Provides leadership by example in reducing pesticide use in Egyptian cotton fields by 90 percent. The SE established schools, an adult education center, and a medical center. Sekem fills an institutional void in Egypt by providing the social structures that people can trust. It also alleviates their poverty trap and helps them gain control over their lives.	Promote sustainable agriculture and economic growth. Provide education, training, and skills for productive employment. Build an infrastructure that was lacking. Promote inclusive and sustainable social health and security programs.

(Younis, 2015). Barriers include lack of funding and inability of existing SEs to scale up their operations. Awareness of civic engagement and social responsibility is now more favorable with an increasing interest in SE among youth (Abdou and El Ebrashi, 2015).	Helm http://www.helmegypt.org Training and employment of people with disabilities	Helm, translating to "dream", is a non-profit to promote social inclusion in employment and accessibility for persons with disabilities. Works to change how Egyptian society perceives disabilities. Encourages private and public institutions to become accessible for everyone. Assists companies to accept and support individuals with disabilities as part of a diverse and productive workforce. Provides career and counseling services as well as internships.	Embrace and enhance every ability, skill, and talent of individuals with disabilities. Provide support, counseling, and training opportunities to vulnerable population as well as foster their ambitions and fulfill their career goals.
France (*EU Member*) Nation is developing SEs, but still has no precise definition or legal status. Some organizations de facto meet the EU operational criteria of SEs. Activities include public utility cooperatives, non-profit organizations (associations and foundations) with commercial activities, and mainstream enterprises pursuing an explicit and primarily social aim (European Commission, 2014c).	Club Med and Agrisud http://www.agrisud.org/en/club-med-agrisud-un-partenariat-durable/ Tourism, hospitality, and agriculture	Club Med has partnered with Agrisud to achieve sustainable development and social responsibility. Agrisud is an SE focused on poverty reduction by helping to form "very small family enterprises." Supports local agriculture by aiding farmers to supply Club Med resorts, thus giving them a more stable economic perspective and encouragement to invest. It encourages farmers to a more sustainable use of land and initiates them to a market economy through commercial, organizational, and management empowerment.	Protect, restore and promote sustainable use of land ecosystems. Sustainability in family farms.
	Petit Bain http://www.petitbain.org Arts	A cooperative for artists and actors located on a floating barge. It has a theater, restaurant, and arts space. It also assists in social integration by easing accessibility to people with reduced mobility, as well as for the deaf and hard of hearing. It fosters socialization of individuals by offering them a job and by training them to help them find sustainable work.	Build resilient infrastructure, and foster innovation. Invest in sustainable facilities that allow universal access and use, especially by persons with disabilities and other disadvantaged groups.

(Continued)

Table 5.1 (Continued)

Mediterranean countries	SE name and activity	Main focus	Social impact
Gibraltar Many new businesses are established each year in all sectors. Tight market means Gibraltar has problems in recruitment and finding affordable office space. The government has been non-interventionist, which attracts entrepreneurs from abroad. Lacking natural resources, the laissez-faire strategy has been among this duty-free port's most important assets (Dana, 2002).	PwC Gibraltar https://www.pwc.gi/about-us/csr.html Accounting and consulting services	The large multinational has initiatives to create a better work environment, including training and development, as well as people-centered employment policies. Established a code of conduct as well as confidential grievance and ethical guidance procedures. Conducts annual survey to share views and opinions focusing on what employees feel are the strongest and weakest areas of their workplaces.	Build a resilient infrastructure; promote inclusive and sustainable business operations that also foster innovation.
	Leisure Cinemas http://www.leisurecinemas.com Entertainment	Local movie theater has equipment suited to the needs of the deaf or hard of hearing as well as for the blind and visually impaired. Headphones provide descriptive audio of what is happening on screen. Wireless captioning glasses for people who are deaf and hard of hearing allow them to view closed captioned text in their line of sight.	Promote inclusive and sustainable participation for all by using innovation. Invest in sustainable facilities and infrastructures that allow universal access and use, especially by persons with disabilities and other disadvantaged groups.
Greece *(EU Member)* Greece lacks policies for SEs and has not yet implemented appropriate standards. It is disconnected from European practices that facilitate SEs (Zoehrer, 2017). Many Greek SEs operate bottom-up, often within the informal economy or function as charitable organizations. Financing is only available for project-based funding and money is from abroad. There are no	OTE https://www.cosmote.gr/otegroup/en_index.jsp Telecommunication	Identified safety and health risks to provide proper training for employees. Provides telephone devices and special discounts to vulnerable people. Funds scholarships and work experience to disadvantaged students. Established recycling program for packaging materials and reduction of waste streams.	Reduce inequality within society, especially during times of economic disruption. Environmental sustainability and effective programs to help mitigate pollution.

support structures such as incubators, mentoring, and counseling (European Commission, 2014d; Morgan, 2015).	Solidarity Salt https://www.solidaritysalt.com Food company	First SE in Greece to empower women newcomers to build a new life for themselves and their families. Goal is to address the lack of employment options for female refugees. Helps overcome the problems derives from the lack of language skills that isolate newcomers in camps, thus making their integration into Greek society challenging. The women take natural sea salt, package it in a handmade bag, and include a personal message from its maker.	Addresses specific issues of refugees with no opportunities for employment or integration. Provides education, skills training, and develops a strong community.
Israel Many options exist in that SEs may be registered as a business or a non-profit organization (NPO). NGOs can establish SEs as a subsidiary that is either a separate NPO or as a business. Businesses can partner with NGOs as owners of joint SEs. Cooperatives may establish their own NPOs. Cooperatives were traditionally regarded as separate, but are now considered as part of the SE field (Abbou et al., 2017).	Juha's Guesthouse http://www.zarqabay.com Tourism and hospitality	A guesthouse in an Arab village with the lowest socioeconomic ranking in Israel. It is the first step in reconstructing the community's image and business infrastructure. The guesthouse attracts attention from tourists and for developing a tourism economy in an overlooked destination. Provides growth for other businesses and initiatives, for positive change in the village. It also has a program to empower local youth, teach them English, and serve as guide tours.	Reduce inequalities within society. Ensure inclusive and equitable quality education and promote learning opportunities. Creates business opportunities for communities and in developing critical work skills.
	Zot Zot www.zotzot.co.il Education	The SE provides training and employment for female ex-convicts in the field of digital printing. They also make a range of products that includes fashion accessories, coasters, cell phone cases, mouse pads, etc.	Achieve gender equality and empower women. Promote sustained, inclusive, and sustainable employment.

(Continued)

Table 5.1 (Continued)

Mediterranean countries	SE name and activity	Main focus	Social impact
Italy *(EU Member)* Italy recognizes two forms of social-based businesses: social cooperatives and SEs. SEs are diversifying into new markets, but there is competition from for-profit companies in markets traditionally served by SEs. Problems in attracting effective managers to because of lower salaries compared to other sectors of the economy (European Commission, 2014e).	Banco Farmaceutico https://www. bancofarmaceutico.org / Charity organization	Organizes a "National Medicine Collection Day." Objective is to salvage medicines from pharmaceutical companies in collaboration with select pharmacies. This involves the recovery of unexpired drugs. The effort provides social welfare charities with a supply of medicines, prescription drugs, supplements, and devices.	Ensure healthy lives and promote well-being. Reduce inequality within society.
	Spazio Aperto Servizi http://www.spazioaper toservizi.org Hostel for at risk individuals	A center for the care of trauma in youth and family. Focus on those with physical and sexual abuse, incest, serial abandonment, and the impacts of a lack of parental skills. The co-op provides sheltered accommodation, with children and caregivers. Helps those with acute trauma, rather than chronic conditions.	Ensure healthy lives and promote well-being for youth. Offers psychological intensive care.
Lebanon People with prior experience in entrepreneurship who shared similar viewpoints about a social issue have started SEs (Halabi et al., 2017). There is interest in the study of women social entrepreneurs engaged in the professional integration of low-skilled women in Lebanon. However, female entrepreneurs remain a minority in Lebanon (Wahidi and Lebègue, 2017).	Sarah's bag https://shop.sarahsbag. com/en/home Handicraft bags	The fashion house SE creates luxury handcrafted bags and accessories. Employs women, particularly those who are illiterate with few options for employment, those from conservative religious backgrounds who cannot work outside their homes despite needing an income to support their families, as well as current and ex-prisoners. Former convicts have used their income to overturn wrongful convictions while current inmates support their families while being incarcerated. Encourages these artisans to train other women in their towns and villages, thus creating additional jobs in their communities.	Achieve gender equality and empower underprivileged women, especially prisoners. Promote inclusive and sustainable economic growth along with full and productive employment. Reduce inequality within societies with morbid-bound traditions of female subordination and subservience.

	Organization	Objective	Outcomes/Aims
	The Food Heritage Foundation http://food-heritage.org Traditional food products	Objective is to increase consumers' awareness and demand for healthy home-cooked local cuisine and produce. Establishes linkages between urban and rural communities so small farmers and producers can promote culinary and agricultural traditions and sell their products. Preserve and revive local food knowledge and traditions. Bridge modern generation and urban populations with food traditions to culinary heritage and benefit small producers and farmers.	Aiming at the conservation of indigenous culinary knowledge through preservation and documentation of traditional food heritage. Promotes the livelihoods of rural producers and processors through the creation of rural-urban linkages. Economic development is through the promotion of local food heritage. Providing professional counseling and adjustment skills. Opportunity for youth-led groups according to the needs in their communities.
Libya Libya has undergone a turbulent and conflicted environment making it difficult to have stable conditions for positive change and thriving social enterprises. Armed conflict and political instability severely impact conditions, but there are initiatives and externally funded projects (OECD, 2014; Mussa, 2017).	The Libya Youth Center https://www.facebook.com/pg/libyayouthcenter/about/?ref=page_internal Youth center	Offers the prospect of a better future to children and adolescents who have suffered from acts of war and their consequences in Libya. The goal is to enable young people to work through their trauma and experiences with professional support. Operates a volunteer staffed psycho-social center as a drop-in center. Leisure and outdoor activities as well as educational programs emphasize the inclusion of parents and families. Teams also work within schools, hospitals, and other community centers to help those affected overcome any inhibitions and fears.	

(Continued)

Table 5.1 (Continued)

Mediterranean countries	SE name and activity	Main focus	Social impact
	Yummy Libya https://www.facebook. com/pg/79yummy/ reviews/?ref=page_ internal Traditional food products	Provides support for women through a food delivery app called Yummy that delivers homemade meals cooked by women in their own kitchens. Offering anonymity options for the cooks, and allows women to take food orders from men without having to speak to them. This is a product of a nationwide movement to encourage entrepreneurial development and help diversify the Libyan economy away from oil.	Achieve gender equality and empower women. Promote productive employment as well as decent work for women. Benefits include increased self-confidence and a positive demonstration effect from female employment in their community.
Malta *(EU Member)* NGOs, voluntary sector organizations, and cooperatives fulfill the functions of SE. They have potential to support and providing services to vulnerable groups in society including the disabled, the long-term unemployed, young people, women, and immigrants. SEs help these groups and have them re-enter the labor market (European Commission, 2014f).	Empower http://www.empower-coop.org Social mission driven organization	Local business people initiated the cooperative to create employment opportunities for those with disabilities and other vulnerable groups. Lobbying for full and active inclusion individuals with disabilities. Production is undertaken under profitable conditions so that the work provided by them will contribute to their integration within society. Examples include sorting of plastic and rubber parts that are then recycled. Various assembly tasks including folding of brochures. Another SE function is a temporary staffing agency for filling various positions, such as data entry, which is supported on location by co-op staff members.	Promote sustained, inclusive and sustainable economic growth, full-time and productive employment. The company encourages the hiring and entrepreneurship especially among vulnerable groups.

As of 2015, SE legislation allows businesses to consider alternative ways of achieving corporate social responsibility (gov.mt, 2015).	Jacob's Brew https://www.jacobsbrew. cafe Coffee Shop	A coffee shop with programs to assist individuals facing hardships or trauma. Paying customers get a token for free coffee that they can pass on to someone going through a trauma. They organize therapy meetings for survivors and help boost the morale of families facing trauma. Other NGOs and SEs can hold fund raising initiatives at the coffee shop. Another project delivers free sandwiches and beverages every Sunday to families in the waiting area at hospital.	Filling emotional and social needs during crisis and trauma situations. Provide support opportunities and therapy mechanisms.
Monaco Monaco's international development policy is on fighting poverty and it supports more than 130 projects in 12 nations, primarily the least developed countries (redherring. com, 2017). Local entrepreneurs have a sustainable vision. Focus on vulnerable populations: children, women, people with disabilities, and refugees.	LeMéridien Beach Plaza http://www. lemeridienmontecarlo. com/green-sustainable- development Tourism and Hospitality	Hotel protects its location facing the Mediterranean. Provides guests options to use less water, energy, and other resources. Reduced energy consumption and sourcing local herbs and plants from environmental friendly farms and menus with regional foods. A portion of property proceeds is donated to the children's program of UNICEF.	Climate action: Take action to combat pollution and its impacts. Support local farming and culinary traditions.
	Monaco Impact https://www.monaco- impact.org Finance managing investment funds	Objective is to connect global citizens, local philanthropists, and investors, through collaboration, education, and opportunities to support the next generation of "Responsible Entrepreneurs or Social Entrepreneurs". Activities contribute to a positive image of Monaco. Has also launched an "incubator" to support young Monaco-based entrepreneurs and business start-ups and encourages them to expand the "social impact" dimension in their business model.	A financial infrastructure for local entrepreneurs and for fostering social innovation.

(Continued)

Table 5.1 (Continued)

Mediterranean countries	SE name and activity	Main focus	Social impact
Montenegro There is a lack of specific regulations on SE activities as well as the legal and funding framework is weak. However, a number of SEs operate in the Montenegro. The funding landscape for social enterprises is limited. Most SEs were set up with funding from local organizations, foundations or international donors and pursue additional donor funding to develop their initiatives (MVCA, 2016; Varga, 2017).	Nova Šansa u Novom http://www.novasansau novom.com Digital printing office	Voluntarily organized, non-profit and non-political organization. The digital printing business has the objective of providing employment and professional training to people with developmental disabilities. The initiative was developed in partnership and with the support of government agencies.	Promote sustained, inclusive and sustainable economic growth, full-time employment. Provide training for persons with special needs. The company encourages the hiring and entrepreneurship especially among vulnerable groups.
	Cooperative Rukatnice http://en.korak-hapi-step.eu/interview-fana-delija/#more-112 Handicraft cooperative	Originally set up to provide employment opportunities and income to women affected by violence. The women's craft cooperative makes products out of recycled textiles. It was started with a grant from international donors and the Employment Agency of Montenegro.	Achieve gender equality and empower women.
Morocco Regulations define SEs as those aiming to address social needs and improve communities, while creating economic growth and jobs. SEs often work to improve or support a community, usually women, or the poorly educated or trained. Personal funds, membership fees, and government funding are most common sources of SE funding. Challenges include lack of technical support, lack of funding, the limitations of the legal framework, the lack of an enterprise culture and mindset,	Eco Hotel Atlas Mountains https://www.changemakers.com/competition/geotourism2008/entries/eco-hotel-atlas-mountains http://www.morocco-travel.com/morocco/DarItrane/	A minimalist lodging establishment that is wholly owned and co-managed by a local family. The hotel was renovated using local and ancient methods and materials. The original building was without electricity, but electric power is now connected for travelers' convenience. A major objective is for visitors to experience the local Berber culture, traditions, and cuisine in an authentic setting. The local community also participates in direct contact with travelers.	Ensure sustainable consumption and production patterns. Implement resource reuse adopt sustainable practices in relation to their supply chain, incorporate sustainability information into their corporate reports and promote local culture and products. Promote awareness among travellers and tourists to make sustainability an attribute of value in the
	Tourism and Hospitality	The enterprise also teaches traditional farming methods without the use of fossil fuels, as well as selling natural cleaning agents and herbal medicines that are used by the Berber people.	choice of destinations, products and tourism services and raise awareness of the importance of their responsible behavior in the destination.

as well as language issues (Angel-Urdinola, 2014; wamda.com, 2014).	MCISE http://www.mcise.org/en/ Consulting, and business incubation	The Moroccan Center for Innovation and Social Entrepreneurship opened co-working space, called Dare that also means "do" in the Moroccan dialect. It is designed develop SE ideas and social innovation training. It has a place for meetings, special events, and art exhibits. Offers computer coding and an innovation lab. Has a business incubation program and offers partnerships with funding organizations and external foundations.	Build an infrastructure for social entrepreneurs and foster innovation. Promotes inclusive and equitable skills and learning opportunities. Offers collaborative space for working and an inspirational place for events.
Slovenia (*EU Member*) Laws are in line with EU definition of SEs, but few public measures have been implemented for SEs. Barriers include; weak business skills among majority of social entrepreneurs, limited understanding of SE concept among the general public, lack of public support and access to finance. Existing SE are in agriculture development, green tourism, organic farming, and herbal medicine. Migrants and asylum seekers work for SEs and allow them to better integrate into the Slovenian society (European Commission, 2014g; EESC, 2017).	Hotel Park Ljubljana http://www.hotelpark.si Tourism and Hospitality	The hotel created a beehive on its rooftop to safeguard sea bees, which are a protected species. Works to encourage their preservation. Organizes tours to its roof for schools and kindergartens to sensitize younger generations on sustainability and wildlife preservation issues.	Environmental sustainability Ensuring sustainable consumption and production patterns Protect, restore, and promote use of ecosystems in urban areas.
	Eco boutique hotel A.M.S. Beagle https://amsbeagle.com Tourism and Hospitality	A certified "Slovenia Green Destination" logging facility in a small town that features a passive-active net zero-carbon, virtually zero-energy building with views of the surrounding mountains. Meals are made from locally sourced natural ingredients, all beverages from reusable glass bottles, etc. The Slovenia Green Brand not only promotes sustainable endeavors, but also enables hotels to evaluate and improve their efforts.	Effort directed for sustainable development of tourism Environmental sustainability Ensuring sustainable consumption and production patterns Protect and promote use of ecosystems in rural areas

(Continued)

Table 5.1 (Continued)

Mediterranean countries	SE name and activity	Main focus	Social impact
Spain (*EU Member*) No formal definition of what constitutes a "social entrepreneurship" and SEs are unregulated. Entities in the social economy are cooperatives, mutual societies, foundations and associations engaged in an economic activity, employee-owned enterprises, work integration enterprises, sheltered employment centers, fishermen's associations, agricultural processing companies and unique entities created under specific rules. Problems include lack of support from the government, limited awareness among public institutions about the concept of SE, lack of practice of social public procurement, and difficulties in access to finance (European Commission, 2014h).	A Puntadas http://www.apuntadas.es/a_puntadas/quienes_somos.html Textile	Manages training workshops in textile confection aimed at women at risk of exclusion. Since its inception the SE incorporated product design and marketing from a business vision, favoring the professionalization of women and the sustainability of project. Received Global Organic Textile Standard (GOTS) certification, a voluntary world standard covering all post-harvest processing (spinning, loom weaving, dyeing, and manufacturing) of clothing and textiles made with organic fibers.	Achieve gender equality and empower women. Promote inclusive and sustainable employment. Developing sustainable consumption and production patterns.
	PortAventura https://www.portaventuraworld.com/en Entertainment, Tourism-Theme park	PortAventura integrated into their operations and strategy the United Nations Global Compact principles on human rights, labor, environment, and anti-corruption. Adapted the amusement park for everyone to access, including disabled visitors. Sustainable use of resources by encouraging reuse and minimal generation of waste. Employees have training and motivational workshops to promote healthy habits such as managing stress, smoking cessation, healthy eating, and regular physical exercise.	Promote inclusive society by access for all. Invest in sustainable facilities and infrastructures. Reduce pollution and its impacts. Promote healthy lives and individual well-being.

State of Palestine People face a daily struggle to survive with a high unemployment rate. Limited heath care with safety and food insecurity compounds problems for the many living in severe poverty. A barrier is to change the state of mind; thus, SEs need to make a difference in society: "leave the talking to the politicians and focus on being active change makers in society" (Yaacoubi, 2016).	Siraj Fund Management Company https://www.siraj.ps Finance managing investment funds	The first private equity fund established in Palestine. Direct equity investments range from start-ups or distressed companies, to large companies. Objective is to release the potential of these businesses, while promoting technological advancements and development; thus spurring economic growth, job creation and innovation in Palestine. SFMC launched Siraj Palestine Fund II and has plans future funds focused on the Palestinian market, thereby contributing to the sustainable development of the country.	Building a financial infrastructure for entrepreneurs and fostering innovation.
Syria For those remaining in Syria, to focus on work requires an effort to rise above the various "distractions" such as worries about Internet access or availability of electricity. However, there has been improvement for females, not only as entrepreneurs, but also as chief breadwinners for the family. Many men have been forced to flee or engage in armed conflicts. (Taylor, 2015)	Daaboul Industrial Group http://www.dig.bz/co2/index.php?lang=en Aluminum & glass industrial	Built an advanced smelter to recycle parts and pieces of damaged aluminum. Uses industrial technology that has the highest efficiency to reduce energy consumption and minimize harmful gas emissions. Waste water is treated and used to irrigate the companies' site. Committed to provide safe and healthy working conditions and atmosphere. They established a separate charity management group (zakat or sadaqa) that distributes about $1.5 million annually. It also has a library open to all employees and their families.	Actions to combat climate change and its impacts. Reduce inequality and promote sustainable economic growth.

(Continued)

Table 5.1 (Continued)

Mediterranean countries	SE name and activity	Main focus	Social impact
Tunisia The nation lacks data and no legal definition of SEs. The term "social enterprise" covers heterogeneous practices and organizational arrangements ranging from non-profits to for-profits. Most organizations that call themselves SEs are actually NGOs that have revenue-generating activities. SEs operate as private enterprises, associations or hybrids (e.g., associations with independent private enterprise ventures or vice versa). In agribusiness and handicrafts, SEs are more likely to adopt the status of cooperatives (World Trade Bank, 2017).	Debbo 52 https://www.facebook.com/debbo52/ Artist cooperative	An artistic incubator in the fields of visual and digital arts. Supplies artists with the technical and logistical means as well as in the search of funding to help them carry out their projects. It is also a platform that gathers artists from different backgrounds and cultures for collaboration. Young artists manage their artistic projects and act as a catalyst for the Tunisian creative industry.	Building a financial infrastructure for entrepreneurs and fostering innovation.
	Kolna Hirfa https://www.facebook.com/KolnaHirfaTabarka/ Handicrafts and livelihoods	Provides training to rural women artisans between 25 and 50 years old in high-end handicrafts techniques and production management. Empowers women to participate in decision-making processes and acquire business skills in managing a handicraft company, including choosing products, raw materials, and pricing.	Achieve gender equality and empower females. Promote sustained economic growth. Benefits include increased self-confidence and a positive demonstration effect from women's employment in their community.

Turkey			
There is no legal and officially recognized definition of SE. Thus initiatives are "ad hoc" or implemented by various legal entities such as charities and associations, cooperatives, and non-profits. Economic growth alone does not bring direct and positive change for the benefit of vulnerable groups. Problems of social cohesion, environment, gender equality, and regional disparities in Turkey are structural. (Türker et al., 2014).	Evreka https://evreka.co R&D company	Evreka Smart Waste Collection System provides a green solution for traditional waste collection. Sensors inside garbage bins collect the fullness data and using M2M technology, transfers them to cloud server. With the help of fill rate information in the trash bins, truck routes can be optimized for collections. After the route optimization process, garbage collection costs can be decreased up to 55 percent.	Action to combat pollution and the impacts of waste.
	Hayata Sarıl "hug life" Foundation http://hayatasaril.org Restaurant	First restaurant in Istanbul that offers free meals for all homeless people during certain hours. The restaurant operates with the slogan of "body, nourish and spirit." It also provides work and life opportunities for homeless people.	Reduce poverty and hunger. Achieve food security and improved nutrition. Reduce inequality within the society

Although some have benefited from direct and indirect public subsidies, these SEs are based on the idea that their activities are market oriented rather than operating as a strictly public or publicly funded organization (Smith, 2012). The examples promote the concept of SEs operating in these countries and in different environments. Many are grassroots innovations that increase the role of civil society in solving social problems as well as providing solutions to challenges and new ways to create added value for the local economy (Ates, Ates and Yülek, 2016).

Discussion and conclusion

Social entrepreneurship is a growing phenomenon in almost all nations (Urbano, Toledano and Soriano, 2010; Wulleman and Hudon, 2016). Although there are many shared attributes between traditional entrepreneurship and SE, Austin, Stevenson and Wei-Skillern (2006) found the greatest differences among them were the sources of financing and the mobilization of human resources. The literature exploring SE encompasses different perspectives as well as a variety of theories and approaches (Venkataraman, 1997), with no common definition of the concept itself (Dees, 2001; Mair and Marti, 2006; Martin and Osberg, 2007). Dees (2001) had already noted that SE has different meanings among people. Nations also do not agree, resulting in different legal forms for SE endeavors. Member nations of the EU have generally harmonized standards, but different political, economic and cultural traditions among them give rise to divergent meanings attached even to the phrase "social entrepreneurship" itself. Early adopters include Italy, where the term social enterprise was already customary in the 1980s (European Commission, 2014e). In France, there is a greater emphasis on the collective dimension of SEs (European Commission, 2014c). In other words, there is diversity in formal policies and legal framework regarding SEs, and there are differences in the efforts to establish legal categories for SE activities. Given the national backgrounds, there is no broad EU delineation of what organizations make up SEs, and there are even gaps among member nations such as in Croatia and Cyprus that do not specify SEs in their statutes (European Commission, 2014a, 2014b).

There is wide latitude in the regulations for SEs and their activities (European Commission, 2014c). Because they can be pursued through various legal vehicles, there are examples of SE forms found among the range of cooperative, non-profit, business and governmental sectors (Austin, Stevenson and Wei-Skillern, 2006; European Commission, 2014d). Moreover, what are considered SE activities can range in meaning, from not-for-profit initiatives that need alternative funding strategies to even describing it as any management scheme to create social value (Austin, Stevenson and Wei-Skillern, 2006). Others catalog any socially responsible practices by commercial businesses as SE, especially when such functions involve cross-sector partnerships (Sagawa and Segal, 2000). Another perspective categorizes SE initiatives as a means to alleviate social problems and to assist in accomplishing social change (Alvord et al., 2004). Moreover, authors that have a positive inclination to SE endeavors have mostly dominated the literature, and they tend to contrast them with traditional purely profit-focused entrepreneurship

(Chell et al., 2016). This perspective leads to studies that emphasize social enterprises as possessing the potential to help solve social problems (Chell et al., 2016). Research by Lubberink et al. (2018) confirms that social entrepreneurs develop important innovative solutions for complex societal challenges.

The motivation to achieve social activities, the resources needed to complete their mission and various influences that may control the decisions made by SEs present unique ethical challenges (André and Pache, 2016; Bacq, Hartog and Hoogendoorn, 2016). Their managers also take entrepreneurial risks to create social change while most often having to function with limited funding and almost always dealing with financial insecurity (Bugg-Levine, Kogut and Kulatilaka, 2012). These constraints, along with competition, sometimes force individuals to make difficult decisions. They may encounter many situations, such as during mission development, resource mobilization and performance management, which can enhance or obstruct their ethical principles. The enterprise's social mission itself provides challenges beyond what is encountered by typical commercial businesses.

Social enterprises operate in risky and dynamic environments that are mostly avoided by traditional profit-driven businesses (Dacin, Dacin and Matear, 2010). The SE movement is growing, with a wide variety of endeavors in many industries, and is conspicuous within the travel and hospitality sector. Moreover, tourism is an economic activity that accounts for 10% of the world's gross domestic product (GDP) and 7% of global trade, and provides 10% of all jobs (UNWTO, 2017). Because of this sector's inescapable influence, tourist-related SE initiatives could be a catalyst to promote and foster solutions to social problems. These include helping the transformations needed to achieve gender equality, building sustainable communities and promoting local culture and products, as well as serving as an employment vehicle for disadvantaged groups and those afflicted with poverty. For example, Iorgulescu and Răvar (2015) reported that SEs have an important role in the development of emerging economies because they not only provide employment opportunities for vulnerable groups but also serve as initiators for projects and services that generally have been offered by governments.

Every enterprise in the tourism sector has an important role in transforming the industry's approach in general, as well as enacting effective sustainability principles and innovative solutions into their operations (Crouch and Ritchie, 1999). Moreover, tourism is facilitated by many businesses, from numerous individual proprietors to large multinational corporations (Getz and Carlsen, 2005). From a structural perspective, the industry involves a complex network of selling chains, transport patterns, attractions, accommodations and technologies (Ryan, 2002). The numerous activities conducted by tourism-related businesses provide many opportunities to align their strategies with sustainability. There are implications for tourism in global economic, social, political, environmental and technological trends that should be noted by policy-makers (Dwyer et al., 2009). A strategy is to promote responsible practices that not only respect the natural, cultural and social environments, but also foster sustainable development of tourism destinations.

The trends into the future not only point to continuing potential of this sector from business opportunities, but also call for innovative enterprises to provide solutions in dealing with the challenges of mass tourism, especially in relation to the problems facing many destinations of sustainable economic growth, inclusive development and environmental preservation (UNWTO, 2016). There are gradually persuasive demands from many groups for the tourism operators and the travel industry in general to embrace more ethical and related positive attitudes within their operations (UNWTO, 2001). This desire for a more ethical approach has been noted in several studies and is especially needed in the ways in which tourism businesses relate not only with their consumers and the natural environment, but increasingly with calls for progressive acts, such as towards indigenous people and especially those who are impoverished, to help empower disadvantaged groups, especially young people and women as well as those in destinations that are suffering human rights abuses (Kinnaird and Hall, 1996; Ashley, Boyd and Goodwin, 2000; Ghodsee, 2003; Vellas, 2011; Lovelock and Lovelock, 2013). These areas of concern are particularly emphasized by social entrepreneurs. An increasing number of social enterprises have evolved within the tourism sectors that focus on responsible tourism by contributing to poverty alleviation and environmental protection (Briassoulis, 2004; von der Weppen and Cochrane, 2012).

Focusing only on the coastal areas of the European Union (EU) member nations provides evidence of these areas as attractive and desirable destinations for many people. All the Mediterranean countries' economies rely on tourism (WTTC, 2017). It is estimated that over half of all of the European hotel bed capacity is concentrated in the regions with a sea border, and this EU coastal and maritime tourism sector provides employment for over 3.2 million people (European Commission, 2018). Most of the focus has been on the advanced EU nations, but the Mediterranean Basin also includes other countries that are less developed and have areas with poverty and conflict (Natalucci, 2016).

The main contribution of this chapter to the literature is as the first analysis of SE in the Mediterranean Basin, using selected functioning examples related to tourism and hospitality to identify and elaborate on their essential components. These enterprises were established with the potential to set in motion new opportunities and bring innovation to their travel destinations. The selected SE examples attempt to achieve transformation within their local economic and social structures. They also illustrate some of the opportunities, experience and challenges with tourism-related projects. However, inquiries in other contexts might have different results. This chapter's objective, to examine social entrepreneurship and provide examples from Mediterranean countries, should also open additional approaches for further study. Analysis of the numerous facets of SE in the tourism sector and in other destinations around the world should also present useful insights.

References

Abbou, I., Gidron, B., Buber-Ben David, N., Greenberg, Y., Monnickendam-Givon, Y. and Navon, A. (2017). Social enterprise in Israel: The swinging pendulum between collectivism and individualism. *Social Enterprise Journal*, 13(4), pp. 329–344.

Abdou, E. and El Ebrashi, R. (2015). The social enterprise sector in Egypt: Current status and way forward. In: D. Jamali and A. Lanteri, eds., *Social entrepreneurship in the Middle East*. London: Palgrave Macmillan, pp. 37–62.

Aliouche, H. and Fernandez, D.B. (2017). Social entrepreneurship and franchising: A panacea for emerging countries? The case of Algeria. In: G. Hendrikse, G. Cliquet, T. Ehrmann, and J. Windsperger, eds., *Management and governance of networks*. Cham: Springer, pp. 75–90.

Alvord, S.H., Brown, L.D. and Letts, C.W. (2004). Social entrepreneurship and societal transformation: An exploratory study. *The journal of applied behavioral science*, 40(3), pp. 260–282.

Amelung, B. and Viner, D. (2006). Mediterranean tourism: Exploring the future with the tourism climatic index. *Journal of Sustainable Tourism*, 14(4), pp. 349–366.

Amin, A. (2009). Extraordinarily ordinary: Working in the social economy. *Social Enterprise Journal*, 5(1), pp. 30–49.

André, K. and Pache, A.C. (2016). From caring entrepreneur to caring enterprise: Addressing the ethical challenges of scaling up social enterprises. *Journal of Business Ethics*, 133(4), pp. 659–675.

Angel-Urdinola, D. (2014). Promoting social entrepreneurship in Morocco. Available at: http://blogs.worldbank.org/arabvoices/promoting-social-entrepreneurship-morocco [Accessed 19 Feb. 2018].

Ashley, C., Boyd, C. and Goodwin, H. (2000). Pro-poor tourism: Putting poverty at the heart of the tourism agenda. *Natural Resource Perspectives*, 51, pp. 1–6.

Ates, S.A., Ates, M. and Yülek, M.A. (2016). Going beyond GDP: The role of social innovation in building a welfare state. In: J.M. Saiz-Álvarez, ed., *Handbook of research on social entrepreneurship and solidarity economics*. Hershey, PA: Business Science Reference.

Austin, J.E., Stevenson, H.H. and Wei-Skillern, J. (2006). Social and commercial entrepreneurship: Same, different, or both?. *Entrepreneurship Theory and Practice*, 30(1), pp. 1–22.

Bacq, S., Hartog, C. and Hoogendoorn, B. (2016). Beyond the moral portrayal of social entrepreneurs: An empirical approach to who they are and what drives them. *Journal of Business Ethics*, 133(4), pp. 703–718.

Banks, J.A. (1972). *The sociology of social movements*. London: MacMillan.

Berenger, V. and Bresson, F. (2013). *Poverty and social exclusion around the Mediterranean sea*. New York: Springer.

Besley, T. and Ghatak, M. (2017). Profit with purpose? A theory of social enterprise. *American Economic Journal: Economic Policy*, 9(3), pp. 19–58.

Bibb, E., Fishberg, M., Harold, J. and Layburn, E. (2004). *The blended value glossary* [online]. Available at: http://impactinvesting.org/wp-content/uploads/2004/02/pdf-blended value-glossary.pdf [Accessed 19 Jan. 2018].

Bidet, E. and Spear, R. (2003). The role of social enterprise in European labour markets. *EMES Network Working Paper*. [online] pp. 1–46. Available at: http://dx.doi.org/10.2139/ssrn.1352411 [Accessed 19 Feb. 2018].

Bloom, P.N. and Dees, G. (2008). Cultivate your ecosystem. *Stanford Social Innovation Review*, 6(1), pp. 47–53.

Bornstein, D. (2004). *How to change the world: Social entrepreneurs and the power of new ideas*. Oxford: Oxford University Press.

Bramwell, B. (2004). Mass tourism, diversification and sustainability in Southern Europe's coastal regions. In: B. Bramwell, ed., *Coastal mass tourism: Diversification and sustainable development in Southern Europe*. Clevendon, UK: Channel View Publication, pp. 1–31.

Brendon, P. (1991). Thomas Cook: 150 years of popular tourism. UK: Secker (Martin) & Warburg Ltd.

Briassoulis, H. (2004). Crete: Endowed by nature, privileged by geography, threatened by tourism. In: B. Bramwell, ed., *Coastal mass tourism: Diversification and sustainable development in Southern Europe*. Clevendon, UK: Channel View Publication, pp. 48–67.

Buchholz, R.A. and Rosenthal, S.B. (2005). The spirit of entrepreneurship and the qualities of moral decision making: Toward a unifying framework. *Journal of Business Ethics*, 60, pp. 307–315.

Bugg-Levine, A., Kogut, B. and Kulatilaka, N. (2012). A new approach to funding social enterprises. *Harvard Business Review*, 90(1/2), pp. 118–123.

Butler, R.W. (1990). Alternative tourism: Pious hope or Trojan horse?. *Journal of Travel Research*, 28(3), pp. 40–45.

Butler-Bowdon, T. (2010). *50 self-help classics: 50 inspirational books to transform your life from timeless sages to contemporary gurus*. Clerkenwell, London: Nicholas Brealey Publishing.

Cabezas, A.L. (1999). Women's work is never done: Sex tourism in Sousa, Dominican Republic. In: K. Kempadoo, ed., *Sun, sex, and gold: Tourism and sex work in the Caribbean*. Lanham, MD: Rowman & Littlefield Publishers, pp. 93–124.

Cacaud, P. (2005). Fisheries laws and regulations in the Mediterranean: A comparative study. Available at: www.fao.org/docrep/008/y5880e/y5880e00.htm#Contents [Accessed 19 Feb. 2018].

Cao, J., Galinsky, A.D. and Maddux, W.W. (2014). Does travel broaden the mind? Breadth of foreign experiences increases generalized trust. *Social Psychological and Personality Science*, 5(5), pp. 517–525.

Chell, E., Spence, L.J., Perrini, F. and Harris, J.D. (2016). Social entrepreneurship and business ethics: Does social equal ethical?. *Journal of Business Ethics*, 133(4), pp. 619–625.

Cho, A.H. (2006). Politics, values and social entrepreneurship: A critical appraisal. In: J. Mair, J. Robinson and K. Hockerts, eds., *Social entrepreneurship*. New York: Palgrave Macmillan, pp. 34–56.

CICOPA-International Organisation of Industrial, Artisanal and Service Producers' Cooperatives (2013). Promoting cooperatives and the social economy in Greece. Available at: www.cicopa.coop/IMG/pdf/Promoting_cooperatives_and_the_social_economy_in_Greece_Sep_2013.pdf [Accessed 19 Jan. 2018].

Cohen, R. and Kennedy, P. (2012). *Global sociology*. London: Palgrave Macmillan.

Coleman, W.D. and Essid, Y. (2012). *Two Mediterranean worlds: Diverging paths of globalization and autonomy*. Vancouver: UBC Press.

Cooney, K. (2013). Examining the labor market presence of US WISEs. *Social Enterprise Journal*, 9(2), pp. 147–163.

Cooper, M. and Hanson, J. (1998). Where there are no tourists . . . yet: A visit to the slum brothels in Ho Chi Minh City, Vietnam. In: M. Oppermann, ed., *Sex tourism and prostitution: Aspects of leisure, recreation and work*. New York: Cognizant Communication, pp. 144–152.

Crick, M. (1989). Representations of international tourism in the social sciences: Sun, sex, sights, savings, and servility. *Annual Review of Anthropology*, 18(1), pp. 307–344.

Crouch, G.I. and Ritchie, J.B. (1999). Tourism, competitiveness, and societal prosperity. *Journal of Business Research*, 44(3), pp. 137–152.

Csapo, J. (2012). The role and importance of cultural tourism in modern tourism industry. In: M. Kasimoglu, ed., *Strategies for tourism industry-micro and macro perspectives.* Croatia: InTech, pp. 201–232.

Dacin, P.A., Dacin, M.T. and Matear, M. (2010). Social entrepreneurship: Why we don't need a new theory and how we move forward from here. *The Academy of Management Perspectives*, 24(3), pp. 37–57.

Dana, L.P. (2002). Entrepreneurship and public policy in Gibraltar. *International Journal of Entrepreneurship and Innovation Management*, 2(1), pp. 38–42.

Daniele, R. and Quezada, I. (2017). Business models for social entrepreneurship in tourism. In: P.J. Sheldon and R. Daniele, eds., *Social entrepreneurship and tourism.* Cham: Springer, pp. 81–100.

Dees, J.G. (2001). *The meaning of social entrepreneurship.* [online] Duke University News. Available at: https://entrepreneurship.duke.edu/news-item/the-meaning-of-social-entre preneurship/ [Accessed 1 Dec. 2017].

Dey, P. and Steyaert, C. (2016). Rethinking the space of ethics in social entrepreneurship: Power, subjectivity, and practices of freedom. *Journal of Business Ethics*, 133(4), pp. 627–641.

Donyadide, A. (2010). Ethics in tourism. *European Journal of Social Sciences*, 17(3), pp. 426–433.

Drayton, W. (2006). Everyone a changemaker: Social entrepreneurship's ultimate goal. *Innovations: Technology, Governance, Globalization*, 1(1), pp. 80–96.

Drucker, P. (1979). *The practice of management.* London: Pan Books.

Drucker, P. (1985). *Innovation and entrepreneurship.* New York: Harper & Row.

Dwyer, L., Edwards, D., Mistilis, N., Roman, C. and Scott, N. (2009). Destination and enterprise management for a tourism future. *Tourism Management*, 30(1), pp. 63–74.

EESC – European Economic and Social Committee (2017). Recent Evolutions of the Social Economy in the European Union. Available at: www.ciriec.ulg.ac.be/wp-content/uploads/2017/10/RecentEvolutionsSEinEU_Summary2017.pdf [Accessed 1 Dec. 2017].

Elkington, J. (1994). Towards the sustainable corporation: Win-win-win business strategies for sustainable development. *California Management Review*, 36(2), pp. 90–100.

Elkington, J. (1997). *Cannibals with forks: The triple bottom line of 21st century business.* Oxford: Capstone Publishing.

Euclid Network (14 April 2017). Gathering to Grow Europe's Social Enterprise Movement. Available at: http://euclidnetwork.eu/2017/04/gathering-grow-mep [Accessed 9 Mar. 2018].

European Commission (2014a). *A map of social enterprises and their eco-systems in Europe. Country Report: Croatia.* Available at: shttp://ec.europa.eu/social/BlobServlet?docId=12991&langId=en [Accessed 4 Feb. 2018].

European Commission (2014b). *A map of social enterprises and their eco-systems in Europe. Country Report: Cyprus.* Available at: http://ec.europa.eu/social/BlobServlet?docId=12992&langId=en [Accessed 4 Feb. 2018].

European Commission (2014c). *A map of social enterprises and their eco-systems in Europe. Country Report: France.* Available at: http://ec.europa.eu/social/BlobServlet?docId=13024&langId=en [Accessed 4 Feb. 2018].

European Commission (2014d). *A map of social enterprises and their eco-systems in Europe. Country Report: Greece.* Available at: http://ec.europa.eu/social/BlobServlet?docId=13026&langId=en [Accessed 4 Feb. 2018].

European Commission (2014e). *A map of social enterprises and their eco-systems in Europe. Country Report: Italy.* Available at: http://ec.europa.eu/social/BlobServlet?docId=13026&langId=en [Accessed 4 Feb. 2018].

European Commission (2014f). *A map of social enterprises and their eco-systems in Europe. Country Report: Malta.* Available at: http://ec.europa.eu/social/BlobServlet?docId=13026&langId=en [Accessed 4 Feb. 2018].

European Commission (2014g). *A map of social enterprises and their eco-systems in Europe. Country Report: Slovenia.* Available at: http://ec.europa.eu/social/BlobServlet?docId=13026&langId=en [Accessed 4 Feb. 2018].

European Commission (2014h). *A map of social enterprises and their eco-systems in Europe. Country Report: Spain.* Available at: http://ec.europa.eu/social/BlobServlet?docId=13026&langId=en [Accessed 4 Feb. 2018].

European Commission (2018). *Coastal and maritime tourism.* Available at: https://ec.europa.eu/growth/sectors/tourism/offer/maritime-coastal_en. [Accessed 4 Feb. 2018].

European Social Enterprise Law Association – ESELA (October 2015). *Social enterprise in Europe: Developing legal systems which support social enterprise growth.* Available at: https://esela.eu/wp-content/uploads/2015/11/legal_mapping_publication_051015_web.pdf [Accessed 9 Mar. 2018].

Fennell, D.A. (2015). Ethics in tourism. In: G. Moscardo and P. Benckendorff, eds., *Education for sustainability in tourism.* Berlin, Heidelberg: Springer, pp. 45–57.

Fisscher, O., Frenkel, D., Lurie, Y. and Nijhof, A. (2005). Stretching the frontiers: Exploring the relationships between entrepreneurship and ethics. *Journal of Business Ethics*, 60(3), pp. 207–209.

Foryt, S. (2002). *Social entrepreneurship in developing nations* [online]. Available at: www.griequity.com/resources/integraltech/GRIMarket/socialentrepcases.pdf [Accessed 4 Feb. 2018].

Francis, J. (2016). Does travel really broaden the mind? *The Independent.* Available at: www.independent.co.uk/travel/news-and-advice/brexit-travel-broaden-the-mind-responsible-ethical-travel-kenya-holiday-spain-holiday-a7136486.html [Accessed 25 Feb. 2018].

Galera, G. and Borzaga, C. (2009). Social enterprise: An international overview of its conceptual evolution and legal implementation, *Social Enterprise Journal*, 5(3), pp. 210–228.

Getz, D. and Carlsen, J. (2005). Family business in tourism: State of the art. *Annals of Tourism Research*, 32(1), pp. 237–258.

Ghiat, B. (2014). Social change and women entrepreneurship in Algeria. *International Review* (1–2), pp. 90–100.

Ghodsee, K., 2003. State support in the market: Women and tourism employment in post-socialist Bulgaria. *International Journal of Politics, Culture, and Society*, 16(3), pp. 465–482.

Gilman, S.C. (2005). *Ethics codes and codes of conduct as tools for promoting an ethical and professional public service.* [online] Washington, DC: PREM, the World Bank, pp. 1–76. Available at: www.oecd.org/mena/governance/35521418.pdf [Accessed 4 Feb. 2018].

Goodwin, H. (1998). Sustainable tourism and poverty elimination. In: *DFID/DETR workshop on sustainable tourism and poverty* (Vol. 13). London: Department for International Development. Available at: www.academia.edu/download/31019248/dfidpaper.pdf [Accessed 12 Feb. 2018].

gov.mt (2015). *Social enterprise legislation allows businesses to consider alternative.* [online] Available at: www.gov.mt/en/Government/Press%20Releases/Pages/2015/June/26/pr151491.aspx [Accessed 10 Mar. 2018].

Groot, A. and Dankbaar, B. (2014). Does social innovation require social entrepreneurship? *Technology Innovation Management Review*, 4(12), pp. 17–26.

Halabi, S., Kheir, S. and Cochrane, P. (2017). *Social enterprise development in the Middle East and North Africa: A qualitative analysis of Lebanon, Jordan, Egypt and Palestine.* Available at: https://wamda-prod.s3.amazonaws.com/resource-url/e2981f10ea87448.pdf [Accessed 12 Feb. 2018].

Haugh, H.M. and Talwar, A. (2016). Linking social entrepreneurship and social change: The mediating role of empowerment. *Journal of Business Ethics*, 133(4), pp. 643–658.

Henderson, V.E. (1984). The spectrum of ethicality. *Journal of Business Ethics*, 3(2), pp. 163–171.

Higgins-Desbiolles, F. (2006). More than an "industry": The forgotten power of tourism as a social force. *Tourism Management*, 27(6), pp. 1192–1208.

Hlady-Rispal, M. and Servantie, V. (2018). Deconstructing the way in which value is created in the context of social entrepreneurship. *International Journal of Management Reviews*, 20(1), pp. 62–80.

Holden, A. (2000). *Tourism and environment.* London: Routledge.

Hunt, S.D. and Vitell, S. (1986). A general theory of marketing ethics. *Journal of Macro-marketing*, 6(1), pp. 5–16.

IED (2016). *Can social entrepreneurship facilitate the inclusion of immigrants in labor market?* [online] Available at: https://ied.eu/can-social-entrepreneurship/ [Accessed 12 Feb. 2018].

Iorgulescu, M.C. and Răvar, A.S. (2015). The contribution of social enterprises to the development of tourism. The case of Romania. *Procedia Economics and Finance*, 32, pp. 672–679.

Jaén, I., Fernández-Serrano, J., Santos, F.J. and Liñán, F., 2017. Cultural values and social entrepreneurship: A cross-country efficiency analysis. In: M. Peris-Ortiz, F. Teulon and D. Bonet-Fernandez, eds., *Social entrepreneurship in non-profit and profit sectors.* Cham: Springer, pp. 31–51.

Jahdi, K.S. and Acikdilli, G. (2009). Marketing communications and corporate social responsibility (CSR): Marriage of convenience or shotgun wedding? *Journal of Business Ethics*, 88(1), pp. 103–113.

Jafari, J. (1974). The socio-economic costs of tourism to developing countries. *Annals of Tourism Research*, 1(7), pp. 227–262.

Jamal, T. and Camargo, B.A. (2014). Sustainable tourism, justice and an ethic of care: Toward the just destination. *Journal of Sustainable Tourism*, 22(1), pp. 11–30.

Jamali, D. (2007). The case for strategic corporate social responsibility in developing countries. *Business and Society Review*, 112(1), pp. 1–27.

Justraveling.com (2016). *Mr. Thomas Cook and the impolite visiting* [online]. Available at: www.justraveling.com/explorers-voyagers/thomas-cook-impolite-visiting/ [Accessed 5 Feb. 2018].

Kettle, M. (2017). Mass tourism is at a tipping point – But we're all part of the problem. *The Guardian* [online]. Available at: www.theguardian.com/commentisfree/2017/aug/11/tourism-tipping-point-travel-less-damage-destruction [Accessed 6 Feb. 2018].

Kidder, R.M. (1995). *How good people make tough choices.* New York: Morrow.

Kim, A.K. and Brown, G. (2012). Understanding the relationships between perceived travel experiences, overall satisfaction, and destination loyalty. *Anatolia*, 23(3), pp. 328–347.

Kinnaird, V. and Hall, D. (1996). Understanding tourism processes: A gender-aware framework. *Tourism Management*, 17(2), pp. 95–102.

Kirzner, I.M. (2009). The alert and creative entrepreneur: A clarification. *Small Business Economics*, 32(2), pp. 145–152.

Laeis, G.C. and Lemke, S. (2016). Social entrepreneurship in tourism: Applying sustainable livelihoods approaches. *International Journal of Contemporary Hospitality Management*, 28(6), pp. 1076–1093.

Lea, J.P. (1993). Tourism development ethics in the Third World. *Annals of Tourism Research*, 20(4), pp. 701–715.

Lever, A. (1987). Spanish tourism migrants: The case of Lloret de Mar. *Annals of Tourism Research*, 14(4), pp. 449–470.

Lewis, P.V. (1985). Defining 'business ethics': Like nailing jello to a wall. *Journal of Business Ethics*, 4(5), pp. 377–383.

Liu, Z. (2003). Sustainable tourism development: A critique. *Journal of Sustainable Tourism*, 11(6), pp. 459–475.

Lordkipanidze, M., Brezet, H. and Backman, M. (2005). The entrepreneurship factor in sustainable tourism development. *Journal of Cleaner Production*, 13(8), pp. 787–798.

Lovelock, B. and Lovelock, K. (2013). *The ethics of tourism: Critical and applied perspectives*. New York: Routledge.

Lubberink, R., Blok, V., van Ophem, J., van der Velde, G. and Omta, O. (2018). Innovation for society: Towards a typology of developing innovations by social entrepreneurs. *Journal of Social Entrepreneurship*, 9(1), pp. 52–78.

MacCannell, D. (1976). *The tourist: A new theory of the leisure class*. Berkeley: University of California Press.

Mahoney, J. (1990). Spheres and limits of ethical responsibilities in and of the corporation. In: G. Enderle, B. Almond and A. Argandoña, eds., *People in corporations*. Dordrecht: Springer, pp. 239–241.

Mair, J. and Marti, I. (2006). Social entrepreneurship research: A source of explanation, prediction, and delight. *Journal of World Business*, 41(1), pp. 36–44.

Martí, I. (2006). Introduction to part I – Setting a research agenda for an emerging field. In: J. Mair, J. Robinson and K. Hockerts, eds., *Social entrepreneurship*. New York: Palgrave Macmillan, pp. 17–21.

Martin, R.L. and Osberg, S. (2007). Social entrepreneurship: The case for definition. *Stanford Social Innovation Review*, 5(2), pp. 28–39.

McGill, R. and Sachs, D. (2013). The rise of social entrepreneurship suggests a possible future for global capitalism. *Forbes*. Available at: www.forbes.com/sites/skollworld forum/2013/05/02/the-rise-of-social-entrepreneurship-suggests-a-possible-future-for-global-capitalism/ [Accessed 24 Feb. 2018].

McKercher, B. (1993). Some fundamental truths about tourism: Understanding tourism's social and environmental impacts. *Journal of Sustainable Tourism*, 1(1), pp. 6–16.

Minnaert, L., Diekmann, A. and McCabe, S. (2012). Defining social tourism and its historical context. In: S. McCabe, L. Minnaert and A. Diekmann, eds., *Social tourism in Europe: Theory and practice*. Clevendon, UK: Channel View Publications, pp. 18–30.

Mitchell, M. (2013). The 5 P's of social entrepreneurship. *The Huffington Post* [online]. Available at: www.huffingtonpost.com/monika-mitchell/the-5-ps-of-social-entrep_b_ 4079248.html [Accessed 26 Feb. 2018].

Morgan, M. (2015). Can social enterprise help fix the Greek crisis? *The Guardian* [online]. Available at: www.theguardian.com/sustainable-business/2015/nov/10/social-enterprise-help-fix-greek-crisis-greece [Accessed 9 Mar. 2018].

Mussa, A.B. (2017). *Libyan entrepreneurship in the time of war*. Available at: www.wamda. com/2017/04/libyan-entrepreneurship-war [Accessed 4 Feb. 2018].

MVCA (2016). *General assembly feat. Christmas cocktail on social entrepreneurship*. Available at: www.mvca.asso.mc/en/eventsrecent-128/general-assembly-feat-christmas-cocktail-on-social-entrepreneurship.html [Accessed 15 Mar. 2018].

Natalucci, M. (2016). The economic and ethical implications of pro-poor tourism. Available at: https://europa.eu/capacity4dev/securityfordevelopment/discussions/economic-and-ethical-implications-pro-poor-tourism [Accessed 1 Mar. 2018].

Neto, F. (2003). A new approach to sustainable tourism development: Moving beyond environmental protection. *A United Nations Sustainable Development Journal*, 27(3), pp. 212–222.

Newey, L.R. (2018). Changing the system: Compensatory versus transformative social entrepreneurship. *Journal of Social Entrepreneurship*, 9(1), pp. 13–30.

Nicholls, A. (2007). *What is the future of social enterprise in ethical markets? A social enterprise think piece for the office of third sector.* Available at: http://webarchive.nationalarchives.gov.uk/+/http:/www.cabinetoffice.gov.uk/media/cabinetoffice/third_sector/assets/future_social_enterprise_ethical_markets.pdf [Accessed 4 Feb. 2018].

OECD (2010). *Social entrepreneurship and social innovation.* Available at: http://ec.europa.eu/internal_market/social_business/docs/conference/oecd_en.pdf [Accessed 24 Feb. 2018].

OECD (2013). *Job creation through the social economy and social entrepreneurship.* Available at: www.oecd.org/cfe/leed/130228_Job%20Creation%20throught%20the%20Social%20Economy%20and%20Social%20Entrepreneurship_RC_FINALBIS.pdf [Accessed 1 Jan. 2018].

OECD (2014). *SME development strategy project for Libya: Consultative meeting for the diagnostic study.* Available at: www.oecd.org/mena/competitiveness/OECD%20meeting%20summary_Libya%20diagnostic%20study_250914.pdf [Accessed 4 Feb. 2018].

OECD (2017). *High level meeting on tourism policies for sustainable and inclusive growth.* Available at: www.oecd.org/cfe/tourism/OECD_High-Level-Meeting-on-Tourism_Meeting-Summary.pdf [Accessed 1 Jan. 2018].

Panwar, R., Nybakk, E., Hansen, E. and Pinkse, J. (2017). Does the business case matter? The effect of a perceived business case on small firms' social engagement. *Journal of Business Ethics*, 144(3), pp. 597–608.

Park, J. (2015). *Europe's migration crisis.* New York: Council of Foreign Relations, pp. 311–325. Available at: www.cfr.org/backgrounder/europes-migration-crisis [Accessed 4 Feb. 2018].

Peredo, B. and Wurzelmann, S. (2015). Indigenous tourism and social entrepreneurship in the Bolivian Amazon: Lessons from San Miguel del Bala. *The International Indigenous Policy Journal*, 6(4), pp. 5.

Perić, J. and Delić, A. (2014). Social entrepreneurship in Croatia: Do regional disparities influence young people's perception of social entrepreneurship as a potential career path?. *Ekonomski Vjesnik/Econviews: Review of Contemporary Business, Entrepreneurship and Economic Issues*, 27(1), pp. 81–92.

Petmesidou, M. and Papatheodorou, C. (2006). *Poverty and social deprivation in the Mediterranean: Trends, policies and welfare prospects in the new millennium.* London: Zed Books.

Pomerantz, M. (2004). Find a balance between mission and money. *Puget Sound Business Journal*, [online] 17, pp. 1–3. Available at: www.bizjournals.com/seattle/stories/2004/05/24/focus22.html [Accessed 4 Feb. 2018].

redherring.com (2017). *We want to promote sustainable entrepreneurship: Monaco's new incubator sets its hopes high* [online]. Available at: www.redherring.com/features/want-promote-sustainable-entrepreneurship-monacos-new-incubator-sets-hopes-high/ [Accessed 10 Mar. 2018].

Richards, G. and Wilson, J. (2006). Developing creativity in tourist experiences: A solution to the serial reproduction of culture?. *Tourism management*, 27(6), pp.1209–1223.

Rondinelli, D.A. (2003). Partnering for development: Government-private sector cooperation in service provision. In: D.A. Rondinelli and G.S. Cheema, eds., *Reinventing government for the twenty-first century: State capacity in a globalizing society.* Bloomfield, CT: Kumarian Press, pp. 219–239.

Ryan, C. (2002). Equity, management, power sharing and sustainability-issues of the new tourism. *Tourism Management*, 23(1), pp. 17–26.

Sagawa, S. and Segal, E. (2000). *Common interest, common good: Creating value through business and social sector partnerships.* Boston, MA: Harvard Business Press.

Scheyvens, R. (1999). Ecotourism and the empowerment of local communities. *Tourism Management*, 20(2), pp. 245–249.

Schumpeter, J.A. (1934). *The theory of economic development.* Cambridge, MA: Harvard University Press.

Sen, P. (2007). Ashoka's big idea: Transforming the world through social entrepreneurship. *Futures*, 39(5), pp. 534–553.

Sethi, S.P. (1979). A conceptual framework for environmental analysis of social issues and evaluation of business response patterns. *Academy of Management Review*, 4(1), pp. 63–74.

Shaw, E. and Carter, S. (2007). Social entrepreneurship: Theoretical antecedents and empirical analysis of entrepreneurial processes and outcomes. *Journal of Small Business and Enterprise Development*, 14(3), pp. 418–434.

Sheldon, P.J., Pollock, A. and Daniele, R. (2017). Social entrepreneurship and tourism: Setting the stage. In: P.J. Sheldon and R. Daniele, eds., *Social entrepreneurship and tourism.* Cham: Springer, pp. 1–18.

Sigala, M. (2016). Learning with the market: A market approach and framework for developing social entrepreneurship in tourism and hospitality. *International Journal of Contemporary Hospitality Management*, 28(6), pp. 1245–1286.

Smith, S.R. (2012). Foreword. In: B. Gidron and Y. Hasenfeld, *Social enterprises: An organizational perspective.* Basingstoke: Palgrave Macmillan, pp. ix–xiii.

Spreckley, F. (1981). *Work aid – social audit: A management tool for co-operative working.* Leeds: Beechwood College.

Stem, C.J., Lassoie, J.P., Lee, D.R., Deshler, D.D. and Schelhas, J.W. (2003). Community participation in ecotourism benefits: The link to conservation practices and perspectives. *Society & Natural Resources*, 16(5), pp. 387–413.

Stitsworth, M.H. (1988). In search of global perspectives. *Journal of Extension*, 26(1). Available at: www.joe.org/joe/1988spring/rb4.php [Accessed 11 Feb. 2018].

Sud, M., VanSandt, C.V. and Baugous, A.M. (2009). Social entrepreneurship: The role of institutions. *Journal of Business Ethics*, 85(1), pp. 201–216.

Swarbrooke, J. (1999). *Sustainable tourism management.* New York: CABI Publishing.

Taylor, S. (2015). How Syrian entrepreneurs are creatively working through war. Available at: www.wamda.com/2015/02/syrian-entrepreneurs-creatively-working-through-war [Accessed 12 Feb. 2018].

Theng, S., Qiong, X. and Tatar, C. (2015). Mass tourism vs alternative tourism? Challenges and new positionings. *Études caribéennes*, pp. 31–32. Available at: http://journals.open edition.org/etudescaribeennes/7708 [Accessed 12 Feb. 2018].

Thomascook.com (2018). *Thomas Cook history* [online]. Available at: www.thomascook. com/thomas-cook-history/ [Accessed 5 Feb. 2018].

Tillmar, M. (2012). Sectoral intertwining at the grass roots level. In: K. Berglund, B. Johannisson and B. Schwartz, eds., *Societal entrepreneurship: Positioning, penetrating, promoting.* Cheltenham, UK and Northampton, MA: Edward Elgar Publishing, p. 35.

Turner, L. and Ash, J. (1975). *The golden hordes: International tourism and the pleasure periphery.* London: Constable.

Türker, D., Özerim, G. and Yıldız, A. (2014). Social enterprises in a developing country context: Analysis of social entrepreneurship models in Turkey. *International conference on entrepreneurship IEC 2014*. Istanbul Aydın University: Conference Proceeding, pp. 117–129.

UNWTO (2001). *Global code of ethics for tourism – Article 1*. [online] Available at: http://ethics.unwto.org/content/global-code-ethics-tourism-article-1 [Accessed 13 Feb. 2018].

UNWTO (2016). *World tourism organization 2016 annual report*. [online] Available at: http://cf.cdn.unwto.org/sites/all/files/pdf/annual_report_2016_web_0.pdf [Accessed 13 Feb. 2018].

UNWTO (2017). *UNWTO tourism highlights 2017 edition*. [online] Available at: www.e-unwto.org/doi/pdf/10.18111/9789284419029 [Accessed 1 Dec. 2017].

Urbano, D., Toledano, N. and Soriano, D.R. (2010). Analyzing social entrepreneurship from an institutional perspective: Evidence from Spain. *Journal of Social Entrepreneurship*, 1(1), pp. 54–69.

Varga, E. (2017). Social enterprise ecosystems in Croatia and the Western Balkans: A mapping study of Albania, Bosnia and Herzegovina, Croatia, Kosovo, FYR Macedonia, Montenegro and Serbia. In: N. Etchart, ed., *NESsT*. Available at: https://static1.squarespace.com/static/58d072963e00bea07a2ca2da/t/599f8968d482e9ac57a09533/1503627672843/2017_SE_Ecosystem_in_the_W_Balkans_web.pdf [Accessed 3 Dec. 2017].

Vellas, F. (2011). The indirect impact of tourism: An economic analysis. *Third meeting of T20 tourism ministers* [online]. Paris, pp. 1–30. Available at: www.academia.edu/download/33144198/Francois_Vellas_The_indirect_impact_of_tourism.pdf [Accessed 25 Feb. 2018].

Venkataraman, S. (1997). The distinctive domain of entrepreneurship research. *Advances in Entrepreneurship, Firm Emergence and Growth*, 3(1), pp. 119–138.

von der Weppen, J. and Cochrane, J. (2012). Social enterprises in tourism: An exploratory study of operational models and success factors. *Journal of Sustainable Tourism*, 20(3), pp. 497–511.

Waddock, S. and Steckler, E. (2016). Visionaries and wayfinders: Deliberate and emergent pathways to vision in social entrepreneurship. *Journal of Business Ethics*, 133, pp. 719–734.

Wahidi, I. and Lebègue, T. (2017). Social entrepreneurs in Lebanon: An exploratory study of women entrepreneurs engaged in the professional integration of low-skilled women. *EUREKA: Social and Humanities* (1), pp. 36–46.

wamda.com (2014). Moroccan social entrepreneurship struggling, MCISE study says [online]. Available at: www.wamda.com/2014/04/report-social-entrepreneurship-morocco [Accessed 20 Mar. 2018].

Wilson, J. (2006). Developing creativity in tourist experiences: A solution to the serial reproduction of culture?. *Tourism Management*, 27(6), pp. 1209–1223.

World Trade Bank (2017). Social entrepreneurship in Tunisia [online]. Available at: https://openknowledge.worldbank.org/bitstream/handle/10986/26396/114408-WP-PUBLIC-P152270-Social-entrepreneurship-in-Tunisia-achievements-and-ways-forward.pdf?sequence=1&isAllowed=y [Accessed 24 Feb. 2018].

WTTC (2017). *Country Reports* [online]. Available at: www.wttc.org/research/economic-research/economic-impact-analysis/country-reports/ [Accessed 14 Feb. 2018].

Wulleman, M. and Hudon, M. (2016). Models of social entrepreneurship: Empirical evidence from Mexico. *Journal of Social Entrepreneurship*, 7(2), pp. 162–188.

Yaacoubi, H. (2016). *Hope beyond the wall: Realizing Palestinian potential through social entrepreneurship* [online]. Available at: www.huffingtonpost.com/huda-yaacoubi/hope-beyond-the-wall-real_b_9832800.html [Accessed 9 Mar. 2018].

Younis, A.A. (2015). The rise of the social entrepreneurs is Egypt's silent revolution. *The Huffington Post* [online]. Available at: www.huffingtonpost.com/alyaa-a-younis/the-rise-of-the-social-en_b_6787054.htm [Accessed 9 Mar. 2018].

Zahra, S.A., Gedajlovic, E., Neubaum, D.O. and Shulman, J.M. (2009). A typology of social entrepreneurs: Motives, search processes and ethical challenges. *Journal of Business Venturing*, 24(5), pp. 519–532.

Ziemnowicz, C. (2013). Joseph A. Schumpeter and innovation. In: E.G. Carayannis, ed., *Encyclopedia of creativity, invention, innovation and entrepreneurship*. New York: Springer New York, pp. 1171–1176.

Zoehrer, K. (2017). Social entrepreneurship in southeastern Europe – Comparative analysis of the cases of Croatia, Serbia and Greece. *6th EMES international research conference on social enterprise* [online]. Louvain-la-Neuve: EMES, pp. 1–40. Available at: https://emes.net/content/uploads/publications/social-entrepreneurship-in-southeastern-europe-comparative-analysis-of-the-cases-of-croatia-serbia-and-greece/Best-PhD-paper-ECSP-6EMES-02.pdf [Accessed 1 Dec. 2017].

6 Corporate social responsibility and sustainable development in the Mediterranean

The case of the Spanish hotel industry in the Barcelona region

*Aysin Pasamehmetoğlu and
Mustafa Mehmet Gökoğlu*

This chapter describes corporate social responsibility(CSR) practices of hotels in the Barcelona region with an aim to understanding business perspectives on sustainable development in the Mediterranean region. From this standpoint, a case study analysis is developed regarding the progress in the implementation of CSR practices leading to sustainable development. The current literature on CSR in the Spanish hotel industry lacks a clear understanding of business perspectives towards sustainability. Specifically, examining CSR practices of hotels in the Barcelona region allows us to describe the progress and problems related to sustainable development. CSR is conceptualized based on internal, external and global dimensions which are characterized by economic, environmental and cultural aspects, respectively. The findings point to an environmentalist business perspective, which traditionally dominates CSR practices in Spain. The hotel industry in Spain is raising its environmental consciousness, and some specific environmental initiatives have been implemented, especially since the early 2000s. By explaining the dynamics of the hotel industry and environment relations in the Barcelona region, this chapter suggests a unique business perspective in the Mediterranean region where environmental solutions are dominated in CSR practices. Present studies in Spain with regard to sustainable development are lacking business perspectives towards environmental initiatives. This chapter aims to fill this gap by examining the CSR practices of hotels based on an environmentalist evaluation of the Barcelona region.

Literature review

This chapter aims at explaining the CSR activities and sustainable development in the Mediterranean region. For that, a case study analysis approach is adopted with Spain as the model country. Sustainable development in the Mediterranean region is regarded as creating a prosperous and peaceful environment where the quality of life is at the highest standards through common objectives and participatory governance (UNEP/MAP, 2016). As for the key issues of sustainable development in the Mediterranean region, ensuring healthy marine and coastal areas, promoting resource management, food production and food security through sustainable forms of rural development, planning and managing sustainable Mediterranean cities, addressing climate change as a priority issue for the Mediterranean, transition towards a green and blue economy and improving governance in support of sustainable development are all on the forefront (UNEP/MAP, 2016). In light of these key issues, the Barcelona region in Spain was selected as the research area for the study.

The impact of corporate social responsibility on governmental activities is growing rapidly (Dahlsrud, 2008; Greenwood, 2007). Specifically, the literature suggests that CSR practices have become a pivotal component of doing business worldwide and of giving back to society (Habisch et al., 2005; Aguilera et al., 2007). CSR seeks to identify and solve problems regarding social development, business government relationships, stakeholder management, corporate social performance and economic, legal and ethical components of organizational performance (Carroll, 1991). CSR practices focus on increasing social welfare of societies, supporting sustainable development and continuous improvement of economic, environmental and cultural heritage (While et al., 2004; Werther and Chandler, 2006). From this standpoint, CSR practices are institutionalized activities of philanthropy that go beyond individual-level benefactions to societal-level development, which result in reducing social and economic problems (Pringle and Thompson, 1999).

Governments, including local, regional and national public sector agencies, are the primary sources of CSR practices in Europe (The European Commission, 2001). However, private sector organizations also play a vital role in the institutionalization of CSR practices which go beyond regulations and add real value to sustainable development (Matten and Moon, 2008). Private organizations help solve social problems by investigating the current issues within their institutional environment and embracing practices that enable government agencies to cooperate with civil society (The World Bank, 2005; The European Commission, 2001). In this vein, European governments treat private sector CSR practices as an essential part of sustainable development and poverty reduction (Matten and Moon, 2008). Moreover, CSR in many European countries is adopted as a way to seek to increase the competitive advantage of organizations through increasing economic, environmental and cultural consciousness (Albareda et al., 2008). Private sector organizations enhance their business competitiveness with the institutionalization of CSR practices that improve organizational reputation and growth of the business (Albareda et al., 2008).

The main research problem is ascertaining what kinds of CSR dimensions dominate the actual practices of hotels which are able to contribute to sustainable development in a unique way. By that, the methodology of the study included a case study analysis with qualitative techniques. Mainly, the content analysis method was adopted and texts regarding the actions and practices within the Barcelona hotels were analyzed through the Nvivo 11 computer program. The results show certain CSR dimensions, appearing in the form of activities in effect, which dominate the business perspectives of hotels in the Barcelona region.

Understanding the CSR from a business perspective

CSR activities by businesses that enable sustainable development are drawing more attention in Europe as businesses and government agencies work together in sharing social responsibility (Aaronson and Reeves, 2002). The importance of support businesses give to social and environmentally sustainable development is recognized throughout Europe and a business perspective which can vary according to different countries is set (Aaronson and Reeves, 2002). For instance, business organizations in Germany have a relatively high interest in employee well-being and employee healthcare issues when implementing their CSR practices (Silberhorn and Warren, 2007). In this vein, CSR practices, which lead to sustainable development, have different dimensions that can be emphasized in different cultures. CSR dimensions can be conceptualized based on economic, environmental and cultural aspects. An internal dimension, which is composed of economic aspects, draws attention to employee well-being and healthcare, improving working conditions and creating an appropriate organizational environment for employee participation along with job satisfaction (The European Commission, 2001). An external dimension, which includes environmental aspects, focuses on ecological balance and what organizations do in decreasing environmental pollution, increasing environmental standards and helping solve environmental issues raised from local and regional projects (The European Commission, 2001). Finally, a global dimension, which consists of cultural aspects, investigates how organizations respond to social problems that appear in the community they are located in and what kind of CSR practices they adopt in order to solve cultural issues (The European Commission, 2001).

This study contributes to the literature on corporate social responsibility by categorizing the specific dimensions of CSR activities. In doing so, the basic preeminence of each dimension along with effects on organizations and practices of CSR dimensions is depicted. Dimensions of CSR are conceptualized from three different aspects that enable researchers to investigate CSR practices in greater detail by highlighting the different characteristics of dimensions belonging to different contexts. Also, this categorization can result in a detailed explanation of the different CSR practices and the basis for the various research carried out in organizations about CSR. The internal, external and global dimensions of CSR practices are summarized in Table 6.1.

Making sense of a business perspective to CSR initially requires investigating the social performance of organizations. Corporate social performance is embedded in CSR activities of organizations. From this perspective, four main aspects of CSR can be identified as:(1) economic responsibilities towards stakeholders and human rights, (2) social responsibilities towards community problems, (3) legal responsibilities towards government agencies and (4) ethical responsibilities towards the environment (Carroll, 1998; Carroll, 1999). This definition extends the scope of CSR practices to include solutions for worker, environment and community issues (Carroll, 1979; Carroll, 1991). Moreover, taking different dimensions of CSR into consideration, Wood (1991) suggests that corporate social

Table 6.1 Dimensions of CSR practices conceptualized from 3 different aspects

CSR dimension	Internal	External	Global
Basic preeminence	Economic values	Environmental values	Cultural values
Effects on organizations	Advancement of employee well-being	Improving environmental standards	Helping solve cultural issues within societies
CSR practices	Increasing job satisfaction and designing wellness programs	Adopting measures that conserve ecological balance	Identifying social problems and participating in community projects

performance requires principles, processes and outcomes of public responsibility programs to be addressed. Principles of CSR arise from organizations' internal affairs and managerial discretion, processes of public responsibility roots in environment, stakeholder and issues management and lastly, outcomes occurring in light of CSR practices which are implemented (Wood, 1991).

As for the CSR practices of organizations located in the Spanish peninsula, societal problems like coping with poverty have been the most significant activity that became widespread by the suburbanization of the middle classes (Martinez, Callejo and Fuentes, 2005). It is argued that because of the high unemployment rate, particularly among young people, social issues are on the rise, and decentralized decision-making structures in Spain enable different regions to embrace specific area-based approaches (BMVBS, 2007; Charnock et al., 2014). For instance, while focusing on economic efficiency, environmental conservation and prevention of social problems for sustainable development, government agencies in the Barcelona region spent the bulk of their development funding in an attempt to renew the city based on ecological principles from 2000 to 2006 (BMVBS, 2007).

Sustainable development in the Barcelona region

Sustainable development can be defined as "development that meets the needs of the present without compromising the ability of future generations to meet their own needs" (WCED, 1987). By embracing sustainable development, countries offer a set of solutions for environmental and societal issues which result in positive change in the everyday lives of people (Moir, 2001; Gibson, 2000). Thus, research on sustainable development generally focuses on environmental and societal dimensions of positive change, while economic aspects are evaluated from a trade-off perspective where environmental and societal protection costs become a significant decision-making determinant (Gibson, 2000). In addition to this, sustainable development is an essential component of international development, with worldwide political partnerships including international relations, law and public administration (WCED, 1987). From this standpoint,

> sustainable development is a process of change in which the exploitation of resources, the direction of investments, the orientation of technological

development, and institutional change are all in harmony and enhance both current and future potential to meet human needs and aspirations.

(WCED, 1987)

On the other hand, being the capital of Catalonia, Barcelona has a rich tourism tradition due to its privileged location that has made it a major Mediterranean center of European community, along with extending its influence over a wide area of the world including Latin America, the Middle East and Far East (Turisme, 2017). Sustainable development and CSR practices are closely linked in Barcelona, which evokes commitment to solving the social problems and protection of the environment (Turisme, 2017). In fact, CSR practices leading to sustainable development are composed of economic, environmental and social dimensions, and these dimensions have been evaluated as the essential part of governance and political decision-making in Barcelona (Spangenberg and Hinterberger, 2002). Analyzing the said dimensions enables local actors to determine key policy objectives that result in reduction of environmental pollution and increase in social cohesion and participation (Spangenberg and Hinterberger, 2002). As for the Barcelona region, the Aalborg Charter, signed by the Barcelona city council in 1995, encourages all parties to adopt the principles of sustainable development, and the local Agenda 21 program works towards implementing sustainability in regional activities (Barcelona City Council, 2009).

Barcelona's hotel industry has grown by 40% over the past two decades, with 56,000 beds available. Hotels' CSR practices have raised the city's prestige around the world through economic and sociocultural projects (Turisme, 2017). From this standpoint, analyzing CSR practices of hotels in Barcelona can be used to understand the perspectives businesses have towards sustainable development. Each organization has three main perspectives towards sustainable development. First, organizations can prioritize improving employee well-being in their practices, which will cause the internal dimension of CSR to dominate the organization. Second, organizations may significantly give their attention to protect ecological balance in their environment, which will make the external dimension of CSR dominate the organization. Lastly, organizations can regard helping solve the social problems in their communities as a top priority of CSR practices, which will lead to the global dimension of CSR to dominate the organization.

Methodology

The universe of the study is the hotel industry in the Barcelona region. A purposeful sampling technique was adopted and the sample of the study was chosen from the hotels which have the highest ratings on TripAdvisor. In this vein, the sample of the study is composed of hotels that were present as the most popular during the time analysis was performed. A total of 34 hotels were included in the study. In order to analyze the perspectives hotels have towards sustainable development, data regarding the actual CSR practices were collected from hotels' official websites and other related websites that explain what is done in Barcelona. An in-depth analysis of the collected data was then performed using the content analysis method (Neuendorf, 2002). Content analysis was performed through the evaluation of selected texts, terms and keywords which attribute importance to related research questions (Neuman, 2006). In this study, the research question included the evaluation of dimensions of CSR that hotels use when engaging in CSR practices which contribute to sustainable development. Analysis of textual data indicates that different dimensions of CSR are adopted in Barcelona, and the business perspectives towards sustainable development varies accordingly. For instance, the following text shows what a selected hotel in Barcelona does for contributing to sustainable development, and by doing so, the dominance of the internal dimension of CSR can be argued to appear in this part of textual data.

> We have recently adopted the Solidarity based economic model. This is a new, more sustainable, and fairer economic model, where the peoples' and employees' social well-being is one of its core principals. The Solidarity Economy Network aims to strengthen this model from a transforming point of view. It includes different organizations that believe in the principles of democracy, transparency, equality, and sustainability. Our organizational structure allows for a constant and direct contact between all the people that are part of our organization. Due to the type of fiscal policy, there is a mild form of hierarchy in our organization. Nevertheless, the relationship between the members of our group is based on transparency and honesty. The founding members of our team make the most important business management decisions, but always taking the other parties' members of the group into account through open communication. In terms of wage equality, all job positions are paid the same per hour. All employment contracts are ongoing, and remuneration as well as the pay scale structure is fair. We believe that cities, especially Barcelona, should work towards a touristic model that is balanced and regulated. We offer our facilities, both lodging as well as common areas, with the intention of sharing our knowledge and experience to the people of the city, going beyond a tourism model centered in consumerism. That is why we are working to become a place of reference in sustainable tourism. By that institutions, associations, international and local businesses meaning social, environmental or cultural institutions, can come to our hotel to develop activities such as workshops, health programs, exchange programs, congresses, festivals and so on.

Additionally, the following text shows what a selected hotel in Barcelona does for contributing to sustainable development and, by doing so, illustrates the dominance of the external dimension of CSR that can be argued to appear in this part of textual data.

> We have been committed to protecting the environment for over 25 years. A big part of that commitment is looking for new and creative ways to enhance the brand's awarding winning Sustainability Partnership platform. A flagship example of this commitment is the luxury hotel brand's Bee Sustainable program. We embrace environmentally sustainable business practices and

continue to seek new ways to proactively green our operations. Our company was founded on an enduring connection to the land and communities where we do business. As a leading travel provider, we are reliant on destination health to be profitable and committed to preserving the places where our guests and colleagues work, live and play. We are resolutely aware of the business impacts associated with the environment and we are taking proactive steps to reduce our carbon output and help mitigate the effects of global warming through the followings; Property level Sustainability Teams who are responsible for executing the Sustainability Partnership Program locally by raising awareness and incorporating sustainability into all department operations and ensuring that the company's various sustainability programs are in place, Reducing our use of energy, water, and waste produced and consumed by our properties through formal programs, Monitoring, recording, benchmarking and setting targets on our environmental performance, Providing necessary training and resources/materials to stakeholders in order to meet our environmental objectives, Incorporating our environmental commitments into key business decisions. We have always been at the forefront of environmental activism within the hospitality sector and known for taking a leadership stance on issues affecting our planet.

Finally, the following text shows what a selected hotel in Barcelona does for contributing to sustainable development and by doing so illustrates the dominance of the global dimension of CSR that can be argued to appear in this part of textual data.

Our Corporate Social Responsibility Report has been produced each year since 2006 and explains our activities in the economic, environmental and social scopes in line with the sustainable approach and commitments with groups of stakeholders. This year, global solidarity project is part of our Social Action Up for the People initiatives, which involves both customers and employees, to help the most vulnerable especially at Christmas time. All the company's employees will be involved voluntarily, collecting and donating toys and non-perishable food to different NGOs. We have chosen Red Cross Spain as it is preferred NGO for channeling donations in Barcelona, because of its action plan for the crisis helping people in situations of extreme vulnerability and its current involvement in various Social Action projects with us. As part of its Corporate Responsibility policy, we have also launched an effective global Social Action strategy that encourages employee involvement, identifies opportunities and promotes a large number of responsible projects. There are three different lines of action in Social Action plan encompassed under the slogan Up for the People. These actions include Up for Opportunities; an international work training and experience program for young people at risk of exclusion and disabled people in the Company's hotels, Up for Volunteering; a Corporate Volunteer proposal which includes this initiative and Up for Hospitality; through which special rates are offered and products and services donated to NGOs and other charitable foundations.

Data analysis

In order to investigate the dimensions of CSR activities of hotels in the Barcelona region, content analysis was adopted and textual data regarding the CSR activities was selected through in-depth analysis. The first phase of this analysis included finding the keywords in textual data which appear to ascribe meaning to certain CSR dimensions. By adopting content analysis, the most frequently used keywords which attribute to the subject investigated were categorized in a coding scheme (Flick, 2007). This coding scheme was then used to discover the frequency of each keyword in the textual data (Flick, 2007). Frequency of keywords can be acquired by uploading the textual data to the Nvivo 11 software program, which analyzes qualitative data according to the number of the keywords relative to the total words counted in a portion of text. Thus, weighted percentages in terms of numbers of occurrences of keywords in the data are gathered. After completing the first phase of data analysis, the coding scheme was obtained as follows.

Coding scheme

CSR Dimensions

Internal Dimension

Employee – people well being, employee – people health, employee – people safety, health programs, safety programs, skills, abilities, talent, positioning, working environment, working conditions, learning with colleagues, commitment, cooperate, optimize, colleague relations, personal relations, business relations, job satisfaction, economic value, rights, justice, fair benefit, laws, human rights, work force, labor force, quality, information, technology, knowledge, production, achievement, occupational health, occupational safety, safety standards, improvement of standards, employee needs, employee wants, promotion, pay, bonus, medical reports, medical screening, care for workers – employees, professional development, help for workers – employees, training for workers – employees, trained staff, training for staff

External Dimension

Climate, earth, planet, nature, green, resource, atmosphere, ecology, ecological balance, environment, sea, wind, river, water springs, biology, greenhouse effect, environmental standards, environmental consciousness, renewable sources, environmental sensibility, environmental impact, environmental problems, environmental – ecological degradation, ecologically balanced, environmental plans, environmental issues, environmental protection, environmental audition, environmental engineering – management, environmental education, forest, tree, plant, planting, energy, efficiency, nature friendly, emission, pollution, acidic, disaster, hazard, waste, recycle, reuse, reutilize, contamination, carbon, soil, greenhouse gases, wild life, endangered species, habitat, natural cycle, conservation, vegetation, natural heritage, natural environment

Global Dimension

Spain, culture, country, native, city, global, local, hometown, community, opportunity, community development, civic leaders, activists, social problems, social assistance, social service programs, social protection, red cross, global codes, grant, family, nursing home, care, education, nursery, equal opportunity, peace, conflict management, global service programs, community service, tradition, custom, manners, values, social skills, aid, help, charity, charitable, caring, social structure, social contribution, social action, donate, relief services, volunteer, social issues, social work, voluntary work, poverty, prosperity, gender equality, empowerment, children, adolescence, people in need, social support, community projects, community partnerships, social platforms, nonprofit organizations, social cause, advocate, public service, social change, cultural change

The second phase of the data analysis included discovering the frequencies of keywords in selected portions of texts. The selection of texts was evaluated based on the characteristics of each text and whether they encompass certain attributes which can be related to CSR dimensions. In doing so, weighted percentages in terms of numbers of occurrences of keywords relative to the total words counted in the textual data are obtained. The CSR dimension with the highest value of weighted percentage was regarded as the dominant CSR form in that portion of data. Sample textual data with weighted percentages and the dominant form of CSR dimensions can be shown as follows (keywords are in bold):

Sample textual data with weighted percentages and the dominant form of CSR dimensions

Internal Dimension: 162 (0.18%) – Dominant Form

External Dimension: 155 (0.17%) Global Dimension: 114 (0.0.15%)

"As a fundamental part of our **positioning** as a company, both at present and in the future, it has become the main pillar of our business, ensuring the sustainable creation of **economic value** for the company. This is how we are planning to **optimize** a sustainable business model, ensuring that our stakeholders opt to be a socially responsible hotel company. We offer the best opportunities for **professional development**, based on the stability of a family company and the strength of a leading international player which knows how to recognize **commitment**, **talent** and **achievements fairly**. Companies can and must play a very important role in people's lives. We know that our work can contribute to our customers and **employees well being**, as well as those whose lives we inadvertently touch. We want to make our customers feel special, and also distinguish ourselves as a socially responsible company towards its **employees needs**. The key to achieving this relies on the ability to demonstrate that the company is caring for our **trained staff** and has a special and unique relationship with its customers, **employees** and with society."

External Dimension: 259 (0.21%) – Dominant Form

Internal Dimension: 141 (0.15%) Global Dimension: 184 (0.16%)

"Looking at a society that is more aware and preoccupied with the **environmental impact** of tourism, in Barcelona we are facing a lack of lodging facilities with principles of sustainability. Even though there are some newer hotels that have a better **environmental management**, most of the improvements made are more on the technological aspects rather than on a more global vision of sustainability. Thus, we have adopted an **Environmental Management System** that has to do with aspects such as **reutilize** and **recycle energy efficiency** and saving **water**, usage of cleaning products that are respectful to the **environment**, team communication and **environmental education** and use of **renewable sources** of **energy**. When we think about sustainable tourism, we often think about rural tourism within **green** and **natural environments**. In fact, many of the **environmentally sensible** lodging facilities in Europe and in Catalonia promoting sustainable tourism are far away from the city smog. But we think that cities most work towards a model of tourism that is **ecologically balanced**, and that is why we think that it is necessary to create accommodation facilities that have sustainability as the core of the project, in order to reduce **environmental impact** and also to integrate themselves into the neighborhood's life . . ."

Global Dimension: 389 (0.31%) – Dominant Form

Internal Dimension: 127 (0.12%) External Dimension: 294 (0.26%)

". . . We actively seek to generate **prosperity** and sustainable development in the **communities** where we are present, respecting and promoting their **culture**, **traditions** and **values**, and paying particular attention to

children and the most vulnerable groups. We are committed to **voluntary work** and **social platforms** and since 2014 we have joined **community projects** to promote a model of innovative **social work** which helps promote the employability of young people through real work experience in a professional environment, providing them with experience, **social skills** and maturity that will help them improve their possibility of entering the labor market. Moreover, since 2007 we have upheld the **global code** of conduct for the protection of **children** and **adolescents** against sexual exploitation in the tourism industry. As a result of our **social action** in line of this code, huge progress in the tourism industry has been accomplished and we have renewed our **social action** commitment in 2013. In 2014, we were considered one of the most important members, together with other **global nonprofit organizations**. Today, our **social action** commitment to sustainable and responsible tourism and to successfully implementing the criteria required by the **global code** in our hotel, is giving us further confidence to participate in new **community projects** that enhance **social development . . .**"

The third phase of the data analysis included exploring the dominant forms of CSR dimensions in Barcelona hotels' CSR practices. In order to do so, each hotel's textual data that reflects the actual activities of CSR and sustainable development was analyzed separately and the highest ranking weighted percentages was obtained. The distribution of frequencies of keywords and weighted percentages in each hotel analyzed is summarized in Table 6.2.

After completing the analysis of textual data, we found that certain CSR dimensions appear in related activities of hotels in Barcelona. Specifically, 24 hotels' CSR activities are dominated by external dimension, 6 hotels' CSR activities are dominated by global dimension and 4 hotels' CSR activities are dominated by internal dimension. From this standpoint, it can be argued that the business perspective of Barcelona hotels towards sustainable development is mainly based on an environmentalist view of CSR. The reason why the environmentalist view of CSR prevails may lie in the characteristics of the tourism industry. As put forth by the City of Barcelona Strategic Tourism Plan, the city's wide range of hotels recently experienced huge proportional growth in Europe (Turisme, 2017). This growth led to a greater responsibility in terms of environmental initiatives because of the Barcelona metropolitan city's distinguished environmental sustainability action plans (Environmental Report, 2013; Turisme, 2017). In addition to emphasizing economic efficiency and social problems prevention for sustainable development, government agencies in Barcelona generally give priority to improving the city standards based on ecological principles (BMVBS, 2007).

Table 6.2 The distribution of frequencies of keywords and dominant weighted percentages in each hotel analyzed

Hotel	Internal dimension	External dimension	Global dimension
1	48 (0.05%)	**171 (0.19%) Dominant**	127 (0.14%)
2	135 (0.15%)	193 (0.21%)	**226 (0.27%) Dominant**
3	**162 (0.18%) Dominant**	155 (0.17%)	114 (0.15%)
4	184 (0.11%)	**280 (0.18%) Dominant**	203 (0.16%)
5	71 (0.06%)	**375 (0.26%) Dominant**	288 (0.20%)
6	**123 (0.19%) Dominant**	101 (0.18%)	98 (0.18%)
7	193 (0.18%)	**372 (0.27%) Dominant**	216 (0.21%)
8	136 (0.12%)	249 (0.22%)	**287 (0.25%) Dominant**
9	141 (0.15%)	**259 (0.21%) Dominant**	184 (0.16%)
10	182 (0.16%)	**403 (0.32%) Dominant**	346 (0.27%)
11	**156 (0.23%) Dominant**	133 (0.18%)	120 (0.17%)
12	58 (0.06%)	**319 (0.25%) Dominant**	207 (0.16%)
13	92 (0.07%)	**251 (0.14%) Dominant**	372 (0.19%)
14	128 (0.12%)	163 (0.19%)	**294 (0.23%) Dominant**
15	96 (0.10%)	**405 (0.32%) Dominant**	249 (0.21%)
16	117 (0.11%)	**352 (0.31%) Dominant**	188 (0.15%)
17	37 (0.02%)	**134 (0.09%) Dominant**	63 (0.04%)
18	79 (0.06%)	**247 (0.17%) Dominant**	221 (0.15%)
19	56 (0.07%)	**257 (0.24%) Dominant**	214 (0.21%)
20	152 (0.11%)	**385 (0.23%) Dominant**	270 (0.18%)
21	123 (0.09%)	406 (0.34%)	**428 (0.36%) Dominant**
22	127 (0.12%)	294 (0.26%)	**389 (0.31%) Dominant**
23	152 (0.17%)	**369 (0.28%) Dominant**	231 (0.23%)
24	67 (0.06%)	**274 (0.27%) Dominant**	202 (0.21%)
25	140 (0.12%)	**365 (0.25%) Dominant**	277 (0.18%)
26	32 (0.04%)	**473 (0.36%) Dominant**	169 (0.12%)
27	138 (0.17%)	201 (0.20%)	**273 (0.24%) Dominant**
28	51 (0.04%)	**284 (0.21%) Dominant**	206 (0.17%)
29	128 (0.13%)	**293 (0.22%) Dominant**	221 (0.18%)
30	85 (0.10%)	**291 (0.19%) Dominant**	194 (0.15%)
31	**136 (0.17%) Dominant**	108 (0.14%)	122 (0.15%)
32	157 (0.12%)	**368 (0.30%) Dominant**	264 (0.21%)
33	184 (0.15%)	**330 (0.27%) Dominant**	298 (0.24%)
34	156 (0.12%)	**342 (0.29%) Dominant**	174 (0.15%)

Discussion

The dimensions of CSR reflect different types of characteristics that can be attributed to the way organizations make sense of their environment (Lockett et al., 2006; Carroll, 2000). In this chapter, the CSR dimensions used by organizations within the hotel industry of Barcelona were analyzed, and a dominant environmentalist view of CSR was found to be the prevailing perspective of the region. From this standpoint, it can be argued that ecological balance and environmental issues have become the organizing principle of sustainable development in Barcelona through political strategies for urban development (March and Ribera-Fumaz, 2016). In fact, Barcelona is the first city to develop the first ecofriendly neighborhood in Spain, which included the construction of urban space following high environmental standards that contained the use of local resources and low carbon emissions (March and Ribera-Fumaz, 2016). As part of the sustainable development plan, these efforts with other various sustainability indicators indicate that Barcelona is a significant role model towards the integration of environmental aspects into activity areas of government agencies as well as private organizations (Spangenberg and Hinterberger, 2002).

Barcelona is searching for ways to further advance in sustainable development through protecting natural spaces and biodiversity, reaching optimal environmental quality levels so as to become a healthy city, preserving natural resources and promoting the use of renewable energies, increasing public awareness of sustainability in the form of environmental education, and actively encouraging sustainable development-oriented business activity (Barcelona City Council, 2009). In order to achieve these goals, the Barcelona City Council is adopting certain measures to improve environmental management, whilst promoting and encouraging private business organizations to embrace similar environmental management standards for making a better world (Barcelona City Council, 2009).

References

Aaronson, S. and Reeves, J. (2002). *The European response to public demands for global corporate responsibility*. Washington, DC: National Policy Association.

Aguilera, R.V., Rupp, D.E., Williams, C.A. and Ganapathi, J. (2007). Putting the S Back in CSR: A multi-level theory of social change in organizations. *Academy of Management Review*, 32(3), pp. 836–863.

Albareda, L., Lozano, J.M., Tencati, A., Midttun, A.and Perrini, F. (2008). The changing role of governments in corporate social responsibility: Drivers and responses. *Business Ethics: A European Review*, 17(4), pp. 347–363.

Barcelona City Council (2009). *Barcelona works towards sustainability*. Barcelona: Ajuntament de Barcelona.

Bundesministerium fur Verkehr Bau und Stadtentwicklung (BMVBS) (2007). Integrated urban Development – A Prerequisite for Urban Sustainability in Europe. Berlin:Federal Ministry of Transport, Building and Urban Affairs.

Carroll, A.B. (1979). A three-dimensional conceptual model of corporate social performance. *Academy of Management Review*, 4(4), pp. 497–505.

Carroll, A.B. (1991). The pyramid of corporate social responsibility: Toward the moral management of organizational stakeholders. *Business Horizon*, 34(4), pp. 39–48.

Carroll, A.B. (1998). The four faces of corporate citizenship. *Business and Society Review*, 100(1), pp. 1–7.

Carroll, A.B. (1999). Corporate social responsibility: Evolution of a definitional construct. *Business Society*, 38(3), pp. 268–294.

Carroll, A.B. (2000). Ethical challenges for business in the new millennium: Corporate social responsibility and models of management morality. *Business Ethics Quarterly*, 10(1), pp. 33–42.

Charnock, G., Purcell, T. and Ribera-Fumaz, R. (2014). City of rents: The limits to the Barcelona model of urban competitiveness. *International Journal of Urban and Regional Research*, 38(1): pp. 198–217.

Dahlsrud, A. (2008). How corporate social responsibility is defined: An analysis of 37 definitions. *Corporate Social Responsibility and Environmental Management*, 15(1), pp. 1–13.

Environmental Report. (2013). *Barcelona: A city committed to combating climate change*. Barcelona: Ajuntament de Barcelona.

Flick, U. (2007). *Designing qualitative research.* London: Sage.

Gibson, R. (2000). Specification of sustainability based environmental assessment decision criteria and implications for determining significance in environmental assessment. Canada: Canadian Environmental Assessment Agency, Research and Development Monograph Series.

Greenwood, M. (2007). Stakeholder engagement: Beyond the myth of corporate social responsibility. *Journal of Business Ethics*, 74(4), pp. 315–237.

Habisch, A., Jonker, J., Wegner, M. and Schmidpeter, R. (2005). *Corporate social responsibility across Europe.* Berlin: Springer.

Lockett, A., Moon, J. and Visser, W. (2006). Corporate social responsibility in management research: Focus, nature, salience and sources of influence. *Journal of Management Studies*, 43(1), pp. 115–136.

March, H. and Ribera-Fumaz, R. (2016). Smart contradictions: The politics of making Barcelona a self-sufficient city. *European Urban and Regional Studies*, 23(4), pp. 816–830.

Martinez, A.W., Callejo, M.B. and Fuentes, F.J.M. (2005). National and city contexts, urban development programmes and neighborhood selection. The Spanish background report. UGIS Urban development programmes, urban governance, social inclusion and sustainability. Madrid: Universidad Complutense de Madrid.

Matten, D. and Moon, J. (2008). Implicit and explicit CSR: A conceptual framework for a comparative understanding of corporate social responsibility. *Academy of Management Review*, 33(2), pp. 404–424.

Moir, L. (2001). What do we mean by corporate social responsibility? *Corporate Governance*, 1(2), pp. 16–22.

Neuendorf, K.A. (2002). *The content analysis guidebook.* Thousand Oaks, CA: Sage.

Neuman, W.L. (2006). *Social research methods*,6th ed. Boston: Pearson.

Pringle, H. and Thompson, M. (1999). *Brand spirit: How cause related marketing builds brands.* New York: Wiley.

Silberhorn, D. and Warren, R.C. (2007). Defining corporate social responsibility: A view from big companies in Germany and the UK. *European Business Review*, 19(5), pp. 352–372.

Spangenberg, J.H. and Hinterberger, F. (2002). Post Barcelona – Beyond Barcelona: Recommendations for the integration of sustainability indicators. Germany: Sustainable Europe Research Institute.

The European Commission (2001). Green Paper: Promoting A European Framework for Corporate Social Responsibility. Brussels: Commission of the European Communities.

The World Bank (2005). Opportunities and options for governments to promote corporate social responsibility in Europe and Central Asia. USA: The Development Communication Division.

Turisme (2017). Strategic Tourism Plan 2020. Tourism Department, Managers Office for Enterprise and Tourism. Barcelona: Ajuntament de Barcelona.

UNEP/MAP (2016). Mediterranean Strategy for Sustainable Development 2016–2025. Valbonne: Plan Bleu, Regional Activity Centre.

Werther, W.B. and Chandler, D. (2006). *Strategic corporate social responsibility: Stakeholders in a global environment.* London: Sage.

While, A., Jonas, A.E. and Gibbs, D. (2004). The environment and the entrepreneurial city: Searching for the urban sustainability fix in Manchester and Leeds. *International Journal of Urban and Regional Research*, 28(3), pp. 549–569.

Wood, D.J. (1991). Corporate social performance revisited. *Academy of Management Review*, 16(4), pp. 691–718.

World Commission on Environment and Development. (1987). *Our common future.* Oxford: Oxford University Press.

7 Customer relationship management and service challenges in the Mediterranean region

Özlem Özbek and Roya Rahimi

The customer relationship management (CRM) concept: definition and components

There is intense competition between businesses producing similar products in the same market. In this competitive enterprise, businesses need to make a difference between similar services in order to increase market share and profits and to ensure customer satisfaction (Lu and Wu, 2012). The important factor is to be able to provide a competitive advantage. These strategies have recently been customer-focused as a result of changes in the marketing techniques and demands of the tourism industry. These changes have also led to the need to look at some insights that exist in traditional marketing. CRM, as an extension of a focus approach, is a technology-dominated form of management that exposes marketing to the whole organization.

Looking at the development of marketing, it is understood that CRM is a concept formed due to changes in customer view. It is seen that the customer-oriented marketing concept developed in the 1990s after product and production-oriented marketing (pre-1930), sales-oriented marketing (1930–1950), the marketing concept (1950–1970) and the social marketing concept (1970–1990) (Celtek, 2013, p. 6). Light (2003) noted that CRM was composed from business processes such as relationship marketing and advanced customer value. Customer Relationship Management (CRM) is based on the principles of Relationship Marketing (RM), an emergent area of modern day marketing (Parvatiyar and Sheth, 2000; Huang, Chou and Lin, 2010; Rahimi and Kozak, 2017). Relationship marketing is a CRM strategy used to constitute strong, lasting customer connections to a brand. The goal is to generate repeat sales, encourage word-of-mouth promotion and collect customer information. The concept of CRM in the tourism sector, where human relations are intense, is beginning to gain momentum. In addition to providing customer satisfaction and loyalty, CRM is a guide to creating customer-specific products. At this point, the concept of customer-specific value is emerging. It is possible to say that sociological, economic and technological innovations are the basis of the customer value. Nowadays, customers are more knowledgeable and conscious because all kinds of knowledge is easily accessible with the developments of technology.

CRM means that communication and feedback are intensely used in all areas of decision-making, from the design of product or service to setting up of partnerships with customers in all units of an enterprise. It is a management approach to fulfill the purpose of the business performance, customer satisfaction and loyalty. CRM is intended to sell more than one product to the same customer and to transform to customer into a loyal customer. CRM helps businesses to develop new business strategies in the light of the information gathered to better understand the expectations of customers. When defining the CRM, two important issues arise. As opposed to general customer definitions, the first is to have the ability to analyze each customer individually, such as customer profile, habits, anticipations, location and region information. The second is to make new work plans on the basis of analysis of the obtained data (Zeng, Wen and Yen, 2003; Gummesson, 2004; Ranjan and Bhatnagar, 2011).

The CRM system can be explained as a process of information that includes all steps in promotion, sale and post sales. In another definition, CRM can be figured as "delivering the right goods and service, the right customer, at the right time and price, at the right spot". CRM applications have been developed to enable companies to improve their relationship with current customers, gain new customers and retain all customers. CRM applications are being successfully used in service points that are being tried to be created widely in today's world, such as call centers. It can be used 24/7 on the intranet within the organization, on private distribution channels for business partners and corporations with the Internet all over the world. In this respect, establishment of efficient organizations and higher customer satisfaction are ensured. In order to achieve an effective CRM process, companies need to build a strong IT system. For an organization to establish a data processing system, concepts such as data warehouse, software customization, process automation, help desk and call centers and Internet influence should be required. CRM is a combination of people, processes and technology, and an integrated and holistic approach between these three components is required for a successful CRM implementation (Mendoza et al., 2006; Rahimi and Gunlu, 2016; Rahimi et al., 2017).

Implementing CRM

In order for successful CRM and creation of customer loyalty, processes need to be well structured. Identification of potential customers and segmentation of existing customers are key considerations for customer loyalty (Stockdale, 2007). In summary, CRM phases consist of customer selection, customer acquisition, customer protection and customer deepening concepts (Turker and Ozaltın, 2010). Expanded CRM consists of eight processes: customer selection, customer acquisition, customer protection and customer deepening, analytical CRM, operational CRM, strategic CRM and interactive CRM (Zengin and Mert, 2002).

- Customer selection focuses on maximizing business and marketing resources. To identify the right market segment allows one to communicate to that segment more deeply and effectively. At this stage, studies such as market segmentation, campaign plans, brand and customer analysis and product promotion are being carried out.

- Customer acquisition is one the most critical factors for business success. Firstly, potential customers are identified, and they are divided into different groups. In the next step, customer expectations and needs are clearly defined.
- Customer protection works to ensure that a client is interested and in company for as long as possible.
- Customer deepening involves the steps necessary to maintain long-term loyalty and profitability of a customer and to increase the share of customer spending.
- Analytical CRM is an analysis system installed on the operational system that includes the ability to identify potential customers and provide services such as individual marketing.
- Operational CRM is the first CRM category that comes to mind. It can be defined as an automation system that integrates all points, channels and business processes in contact with the customer. In particular, it enables personnel working in sales, marketing and service departments to see the customer in department.
- Strategic CRM is the phase in which CRM strategies are determined for the company. It measures the performance of existing CRM applications. Competitors are examined for the appropriate CRM strategy, and strategy components are determined.
- Interactive CRM decides a suitable channel to communicate with customers. Interactive CRM is comprising channel management, external message management, customer perception and corporate behavioral model.

For successful completion of all these processes, the following approaches are required: cross selling; customer differentiation; customer loyalty; customer valuation; learning relationship; actual, lifetime and strategic customer value; most growable customers; most valuable customers, pareto efficiency, one-to-one marketing, and personalization. They are the most important points for CRM processes (Rahimi and Gunlu, 2016). The benefits CRM provides to businesses are cost savings, customer satisfaction and loyalty, increased profits, increased internal commitment, employee satisfaction and improved business intelligence (Rahimi and Kozak, 2017). Satisfied and loyal customers offer word-of-mouth marketing opportunities for businesses. Loyal customers are less sensitive to price. Loyal customers are increasing the profitability of the business in a highly competitive business circle. At the same time, CRM increases the satisfaction rate of the employees and decreases the loss rate of employees. All of these reflect profitability in business. Participative CRM systems are functions based on the idea of sharing information about customers with business partners, channels and suppliers and further elaboration of customer special services (Gustafsson, Johnson and Roos, 2005; Mithas, Krishnan and Fornell, 2005).

At the present time, customers obtain information by the Internet, which increases the e-CRM concept (Chen and Chen, 2004). The advantages of e-CRM for customers are interactive, personalized and concerned communication with customers through both electronic and traditional channels. E-CRM provides tips on how to communicate with the customer, allowing you to obtain detailed information about the customer (Milovic, 2011). In the context of Internet-based marketing in the hospitality industry,

> E-CRM is a management strategy supported by web technologies that enables hotels to engage guests in strong, personalized and mutually beneficial interactive relationships, and thereby increasing profitability and sales effectiveness. E-CRM is the latest technique that companies use to increase and improve their marketing skills and capabilities. Integrating technological and marketing elements, E-CRM covers all aspects of online user experience throughout the transaction cycle: pre-purchase, purchase and post-purchase.
>
> (Alhaiou, Irani and Ali, 2009)

CRM in the tourism and hospitality industry

With the development of online marketing, many changes have occurred in the tourism sector. It has become a habit for customers to explore social media channels about destinations before their travels. According to International Tourist Research Centers, 88% of tourism businesses use social media in their promotions, and 70% of the customers rely on information providers in social media. And it is stated that social media is a sustainable word-of-mouth marketing tool for sharing experiences and knowledge of different customers (Jashi, 2013). Implementing CRM in hotel companies help create a better image among the guests, consequently resulting into positive word of mouth, more guest retention and more revenue. CRM applications help with anticipating the needs of a hotel's current and potential guests, and optimize the hotel's revenue by providing optimum guest satisfaction (Brown, 1999; Rahimi, 2017b). Facebook, Instagram, YouTube, Twitter, Pinterest and travelshake are the most used social media circles in the tourism sector. The relationship of social media with CRM concerns the acquisition of information about customers' expectations by social media channels in the tourism enterprise. Business can increase both their recognition rates and their credibility with the social media channel. Another advantage of social media in terms of tourism businesses is that it reduces the marketing costs of businesses. In this context, it is understood that social media is a comprehensive source of knowledge for both businesses and potential tourists (Hall, 2004; Sin, Tse and Yim, 2005).

Besides, it is very beneficial to be able to communicate with the customer through online marketing channels and to be able to advertise and inform with personal messages. With the development of the Internet, hotel managers have realized how important website designs are in terms of marketing. Website design is a basic factor of retaining customers online and must also support the self-service environment of the online travel industry that is largely web based (Stockdale, 2007).

CRM in the tourism and hospitality industry can be defined as a set of customer-focused strategies created by businesses to reduce sales costs, increase revenues, create new markets, expand sales and service channels, increase customer engagement and provide customer loyalty and satisfaction (Bowen and Chen, 2001; Wang and Feng, 2012). The difference in the business is no longer sufficient for competition nowadays; businesses prefer CRM as a new marketing approach in the tourism enterprise. It is impossible to copy special products created after CRM applications. In CRM applications, the main objective is to provide customers with specific products by anticipating the customers' needs, desires and expectations. Since the relationship established with the customers will be much more difficult to copy by competitors, it provides a competitive advantage for the hospitality enterprise. CRM has proven to be a key strategy for improving customer satisfaction, retention and profitability in the hotel businesses (Lo, Stalcup and Lee, 2010; Rahimi, 2017b).

Research in tourism enterprise indicates that majority of dissatisfied customers leave without having expressed their complaints (Burton and Burton, 1997, p. 3). The next preference of customers who do not voice complaints is most likely a different business. The importance of CRM is coming to exist at this point. Information getting by CRM applications is used for private offerings or services to customers. Tourism businesses that decide to implement this management process must be able to collect data on and analyze different customer needs (Power and Douglas, 1997). It is not enough to have advanced technology to do this; it is necessary to establish an organizational structure to enable a learning relationship with the customer (Pepper and Rogers, 1998). There are a number of problems about detection of customer satisfaction in tourism enterprise, which are caused by the fact that products are abstract. The satisfaction level of a service differs according to each customer. Or the satisfaction of the same customer may change over time. Unlike other marketing types, CRM focuses on the satisfaction level of each customer. Like large organizations, many small and medium-sized enterprises have been carrying out CRM. The benefits of CRM applications in the tourism industry are greater success for business professionals, more professional customer service and increasing business sense. Customers feel strongly supported by the tourism company. With the professionalism of customer service, tourist confidence in products and services is increasing. Tourism companies must update and complete their databases. In this way, companies will be able to determine customer expectations in the best possible way.

CRM implications and its process

Within the scope of the contemporary tourism approach, power is nowadays in the hands of consumers, not with businesses. The businesses have to change from being product-centered, the structures consisting of functional units that are not integrated to one another, to being customer-oriented, and that can confront the customer as bodily. This is not just a one-time change; it must be sustainable in parallel with the constantly changing customer demands. In this sense, instead of traditional marketing based on narrow functional CRM, a new form of cross-functional marketing has begun to be preferred. The traditional marketing approach has been increasingly questioned in recent years (PAYNE, 2004).

Although customers have a positive hold on the company and its products, buying behavior has a high degree of situational character. CRM requires managing this relationship, so that it will be profitable and mutually beneficial. The CLV (customer lifetime value) is a tool for measuring this relationship. The customer's lifetime value can be calculated as follows. Monthly or yearly fixed costs are deducted from a customer's monthly or yearly earned money, and the resulting monthly or annual net profit is multiplied by the estimated life of the customer, resulting in the total value of the customer for the company. From this total value, the advertising expenditures to obtain the customer, and the expenditures and investments made to keep the customer, are deducted. The result is a customer's lifetime value (Firat, 2000, p. 156).

The CRM process begins with listening to customers, and doing so continues to determine their expectations from the company, the company's products and how they want those products delivered to them. As the outlines of expectations show, customers continue to allocate microsegments. Then it will continue with determination of profitable and non-profitable customers. It is a much smarter way to send customers who are harming or not making a profit to your competitors. Thereafter, customers at each stage in these different microsegments can obtain detailed information on their needs, such as how they expect a tourism service. And it continues to keep them so that each individual can reach the customer very quickly (Kirim, 2001, p. 52). The CRM project implementation process develops as follows (Kiral, 2004):

STAGE 1:

- Analysis of current situation
- Creation of CRM vision
- Determination of strategy and needs
- Establishment of work processes

STAGE 2:

- Solution implementation according to the need determined
- Testing processes
- Education
- Support

STAGE 3:

- Assessment of the situation
- Identification of new or changing needs.

The main outcome of CRM is that today's customers have become sophisticated. The share of customers is more important for businesses in CRM; that is, the importance of customer value for a lifetime. When mass marketing and CRM are compared, the main points and opposite points are (Kurban, 2002, p. 83):

- Against average customers to individual customers
- Against customers names to customer profile
- Against mass production to individual production
- Against mass advertisements to individual messages
- From one-way messages to two way messages
- Against market segmentation to segmentation of customers
- Against all customers to lucrative customers
- Customer retention strategy against customer withdrawal strategy.

Some of the CRM projects that were passed on during the past were aimed at eliminating certain problems seen in the processes of seeking operational downturn solutions.

Conclusion

In a highly competitive environment, tourism enterprises that try to survive should benefit from contemporary approaches and techniques. It is apparent that CRM is an effective process to ensure a sustainable relationship with customers. The CRM system works to increase the number of constant customers, who are much more advantageous for companies (Dowling, 2002). CRM is an important application in terms of the performance of businesses.

Correctly established and operated customer relations programs create benefits in many areas for businesses. Some of the most important ones are: sales increase; cost decrease; increases motivation in employees; customers are better known; increases customer satisfaction; increases number of loyal customers; increases the chance of planning to the future. CRM can be defined as a business strategy that enables companies to establish long-term and sustainable relationships with their customers and to provide both company and customer value from these relationships. Except for cost or benefit scaling, the most fundamental problem is trained manpower who knows the products in the CRM market and technological infrastructure of the industry.

As a result, it is a useful application for predicting demand content more effectively and taking the concept of quality one step further. In addition to being a system where customer preferences are guided, it is a personnel and resource automation where the company activities can be analyzed from a center. CRM is a system that serves as market segmentation for the most valuable customers of today and the future. Marketing strategies are made according to these segments and it makes customer loyalty management very easy.

References

Alhaiou, T., Irani, Z. and Ali, M. (2009). The relationship between eCRM implementation and e-loyalty at different adoption stages of transaction cycle: A conceptual framework and hypothesis. *Proceedings of the European and Mediterranean conference on information systems*. Crowne Plaza Hotel, Izmir: EMCIS.

Bowen, J.T. and Chen, S.L. (2001). The relationship between customer loyalty and customer satisfaction. *International Journal of Contemporary Hospitality Management*, 1(2), pp. 213–217. Available at: http://dx.doi.org/10.1108/09596110110395893

Brown, S.A. (1999). *Strategic customer care: An evolutionary approach to increasing customer value and profitability*. Toronto, Canada: John Wiley and Sons.

Burton, J. and Burton, L. (1997). *Interpersonal skill for travel and tourism*. Malaysia: Addison Wesley Longman.

Celtek, E. (2013). *Turizm İsletmelerinde Elektronik Müsteri İliskileri (E-Miy)*. Ankara: Detay Yayıncılık.

Chen, Q. and Chen, H.M. (2004). Exploring the success factors of eCRM strategies in practice. *Journal of Database Marketing & Customer Strategy Management*, 11(4), pp. 333–343.

Dowling, G. (2002). Customer relationship management: In B2C markets, often less is more. *California Management Review*, 44(3), pp. 87–104.

Firat, E. (2000). En Değerli Müşteri Kimde? *Capital, Kasım 2000*, ss. 152–156.

Gummesson, E. (2004). Return on relationships (ROR): The value of relationship marketing and CRM in business-to-business contexts. *Journal of Business & Industrial Marketing*, 19(2), pp. 136–148.

Gustafsson, A., Johnson, M.D. and Roos, I. (2005). The effects of customer satisfaction, relationship commitment dimensions, and triggers on customer retention. *Journal of Marketing*, 69(4), pp. 210–218.

Hall, J. (2004). Business intelligence: The missing link in your CRM strategy. *Information Management*, 14(6), p. 36.

Huang, C.-Y., Chou, C.-J. and Lin, P.-C. (2010). Involvement theory in constructing bloggers' intention to purchase travel products. *Tourism Management*, 31(4), pp. 513–526. DOI: 10.1016/j.tourman.2009.06.003.

Jashi, C. (2013). Significance of social media marketing in tourism. 8th Silk Road International Conference. In: *Development of tourism in black and Caspian seas regions*. 24–26 May. Georgia: Tbilisi-Batumi.

Kiral, C. (2004). *Türkiye' de CRM*. Available at: www.crminturkey.org/crm/archive [Accessed 9 Mar. 2018].

Kirim, A. (2001). Strateji ve Bire Bir Pazarlama (CRM). Istanbul: Sistem Yayincilik.

Kurban, E.P. (2002). Küresel Rekabet Aracı Olarak Müşteri İlişkileri Yönetimi ve Halkla İlişkilerin Rolü, Ege Üniversitesi, Sosyal Bilimler Enstitüsü. İzmir: Yayımlanmamış Yüksek Lisans Tezi.

Light, B. (2003). CRM packaged software: A study of organisational experiences. *Business Process Management Journal*, 9(5).

Lo, A.S., Stalcup, L.D. and Lee, A. (2010). Customer relationship management for hotels in Hong Kong. *International Journal of Contemporary Hospitality Management*, 22(2), pp. 139–159.

Lu, C. and ve Wu, S. (2012). The relationship between CRM, RM, and business performance: A study of the hotel industry in Taiwan. *International Journal of Hospitality Management*, 31(1), pp. 276–285.

Mendoza, L.E., Marius, A., Pérez, M. and Grimán, A.C. (2006). Critical success factors for a customer relationship management strategy. *Information and Software Technology*, 49(8), pp. 913–945.

Milovic, B. (2011). *Razlike CRM i eCRM poslovne strategije. X međunarodni naučno-stručni Simpozijum INFOTEH-JAHORINA 2011*. Sarajevo: Elektrotehnički fakultet Istočno Sarajevo, pp. 720–724.

Mithas, S., Krishnan, M.S. and Fornell, C. (2005). Why do customer relationship management applications affect customer satisfaction?. *Journal of Marketing*, 69(4), pp. 201–209.

Parvatiyar, A. and Sheth, J.N. (2000). The domain and conceptual foundations of relationship marketing. In: J.N. Sheth and A. Parvatiyar, eds., *Handbook of relationship marketing*. Thousand Oaks, CA: Sage, pp. 3–38.

Payne, A. (2004). *Customer relationship management*. Cranfield: Cranfield University. Available at: www.ebusinessforum.gr/content/downloads/ap0011.pdf. 09.03.2018

Peppers, D. and ve Rogers, M. (1998). Converting ratepayers into loyal customers. *American Gas*, 80(7), pp. 27–30.

Power, A. and Douglas, J. (1997). Manufacturing the future. *Best Review: Life-Health Insurance Edition*, 98(4).

Rahimi, R. (2017a). Customer relationship management (people, process and technology) and organisational culture in hotels: Which traits matter? *International Journal of Contemporary Hospitality Management*, 29(5). DOI:10.1108/IJCHM-10–2015–0617.

Rahimi, R. (2017b). Organizational culture and customer relationship management: A simple linear regression analysis. *Journal of Hospitality Marketing & Management*, 26(4), pp. 443–449. DOI: 10.1080/19368623.2017.1254579.

Rahimi, R. and Gunlu, E. (2016). Implementing customer relationship management (CRM) in hotel industry from organizational culture perspective. *International Journal of Contemporary Hospitality Management*, 28(1), pp. 89–112. DOI:10.1108/IJCHM-04–2014–0176d

Rahimi, R., Köseoglu, M., Ersoy, A. and Okumus, F. (2017). Customer relationship management research in tourism and hospitality: A state-of-the-art. *Tourism Review*, 72(2), pp. 209–220. Available at: https://doi.org/10.1108/ TR-01–2017–0011

Rahimi, R. and Kozak, M. (2017). Impact of customer relationship management on customer satisfaction: The case of a budget hotel chain. *Journal of Travel & Tourism Marketing*, 34(1), pp. 40–51. DOI: 10.1080/10548408.2015.1130108.

Ranjan, J. and Bhatnagar, V. (2011). Role of knowledge management and analytical CRM in business: Data mining based framework. *The Learning Organization*, 18(2), pp. 131–148.

Sin, L.Y., Tse, A.C. and Yim, F.H. (2005). CRM: Conceptualization and scale development. *European Journal of Marketing*, 39(11/12), pp. 1264–1290.

Stockdale, R. (2007). Managing customer relationships in the self-service environment of e-tourism. *Journal of Vacation Marketing*, 13(3), pp. 205–219.

Turker, A. and Ozaltın, G. (2010). Konaklama Isletmelerinde Musteri İliskileri Yönetimi: Izmır Ilı Ornegi. *Mugla Universitesi Sosyal Bilimler Enstitüsü Dergisi* (25), pp. 81–104.

Wang, Y. and Feng, H. (2012). Customer relationship management capabilities: Measurement, antecedents and consequences. *Management Decision*, 50(1), pp. 115–129.

Zeng, Y.E., Wen, H.J. and Yen, D.C., 2003. Customer relationship management (CRM) in business-to-business (B2B) e-commerce. *Information Management & Computer Security*, 11(1), pp. 39–44.

Zengin, H and Mert, K. (2002). Bilgi Yönetimi Analiziyle Müsteri Sadakatinin Saglanmasında Yeni Bir Yontem: CRM. *Verimlilik Dergisi*, pp. 803–806.

8 Freshwater and wastewater management in Mediterranean hotels and resorts

Owner-operator issues

Willy Legrand and Nicolas Dubrocard

Introduction

In a megatrends report published by Skift, a global online trade magazine, gathering intelligence on the travel and hospitality industry, the following introductory statement to a chapter on climate's role in shaping the management of destination stated: "Extreme weather is the new normal. It's changing destinations for the worse, and it's not going to get better any time soon" (Peltier, 2018, p. 48). In a study conducted by Guiot and Cramer and published in *Science*, the authors discussed the vegetation and pollen cores from sediments. The authors demonstrate that Southern Europe risks becoming a desert by the end of the century due to climate change (Guiot and Cramer, 2016). If the temperature increases above 1.5 degrees in relation to pre-industrial level, many cities and tourist magnets around the Mediterranean will be inhospitable by the year 2100. In addition, the World Economic Forum (WEF) 2017 Travel and Tourism Competitiveness Report states that

> although this relationship is complex [. . .] the more pristine the natural environment of a country, the more tourists are inclined to travel there, and the more they are willing to pay to access well-preserved areas. Consequently, as the natural capital depletes, destinations lose revenue.
>
> (2017, p. 6).

Finally, the Intergovernmental Science-Policy Platform on Biodiversity and Ecosystem Services (IPBES), an independent intergovernmental body providing scientific assessment on biodiversity and ecosystems, warns that "biodiversity continues to decline in every region of the world, significantly reducing nature's capacity to contribute to people's well-being" (IPBES, 2018). The combination of all these factors and scenarios with the increased tourism arrivals in vulnerable destinations is creating unprecedented challenges and pressure on resources. One such resource is critical to the travel and hospitality industry as well as to local communities: *freshwater*.

This chapter looks at the issues of poorly managed water and wastewater resources in hotels and resorts and the consequences for the local communities around the Mediterranean Basin, which are particularly prone to water security issues. A strategic framework with hands-on actions for those properties based on best practices is consequently developed. With the basic Paris agreement equation of *"mitigation + adaption + support"*, the goal is to pave the way to an effective and efficient water management in those areas prone to dire climate change consequences.

Literature review

Global water problem definition

The grand challenges humanity is facing are clearly described within the 17 United Nations Sustainable Development Goals (UN SDGs) established in 2015 (United Nations, 2015a). From ending poverty to ensuring affordable and clean energy or providing access to quality education, all goals come with their own set of challenges in ensuring that all of the 169 targets (over 17 broader goals) are met by 2030 (United Nations, 2015a). Goal 6 stipulates that everyone should have access to water and proper sanitation (United Nations, 2015b).

The facts around water are unambiguous; the challenges lie in terms of both the quality and the quantity of water available across regions. Moreover, water is linked to all aspects of life, from food supplies, health and education to regional economic development. Globally, the United Nations estimates that "2.4 billion people lack access to basic sanitation services, such as toilets or latrines" (United Nations, 2015c, p. 1) and that "water scarcity affects more than 40 per cent of the global population" (United Nations, 2015b, p. 1). Additionally, most of the wastewater (more than 80%) is discharged without treatment, worsening the overall environmental impacts (United Nations, 2015b, p. 1). Water is a precious but diminishing commodity. However, many private and industrial users regard it as just another cost, with little incentive to conserve or use wisely. This in turn is partly due to the price tag in many developed countries – it is still largely negligible, though in constant increase.

Water plays a role on all three pillars of sustainable development, namely the (1) social, (2) economic and (3) environmental pillars.

Social

Sufficient water supply "is critical for a family's health and social dignity" (UN Water, 2015, p. 2). Additionally, access to safe drinking water is a human right. The 2010 Resolution 64/292 from the United Nations General Assembly unequivocally "recognizes the right to safe and clean drinking water and sanitation as a human right that is essential for the full enjoyment of life and all human rights" (United Nations, 2010).

Economic

The role of water in economic development of communities, regions and countries is undeniable. The United Nations Educational, Scientific and Cultural Organization (UNESCO) stated in a report on *The Role of Water in Socio-Economic*

Development (UNESCO, 1987) that "many of man's major achievements have involved improvements in water resource utilization" (p. 3) from foodstuff production via irrigation systems to energy production via hydroelectric power development, to name a few examples. Interestingly, the report also analyzed some of the key features in the collapse of societies and concluded that "notable setbacks [. . .] often have been directly related to the inability to overcome water-related problems" (p. 3). Investment in water infrastructure is a critical component since "many benefits may be gained by promoting and facilitating use of the best available technologies and management systems in water provision, productivity and efficiency, and by improving water allocation mechanisms" (UN Water, 2015, p. 3).

Environmental

The long list of environmental challenges linked to the management of freshwater and wastewater is beyond the scope of this chapter. However, as reported by the United Nations World Water Assessment Programme, "most economic models do not value the essential services provided by freshwater ecosystems, often leading to unsustainable use of water resources and ecosystem degradation" (UN Water, 2015, p. 3). From climate change to food security, humans have only started to realize the critical role of water on biodiversity and the balance of entire ecosystems.

THE MEDITERRANEAN BASIN WATER PROBLEM DEFINITION

The Mediterranean Basin can be defined, at least geographically, as the area surrounding the Mediterranean Sea surpassing three continents: Europe, Asia and Africa. Geopolitically, 22 countries and territories surround the sea, home to 480 million people (EEA, 2015, p. 1). According to the European Environment Agency, "65% of the population (around 120 million inhabitants) is concentrated in coastal hydrological basins, where environmental pressures have increased" (EEA, 2015, p. 1). Interestingly, the region has, comparatively, relatively low levels of greenhouse gas emissions but suffers first hand from changes in climate (EEA, 2015). A drop of 20% in rainfall has been recorded since 1970 in Southern Europe (EEA, 2015). The Water Exploitation Index (WEI) which is "defined as the mean annual total demand for fresh water, divided by the long-term average freshwater resources, shows that southern countries are among the most water-stressed Mediterranean countries, with many having a WEI higher than 40%" (EEA, 2015, p. 3). Some countries, such as Egypt, Israel, Syria and Libya, have a WEI surpassing 80% (EEA, 2015). Along the same line, the Atlas of Water shows a series of countries, including Mediterranean coastal tourism magnets, to be short on water by 2050 (Black and King, 2009). A large section of the Mediterranean population (around 250 million people) is forecasted to become "water-poor" over the next 20 years (UNEP/MAP, 2013). Being "water-poor" is part of a "water stress index" and is defined as an individual who has access to less than 1,000 cubic meters of water per year (Falkenmark, Lundquist and Widstrand, 1989). This is also better known as *water scarcity*. Absolute water scarcity is defined as having access to less than 500 cubic meters of water per person per year (Falkenmark, Lundquist and Widstrand, 1989). A series of other measures of water scarcity have been developed over the years, including the International Water Management Institute (IWMI) Measure of Water Scarcity, and the Water Poverty Index as reported by the Global Water Forum (2012). The explanation of those is beyond the scope of this chapter. However, it is important to realize that different measures will capture different components linked to water pressure. Independent of the measurement chosen, all corroborate to the fact that the Mediterranean Basin faces grave challenges, with regional differences. A similar scenario is depicted by the European Commission in a report on Mediterranean water scarcity and drought, where the "risks of water shortage are generally ascribable at high level and the growth of demand despite limited renewable water resources- and mainly irregular and unequal qualities – thus with availabilities that rarefy" (European Commission, 2007, p. 2). Overall, the Mediterranean Basin "has been identified as one of the main climate change hotspots due to water scarcity, concentration of economic activities in coastal areas, and reliance on climate-sensitive agriculture" (EEA, 2015, p. 3). This concentration on economic and human activities translates into an entire region, which is under tremendous pressure. Additionally, the unique combination of diverse cultures and rich history with a clement climate and beautiful coastline makes the Mediterranean region the number one destination in the world. International tourism arrivals increased significantly from 220 million at the turn of the millennium to 320 million by 2015, almost a third of the world's international tourists (MGI, 2017). The tourism industry is a significant economic driver of smaller villages and communities; however, it is causing severe threats to the natural habitats. As a result, the European Commission, in a Natura 2000 report, states that the "much of the Mediterranean coastline has disappeared under concrete [faced with] chronic water shortages and a constant threat of forest fires" (European Commission, 2018). The UNWTO forecasts more than 1.8 billion international arrivals by 2030, with 500 million in the Mediterranean region alone (UNWTO, 2015; UNWTO, 2017). As German author Hans Magnus Enzenberger ironically stated, "tourists destroy what they seek by finding it . . ." (in German: *Der Tourist zerstört, was er sucht, indem er es findet*). Greenpeace comes to a similar conclusion when discussing the fate of the Mediterranean region if no actions are taken, whereby "it is inevitable that the tourists will leave the Mediterranean as it becomes more depleted of its natural beauty" (2009).

HOSPITALITY INDUSTRY PROBLEM DEFINITION

When a hotel guest checks into a room and turns the water tap on or decides to take a shower, the expectation is that the water flows. Additionally, the water should be colorless, odorless and potable. Failure to reach those basic hygiene factors results in dissatisfaction and complaints. Water in hotels is a critical resource. During the summer months, which is the peak visitation time of the year along the Mediterranean coast, water supplies are exacerbated from the combination of tourist daily usage, swimming pools and golf courses. A tourist "consumes between 300 and 850 litres of water per day" (De Stefano, 2004, p. 4), which is two or three times more than a local resident. As a measure of comparison, globally it is estimated that domestic water usage amounts to 160 liters per person per day (Gössling, 2006). It is important, however, to consider the fact that tourists are not directly responsible for the amount of water used and wasted by hospitality facilities via the maintenance of swimming pools, laundry practices and cleaning duties, especially if those do not operate with water efficiency in mind. Summer is also the time of the year when water availability is at its lowest in the Mediterranean Basin. And while the construction of dams and the extraction of groundwater have been a *quick fix* set of solutions to the tourism water problems, the consequences are dire. As reported by the World·Wildlife Fund (WWF), "tourism is making a major contribution to the degradation and destruction of water ecosystems as rivers are being fragmented, groundwater levels are sinking and wetlands are drying out" (De Stefano, 2004, p. 4). This in turn translates into habitat loss and more water treatment needed for drinking and irrigation due to low level of groundwater and higher salinity (De Stefano, 2004). Accommodating an increased number of tourists also means a growth in urban centers, "likely destroying in the process the few remaining coastal wetlands and lagoons" (De Stefano, 2004, p. 4). Table 8.1 provides a summary of the major categories of impacts due to tourism activities around the Mediterranean Basin. Table 8.2 provides a summary of the causes linked to those impacts.

HOTEL WATER USAGE AND COST

As discussed in the previous section, water consumption per guest per night is between 300 and 850 liters (De Stefano, 2004, p. 4). Although, according to an international review of the literature on tourism and water use conducted by Gössling et al. (2012), "water consumption rates [were] in a range between 84 and 2000 L (liters) per tourist per day, or up to 3423 L per bedroom per day" (p. 7). Higher-standard accommodation sectors tend to have greater usage of water than their budget or guesthouse counterparts. This can be explained due to the facilities available (e.g. swimming pools, spas, water parks) and landscaping surrounding the hotel (e.g. parks and gardens) as well as the activities (e.g. golf courses) and food choices of tourists. Quite a few studies have tried to quantify water use by hospitality facilities, in particular hotels within the Mediterranean Basin. Here too, daily water use per tourist ranges from 84 to 145 liters for campsites (Rico-Amoros, Olcina-Cantos and Sauri, 2009, cited in Gössling et al., 2012), 174 to 300 liters for budget to mid-scale hotels (Rico-Amoros, Olcina-Cantos and Sauri, 2009; Eurostat, 2009, cited in Gössling et al., 2012) and from 361 to 1,000 liters for high-end and luxurious-properties hotels (Rico-Amoros, Olcina-Cantos and Sauri, 2009; Antakyali, Krampe and Steinmetz, 2008, cited in Gössling et al., 2012).

In terms of water use within a hotel facility, Table 8.3 shows water usage in relation to total water used based on a Mediterranean climate. The data presented are based on one particular hotel example without a pool and thus should be understood as an indicator of water usage rather than industry averages.

Table 8.1 Overview of impacts of tourism on freshwater in the Mediterranean

Impacts	Definition/explanation	Status Mediterranean Basin
Overexploitation of groundwater	"[O]ccurs when the volume of abstracted groundwater exceeds the average annual renewal of the groundwater body" (De Stefano, 2004, p. 5).	Considerable overexploitation of groundwater in many Mediterranean countries due to concentration of agriculture and tourism in coastal areas.
Construction of new reservoirs or water transfer schemes	"[G]rowth of tourism is often associated with the search for complementary water sources to satisfy the great demands on water for this economic sector" (De Stefano, 2004, p. 5).	Significant construction of dams altering river flows and habitat (International Rivers, n.d.).
Exploitation of non-renewable groundwater resources	Groundwater is stored in aquifers. Aquifers provide the main source of water for the food industry via irrigation (Clark Z and Briar, 2001).	Resources in Saharan aquifers in serious depletion (Libya, Egypt, Tunisia and Algeria in particular) (De Stefano, 2004, p. 7) and Morocco as well, in areas surrounding Marrakech where multiple golf courses are being built or in planning.
Pollution of surface and groundwater	Often as a result of "insufficient, inefficient or non-existent waste water treatment systems" (De Stefano, 2004, p. 7). Pollution has a direct impact on quality of water and surrounding ecosystems.	It is estimated that within the Mediterranean basin, 37% of settlements with 2000 inhabitants or more do not operate a wastewater treatment plant before discharge (GRID-Arendal, 2013). Municipal wastewater from coastal towns receives no treatment before discharge. There are reports of hotels along the Mediterranean coast not connected with any sewage systems or with ineffective autonomous treatment (De Stefano, 2004; Gabarda-Mallorqui et al., 2016).
Occupation and degradation of wetlands areas	"[A]reas where water covers the soil, or is present either at or near the surface of the soil all year or for varying periods of time during the year" (EPA, 2017).	Coastal overdevelopment to make room for new resorts, hotels and recreational facilities directly impacts the Mediterranean wetlands, affecting the rich and diverse fauna and flora. Wetlands are also considered tourist attractions for recreational use, with considerable degradation as a direct effect. In fact, "wetland disappearance or degradation contributes to the decline of species that depend on them to survive" (De Stefano, 2004, p. 9).

Source: Adapted from De Stefano (2004).

Table 8.2 Freshwater usage and wastewater production due to tourism in the Mediterranean

Cause	Explanation
High water consumption due to population increase	Peak demand during dry season for both tourism purposes (freshwater consumption) and agriculture (irrigation).
Higher consumption of water for associated facilities and leisure	Swimming pools, water parks, golf courses, but also laundry facilities (extra towels from swimming pools) and gardens are all contributing to peak demand (Gössling et al., 2012).
Water embodied in food consumption	As reported by Legrand, Sloan and Chen (2017) as well as Gössling et al. (2012), water is present in great amount in the food consumed by tourists. That amount will vary greatly on the type of food, the agricultural practices and the transport and packaging associated with the food.
Peaks in wastewater volumes, inefficient or non-existent wastewater treatment facilities	Linked to the increased consumption of freshwater is the production of wastewater. The consequence is "large volumes of sewage discharged to sewage treatment plants, or to the sea and rivers, because many tourist facilities are in isolated areas and are not connected to the water treatment network" (De Stefano, 2004, p. 11). Water untreated or disposed correctly results in increased water pollution.
Urban development associated with tourism	All facilities, which are rendering various services to the tourists at location, will in turn have an impact on water usage and wastewater disposal. Those facilities may include hospitality, waste treatment facilities, restaurants and cinemas as well as the construction of second homes on the Mediterranean coastline, for example.
Transport infrastructures associated with tourism	All goods requiring transportation (e.g. food) as well as the movement of tourists at the destination require further infrastructures (e.g. roads, tunnels, bridges) with direct consequences on the water systems and environment.

Source: Adapted from De Stefano (2004).

Table 8.3 Hotel water usage based on activity

Department/activity	Percentage of total water use
Guestrooms	33.3%
Kitchen/dishwashing	16.8%
Landscaping	4.2%
Laundry	4.7%
Heating, ventilation, air conditioning	2.4%
Other/not metered	18.7%

Source: Adapted from ITP (2014).

The cost of water, however, is difficult to estimate, as it varies greatly with the Mediterranean Basin. For example, domestic drinking water price is set at €0.09 per cubic meter (m³) in Algeria but at €0.52/m³ in Spain and €1.36/m³ in France (Chohin-Kuper and Strosser, 2008). It is estimated, however, that water "accounts for 10% of utility bills in many hotels [and] most hotels pay for the water they consume twice – first by purchasing fresh water and then by disposing of it as waste water" (Green Hotelier, 2013).

Considering the impacts, causes and costs as presented here, hoteliers have started to actively implement various water management programs to reduce the overall usage of freshwater and disposal of wastewater.

WATER MANAGEMENT IN MEDITERRANEAN HOTELS

When looking into water management in Mediterranean hotels, there are three areas to consider: (1) water conservation practices, (2) implementation of technologies and (3) wastewater management. However, before a hotel dives into implementation of any of these areas, it is of paramount importance to understand the exact water footprint of the property. A few free-of-charge tools are available for hoteliers, such as the Hotel Water Measurement Initiative (HWMI) developed by the International Tourism Partnership and member hotel companies (ITP, 2018) as well as the Kuoni Water Management Manual for Hotels by the Kuoni Group (Kuoni, 2014). While neither initiative is based on or developed for the Mediterranean Basin in particular, both provide excellent methodologies for measuring and reporting on water consumption in hotels in a consistent manner. This means that in practice, hotels will be involved in the seven steps (based on Kuoni, 2014 and ITP, 2014):

1 Planning: preparing for successful water management means involving employees, which have an impact on water issues and deciding on roles and responsibilities.
2 Data collection: gathering data on water consumption as well as water costs is critical to establish a baseline and examine the areas that are particularly prone to high consumption.
3 Cost-benefit analysis: action can be taken according to importance and based on cost-benefit analysis whether it is about change in operations practices in housekeeping or fixing plumbing in the hotel for example.
4 Action plan: once the cost-benefit analysis is completed, an action plan based on short-, medium-, and long-term goals can be developed with appropriate responsibilities.
5 Monitoring: this will ensure that corrective actions are taken if monitoring shows deviance from goals set in the action plan.
6 Staff training: action plans will work best only if and when staff is involved at every stage.
7 Customer awareness: informing hotel guests about initiatives to manage scarce resources shows responsibility.

An additional step may include looking for funding or government loans when investing in new technologies that help reducing water usage.

Table 8.4 shows the areas of (1) water preservation/conservation practices, (2) technology implementation and (3) wastewater management and associated

Table 8.4 Hotel water usage in relation to total water used based on Mediterranean climate

Water preservation/conservation practices	Technology implementation	Wastewater management
Plumbing system • Fixing leaks	**Plumbing system** • Check water pressure; a reduction means reduced water usage	**Rainwater collection system** • Rainwater can be collected from roofs, following filtration can be channelled into a cistern or rainwater tank for storage and used in gardening or toilet flushing
Sinks and showers • Guest information on water usage	**Sinks and showers** • Install water-efficient fixtures (e.g. flow controllers, tap aerators, low-flow shower heads, push button, infra-red sensors)	**Sinks and showers** • Recycling of gray water • Reuse after treatment for toilets or gardening
Toilets and urinals • Train housekeeping staff on cleaning methods (e.g. maximum number of flush necessary for cleaning)	**Toilets and urinals** • Install water-efficient fixtures (e.g. tank restrictors, dual-flush toilets, gravity toilets, pressure-assisted toilets, dry composting toilets)	**Toilets and urinals** • Recycling of black water (however, contains harmful pathogens and must be properly treated before being discharged into the environment)
Laundry • Involve guests in towel and linen programs • Reward guests for participation	**Laundry** • Implement sub-meters • Use water-efficient equipment (e.g. front-loading machines) • Outsource to launderers using water-efficient methods	**Laundry** • Reuse of first rinsing water • Recycling of gray water
Swimming pools and spas • Create and promote natural pools • Control leaks and evaporation by implementing sub-meters	**Swimming pools and spas** • Use pool covers to slow evaporation	**Swimming pools and spas** • Recycling of gray water
Gardens and water features • Use indigenous plants adapted to local climate and soil conditions • Implement a watering schedule according to time of the day where evaporation is at its lowest	**Gardens and water features** • Implement sub-meters • Use indigenous plants adapted to local climate and soil conditions	**Gardens and water features** • Indigenous plants will require less or no fertilizers and pesticides, reducing wastewater runoffs and further treatments • Use of gray water for fountains and water features

Kitchen/food and beverage
- Train proper dishwasher loading techniques/full loads only
- Plate leftovers discarded with scrapers only
- Use sink-dip method when manually washing rather than running water
- Detect and fix any leakages

Kitchen/food and beverage
- Replace and/or upgrade equipment to water-efficient models (e.g. dishwashers, ice machines, steam cookers)
- Install automatic sensors on faucets, toilets
- Install low-flow pre-rinse spray nozzles

Kitchen/food and beverage
- Reuse gray water produced in kitchen processes for irrigation purposes

Source: Adapted from Legrand, Sloan and Chen (2017).

tactics, which can be implemented in hotels based in the Mediterranean basin as well as in hotels in other geographical locations.

Owner-operator challenges and water management

Hotel owner-operator challenges

While all the practices mentioned in the last section seem relatively straightforward, these are still not considered standard operating procedures (SOPs) in most Mediterranean hotels. The question remains: Why? Considering that not only does water wastage or water mismanagement have an ethical facet, it inherently carries a cost factor for the hoteliers, which is on the increase in most countries around the Mediterranean. Water, in some regions, is the new gold (Sheridan, 2014). Or, perhaps, it is now more appropriate to mention that "water [is] set to become more valuable than oil" (Ward, 2017). The fact that proper water management is not part of a hotel set of SOPs comes down to multiple factors, one of which is of particular relevance and importance: the owner-operator gap. As reported by Melissen, van Ginneken and Wood (2016), in certain circumstances, the owner of the actual land and property may be the hotel operator. In such cases, investments into the facilities as well as the costs of operation are related to one entity only. However, in other circumstances, the owner of the land and building is a separate entity from the operator. Therefore, contractual arrangements (such as management contracts and franchise agreements) will dictate which entity is responsible for what. In many cases, the owner bears the costs linked to facility improvements and any other capital investments related to the property. The operator, however, bears the costs of operations, which includes the cost of utilities such as energy and water, for example (Stipanuk, 2015). Under certain management contract situations, provisions are made by the operator to fund future maintenance, repairs and other building-related investments (Stipanuk, 2015). Those funds are usually related to investments in furniture, fixtures and equipment (FF&E). It is rather uncommon in the industry for an operator to create a fund reserve for non-FF&E investment. In any case, prior approval from the owners is a requirement for any building-related expenditure (Stipanuk, 2015). Under franchise agreements, a similar scenario exists. The franchisor will "require that facilities be developed and operated in accordance with the franchisors' operating manual" (Stipanuk, 2015, p. 20), which usually sets the minimum standards in terms of construction, equipment and operating procedures.

Over the past decade, hotel companies have increasingly pursued an asset-light strategy (Melissen, van Ginneken and Wood, 2016; Hotel Analyst, 2017; Kwok, 2017). While the reasons for "going asset-light" are beyond the scope of this chapter, this may explain in part the challenges faced by hoteliers in installing a comprehensive sustainability plan (Melissen, van Ginneken and Wood, 2016), including the development and construction of water-efficient buildings and necessary water-efficient retrofittings for existing hotel properties. The situation is even more difficult when communication between owners, and operators is difficult or non-existent. Kang and Ricaurte report that "when timelines and budgets have already been set, nobody wants to further delay an opening with a sudden interjection of efficient design, equipment, or FF&E, much less anything futuristically innovative" (2017, p. 18). Additionally, and to "add water to the fire", it is not unusual to have an owner conducting lengthy discussion and planning with important design and construction partners including architects, developers, contractors, lenders and designers before even searching for an operator or a brand (Kang and Ricaurte, 2017). The result is the construction of inefficient hotel buildings, with cost-cutting practices often being the norm. To exemplify the situation, the authors have audited a hotel in the Mediterranean Basin where it was known to the hotel management team that the swimming pool had a leak culminating to 5 cubic meters per day (5,000 liters). The leak was left unfixed due to the following reason: the contract between the hotel operator and the tour operator (the source of a majority of hotel guests) clearly stipulated that under no circumstances should the pool be closed. The fact that the hotel is located in a water-stressed region with the known consequences listed in this chapter combined with the costs of water usage carried by the hotel operator did not change the situation, and the swimming pool remained open to hotel guests but leaking. This is one of many situations that exemplify the multiple stakeholder's dichotomy with irresponsible consequence.

Owner-operator challenges and water management

Referring to Table 8.3, the following pyramid of priority has been developed in accordance with ownership status (see Figure 8.1).

The strong suggestion closing this paper is for all stakeholders to align their interests with *efficiency* in mind. Owners would benefit from a plus-value when

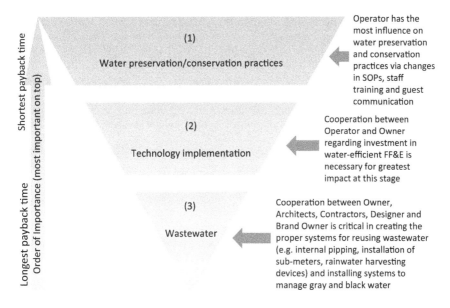

Figure 8.1 Owner-operator water management priority pyramid

the property is energy and water efficient. Architects and designers can propose buildings that keep their value over the lifetime usage via sustainability-thinking. Operators would operate in a cost-efficient manner and market this efficiency to guests. Finally, the authors advocate including the cost of external, indirect impacts of water wastage into the pricing of water. Only then will the Mediterranean region have a realistic chance to face the water challenge of the 21st century.

Limitations and future research

This chapter is based on publicly available data. This means at the time of publication that data, for example on water usage, may be a few years old and potentially outdated. Research on water in general is widely available; however, research on water and hotels is still limited or specific to certain regions or companies – via yearly sustainability reports only. We strongly suggest continuing research on water usage, in particular on gathering data for hotels which are not under the umbrella of a large brand and thus may not have access to the expertise from headquarters. We still do not know precisely either the impacts or the mitigation or adaptation strategies taken by those hotels, even though they make up the bulk of hotels in the Mediterranean Basin.

References

Antakyali, D., Krampe, J. and Steinmetz, H. (2008). Practical application of wastewater reuse in tourist resorts. *Water Science and Technology*, 57, pp. 2051–2057.

Black, M. and King, J. (2009). *The atlas of water, mapping the world's most critical resource.* London: Earthscan.

Chohin-Kuper, A. and Strosser, P. (2008). Water pricing in Europe and around the Mediterranean Sea: Issues and options. 4th EWA Brussels Conference. *European water management and the economic aspects of the water framework directive.* Available at: www. dwa.de/portale/ewa/ewa.nsf/C125723B0047EC38/90E45AEC74290744C1257563003 484E7/$FILE/EWA2008_Chohin_Strosser_conf.pdf

Clark, D.W. and Briar, D.W. (2001). *What is ground water?* U.S. Geological Survey Water Resources Division. Available at: https://pubs.usgs.gov/of/1993/ofr93-643/pdf/ofr93-643.pdf

De Stefano, L. (2004). *Freshwater and tourism in the Mediterranean*, WWF Mediterranean Programme. Available at: http://assets.panda.org/downloads/medpotourismreport final_ofnc.pdf

EEA (2015). *Mediterranean sea region briefing – The European environment – state and outlook 2015.* European Environment Agency. Available at: http://ec.europa.eu/ environment/nature/natura2000/biogeog_regions/mediterranean/index_en.htm

EPA (27 February 2017). *What is a wetland?* United States Environmental Protection Agency. Available at: www.epa.gov/wetlands/what-wetland

European Commission (April 2007). *Mediterranean water scarcity and drought report.* Available at: www.emwis.net/topics/WaterScarcity/PDF/MedWSD_FINAL_Edition

European Commission (30 January 2018). The Mediterranean region. *Natura 2000.* Available at: http://ec.europa.eu/environment/nature/natura2000/biogeog_regions/mediterra nean/index_en.htm

Eurostat (2009). *Medstat II: 'Water and tourism' pilot study*. Eurostat, European Commission. Available at: http://epp.eurostat.ec.europa.eu/cache/ITY_OFFPUB/KS-78-09-699/EN/KS-78-09-699-EN.PDF

Falkenmark, M., Lundquist, J. and Widstrand, C. (1989). Macro-scale water scarcity requires micro-scale approaches: Aspects of vulnerability in semi-arid development. *Natural Resources Forum*, 13(4), pp. 258–267.

Gabarda-Mallorqui, A., Fraguell, R.M., Pavón, D. and Ribas, A (2016). Tourist development and wastewater treatment in the Spanish Mediterranean Coast: The Costa Brava Case Study. *International Journal of Sustainable Development and Planning*, 11(3), pp. 245–254.

Global Water Forum (7 May 2012). *Understanding water scarcity: Definitions and measurements*. Available at: www.globalwaterforum.org/2012/05/07/understanding-water-scarcity-definitions-and-measurements/

Gössling, S. (2006). Tourism and water. In: S. Gössling and C.M. Hall, eds., *Tourism & global environmental change: Ecological, social, economic and political interrelationships*. Abingdon: Routledge, pp. 180–194.

Gössling, S., Peeters, P., Hall, C.M., Ceron, J.-P., Dubois, G., Lehmann, L.V. and Scott, D. (2012). Tourism and water use: Supply, demand, and security. An international review. *Tourism Management*, 33, pp. 1–15.

Green Hotelier (22 March 2013). *Water management and responsibility in hotels*. Available at: www.greenhotelier.org/know-how-guides/water-management-and-responsibility-in-hotels/

Greenpeace (6 May 2009). *Other threats in the Mediterranean*. Available at: www.greenpeace.org/seasia/ph/What-we-do/oceans/marine-reserves/the-mediterranean/mediterranean-other-threats/

GRID-Arendal (2013). *Wastewater treatment in the Mediterranean coastal cities*. State of the Mediterranean marine and coastal environment. GRID-Arendal. Available at: www.grida.no/graphicslib/detail/wastewater-treatment-in-the-mediterranean-coastal-cities_effa

Guiot, J. and Cramer, W. (2016): Climate change: The 2015 Paris agreement thresholds and Mediterranean basin ecosystems. *Science*, 354(6311), pp. 465–468.

Hotel Analyst (24 August 2017). *Luxury pushes asset light*. Available at: http://hotelanalyst.co.uk/2017/08/24/luxury-pushes-asset-light/

International Rivers (n.d.). *Environmental impacts of dams*. Available at: www.internationalrivers.org/environmental-impacts-of-dams

IPBES (23 March 2018). *Biodiversity and nature's contributions continue dangerous decline, scientists warn*. Available at: www.ipbes.net/news/biodiversity-nature%E2%80%99s-contributions-continue-%C2%A0dangerous-decline-scientists-warn

ITP (2014). *Environmental management for hotels*, 3rd ed., digital release. International tourism partnership. Available at: www.greenhotelier.org/wp-content/uploads/2014/09/3-Water-for-web-1-1.pdf

ITP (2018). *Water Stewardship*. International tourism partnership. Available at: www.tourismpartnership.org/water-stewardship/

Kang, G. and Ricaurte, E.E. (2017). Hotel owners for tomorrow: The call to action. In: W. Legrand, W. Wade and H. Roelings, eds., *The hotel yearbook special edition sustainable hospitality*. pp. 18–19. Grandvaux, CH: Wade & Company SA. Available at: www.hotel-yearbook.com/edition/37000021.html

Kuoni (2014). *Kuoni water management manual for hotels: Thailand*. Kuoni Group. Available at: http://cr.kuoni.com/docs/water_manual_hotels_thailand_0_0_4.pdf

Kwok, K. (8 November 2017). More hotels are adopting the "asset-light" strategy. *Multibriefs Exclusive*. Available at: http://exclusive.multibriefs.com/content/more-hotels-are-adopting-the-asset-light-strategy/travel-hospitality-event-management

Legrand, W., Sloan, P. and Chen, J.S. (2017). *Sustainability in the hospitality industry: Principles of sustainable operations*, 3rd ed. London: Routledge.

Melissen, F., van Ginneken, R. and Wood, R.C. (2016). Sustainability challenges and opportunities arising from the owner-operator split in hotels. *International Journal of Hospitality Management*, 54, pp. 35–42.

MGI (9 August 2017). *Tourism in the Mediterranean. Mediterranean growth initiative.* Available at: www.mgi.online/content/2017/8/4/tourism-in-the-mediterranean

Peltier, D. (2018). Extreme weather is creating travel upheaval. *Skift Magazine, Megatrends Defining Travel in 2018*, 8, pp. 48–50. Available at: https://skift.com/2018/01/17/the-megatrends-defining-travel-in-2018/

Rico-Amoros, A.M., Olcina-Cantos, J. and Sauri, D. (2009). Tourist land use patterns and water demand: evidence from the western Mediterranean. *Land Use Policy*, 26, pp. 493–501.

Sheridan, P.M. (24 April 2014). Water becoming more valuable than gold. *Cable News Network (CNN Money)*. Available at: http://money.cnn.com/2014/04/24/news/water-gold-price/index.html

Stipanuk, D. (2015). *Hospitality facilities management and design*, 4th ed. Lansing, MI: American Hotel & Lodging Educational Institute.

UN Water (2015). The United Nations world water development report 2015: Water for a sustainable world. *United Nations world water assessment programme*. Available at: http://unesdoc.unesco.org/images/0023/002318/231823E.pdf

UNEP/MAP (2013). *State of the Mediterranean marine and coastal environment*. Available at: http://195.97.36.231/publications/SoMMCER.pdf

UNESCO (1987). *The role of water in socio-economic development*. Report 1 of IHP-II Project C1. Available at: http://unesdoc.unesco.org/images/0007/000776/077659eo.pdf

United Nations (2010). Resolution adopted by the general assembly on 28 July 2010– 64/292. The human right to water and sanitation. *United Nations General Assembly*. Available at: www.un.org/es/comun/docs/?symbol=A/RES/64/292&lang=E

United Nations (2015a). *Goal 6: Ensure access to water and sanitation for all.* Available at: www.un.org/sustainabledevelopment/water-and-sanitation/

United Nations (2015b). *Sustainable development goals*. Available at: www.un.org/sustainabledevelopment/sustainable-development-goals/

United Nations (2015c). *Clean water and sanitation. Why it matters*. Available at: www.un.org/sustainabledevelopment/wp-content/uploads/2016/08/6_Why-it-Matters_Sanitation_2p.pdf

UNWTO (27 May 2015). UNWTO conference to address quality in Mediterranean destinations. *Press release*. Available at: http://media.unwto.org/press-release/2015-05-27/unwto-conference-address-quality-mediterranean-destinations

UNWTO (August 2017). *UNWTO tourism highlights 2017 editions*. Available at: www.e-unwto.org/doi/pdf/10.18111/9789284419029

Ward, A. (19 March 2017). Water set to become more valuable than oil. *Financial Times*. Available at: www.ft.com/content/fa9f125c-0b0d-11e7-ac5a-903b21361b43

WEF (2017). The travel & tourism competitiveness report 2017. *World economic forum*. Available at: www.weforum.org/reports/the-travel-tourism-competitiveness-report-2017

9 Food tourism and foodies in Italy

The role of the Mediterranean diet between resilience and sustainability

Alessio Cavicchi and Cristina Santini

Introduction

Italy is recognized worldwide as one of the most preferred destinations by foodies. This reputation has been confirmed by the UNWTO Global Report on Food Tourism (2012), which acknowledged the primary role of Italy as an influential destination for food lovers. Italy's forerunner position has been recently recognized by the inclusion of the Mediterranean diet in the UNESCO's list of Intangible Cultural Heritage of Humanity by emphasizing the role of food and wine festivals. Conviviality and sharing of food is part of this cultural asset to promote a destination: during festivals, product knowledge is spread among participants, and local communities and local products become a powerful tool for disseminating the culture of a place.

Nevertheless, this cultural treasure cannot be taken for granted. During the last years, food shopping practices change as the number of Mediterranean diet followers decline (Euromonitor, 2017). Thus, the whole culinary and gastronomic heritage can be threatened by the fast-changing consumption habits.

In May 2018, *The Guardian* published an article titled "The Mediterranean Diet Is in Retreat Even in Italy. What Now for the Foodies' Ideal?" (Gray, 2018). The author reported some insights from the WHO European Childhood Obesity Surveillance Initiative (or COSI), a survey that for over ten years has measured trends in weight gain and obesity among primary-school-aged children in Europe. From this data, a worsening of eating habits is evident, with an impact on weight for many children. It is almost evident that traditional food-related lifestyles cannot just be considered ending anymore in France, Greece and Italy. The evidence is that nowadays, the Mediterranean diet does not seem to be so popular among families in the South of Europe.

The World Expo hold in Milan in 2015, whose title was "Feeding the Planet, Energy for Life", has been the opportunity to spread an impressive bundle of research on gastronomic, food and wine tourism in Italy. But first of all, it represented a good chance to promote a debate in Italy on the linkages between agrifood, health and tourism sectors and, as a conceptual umbrella, the crucial role of the Mediterranean diet as a lever for economic development, with a particular emphasis on rural areas.

The aim of this chapter is twofold. Through desk research and analysis of secondary data we want to provide a short overview of the huge number of traditional food products and their producers, initiatives and associations that are conveying the principles of Mediterranean diet to young generations and that represent the assets of Italy as a destination for foodies (Agriturismo-Sicilia.it, 2012). On the other side, through in-depth interviews with key informants, we aim to outline the changes occurring in the agrifood sector and in consumption habits during the last two decades that are transforming the context in which the Mediterranean diet has been codified.

Then, after the exploration of these conflicting forces, we discuss how this context can impact on Italy as a gastronomic destination, and we explore the role of education to maintain food culture and to increase awareness and reputation of Italy as a destination for foodies.

Background context: Italy, the land of food and foodies – some key organizations

Despite the lack of an official register of public gastronomic events and festivals at the national level, Santini, Cavicchi and Belletti (2013) roughly estimated the presence of more than 7,000 food and wine festivals in the whole country, covering all the seasons and offered by a titanic and unrivaled presence of gastronomic associations, movements, organizations and public-private partnerships.

The private sector is extremely active. Many young entrepreneurs, after the economic crisis in 2007, decided to "go back to the land", and they became crucial to boost innovation in the field of traditional food products (new packaging for wines, food with enriched and fortified nutritional components, new marketing and advertising channels and so forth). Nowadays, local food production brings to the market more than 4,400 traditional food products officially registered by the Ministry of Agriculture (https://www.politicheagricole.it), among which we can find 523 quality wines produced in designated regions or with a typical geographical indication, as well as 294 protected designations of origin (PDO) and protected geographical indications (PGI) for food products (for example, Parma ham).

Public administration has played an active role in the promotion and management of gastronomic tourism in Italy, despite being unevenly coordinated. For instance, "Res Tipica" (https://www.borghiautenticiditalia.it) is a national organization founded in 2003 by the National Association of Municipalities (ANCI) with the aim of coordinating the activities taking place at the local level (https://www.borghiautenticiditalia.it/lassociazione). Today, it is possible to find about 480 wine cities, (http://www.cittadelvino.it) 320 olive oil cities (https://www.cittadellolio.it), 225 almond cities (https://www.fondazioneslowfood.com/it/presidi-slow-food/mandorla-di-noto/) and 192 organic farming cities (http://www.cittadelbio.it), just to cite a few examples. Considering the whole bundle of food and wine cities, the total number of public bodies involved is 2,022.[1]

In addition, a widespread presence of local associations working on a volunteer basis, called "pro loco", is relevant for the events and performances they can organize. UNPLI stands for "Unione Nazionale Pro Loco Italiane" and indicates the national association for the promotion of local areas. In Italy, the Pro Loco number almost 6,000, well diffused even in small villages; there are 650,000 members and 20,000 organized events and performances (Santini, Cavicchi and Belletti 2013).

Farmers' unions bring their contribution to foodies through their specific associations devoted to the promotion of food and wine tourism in rural areas. Terranostra (Coldiretti) is a national association that groups 18 regional and 96 provincial associations through the guide for rural tourism published on a yearly basis; Turismo Verde is an association created in 1981 by the Italian agricultural confederation that promotes hundreds of farms through its guide "Agriturismo in Italia". Turismo Verde also has some regional websites for promoting educational farms and "open farms" operations, "Agriturist" is the oldest rural tourism association, created in 1965, promoting around 200 farms.

Slow Food is well known at the global level: a non-profit, member-supported eco-gastronomic organization which was founded in 1989 to counteract fast food and fast life, the disappearance of local food traditions and people's dwindling interest in the food they eat, where it comes from, how it tastes and how food choices affect the rest of the world. Nowadays, Slow Food is a movement that is active through international networks and involves producers, consumers and educational institutions. Slow food has recognized 500 presidia worldwide, and 250 are Italian: "The Presidia sustain quality production at risk of extinction, protect unique regions and ecosystems, recover traditional processing methods, safeguard native breeds and local plant varieties" (from Slow Food website). More than 13,000 producers are associated with Slow Food in the world, and the movement has seen a growth and continuous improvement in Italy and at a global level over the last decade.

Strade del Vino, or wine routes, are widespread in Italy. Gatti and Incerti (1998) define a wine route as a kind of cultural itinerary; along a sign-posted itinerary, visitors can discover products and wines in a specific region by visiting wineries. Once a wine route is established in a specific area, wineries can decide to join the wine route network. As well as wine routes, the Strade dei Sapori – which means flavor routes – provide tourists with a gastronomic itinerary. In some areas, under the aegis of regional administration, the Strade del Vino and the Strade dei Sapori are jointly promoted.

The Movimento Turismo del Vino (Wine Tourism Movement) was established in 1993 with the aim of encouraging "Italian wineries to open their doors to visitors". The main event is Cantine Aperte (open cellars), which is organized every year in Italy during the last Sunday of May (Santini, Cavicchi and Canavari, 2011).

This census is far from being complete, but it can be considered a first rough picture to understand the incredible bundle of opportunities that foodies have in Italy to satisfy their expectations.

A strong culinary tradition is diffused in Italian families, and during the last years, those who can be defined as foodies have reached 5 million, with an increase of 250,000 persons per year (Episteme, 2013). Even in this case, it is tough to define the boundaries of this emerging trend exactly. For this reason, analogously to what has been said about rural tourism in Italy, we can call it a "sleeping giant". The first research carried out to understand the phenomenon in Italy was performed in 2009 by GPF research for the agri-food company Negroni. They discovered that 4.5 million Italians, corresponding to 9% of the whole population

(65% men, 35% women), could be considered foodies. The identikit revealed a class of medium-high income and a higher education qualification. Moreover, if for almost half (53%) the foodie is married with children, the concentration is above average among singles and couples without children, mostly living in the northwest of the country and with a low penetration in central Italy. Interested in the new and the cuisine of other countries, the foodies are sensitive to the multi-sensory experience of food, they give importance to the impression that they get looking, touching and feeling the flavors of food (Mark-up, 2009).

According to Unioncamere (2017),[2] 110 million tourists traveled to Italy with food and wine as their main motivation in 2017; 43% of these were Italian tourists. The main activities undertaken by food and wine tourists were: to take part in local events (6.6%), to taste (13%) and to buy typical wines and food (8.6%).

Food and wine tourism has grown over the years,[3] rising from 21% of tourism in 2016 to 30% in 2017. Coldiretti states that the 35% of the holiday budget of tourists (Italians and Internationals) is addressed to food; the economic impact in 2018 is around €30 billion (with Italians accounting for 60% of the total). In 2016 Istat[4] has recorded a heavy presence of German tourists in Italy (the 14% of foreign tourists); also French and British tourists, respectively, represent 3% of the total of international tourist flow.

From these studies (Cavicchi, 2014), it emerges that the most relevant factors that increase visitors' enogastronomic experience are the atmosphere linked to local identity, the cordiality and friendliness of local people and the overall satisfaction with food and wine quality.

In order to anticipate the experience of tourists, during recent years many initiatives for foodies have been mainly promoted through the web, with many committed food bloggers who became ambassadors of dedicated appointments. Furthermore, the publishing industry, well developed in Italy with hundreds of wine, food and restaurant guides published every year, has followed this trend and launched new products. The most relevant is the *Foodies' Guide to Italy* that the groups Negroni and Gambero Rosso launched in 2011. The authors recognize that foodies find the Internet and word of mouth far more reliable sources of information than traditional gourmet guides. Thus, this book is differently structured: it is a sort of travel guide that shows readers where to find the best bakeries, cheese specialists, wine merchants, chocolate stores, gourmet delis, farmers markets and a lot more throughout Italy, with more than 1,200 addresses. As stated by the vice-executive director of Gambero Rosso, Laura Mantovano, a foodie is different from a gourmet, in that "without any preconceived notion, he/she wants to learn everything about food, both the best and the ordinary, and about the science, industry, and personalities surrounding food".

In light of this arising interest shown both by a huge part of the Italian population and by international tourists, in 2007 a new kind of shopping experience was launched in Turin: EATALY. Founded by an entrepreneur, Oscar Farinetti, formerly owner of a chain of consumer electronics product stores, this place is a food market/mall including restaurants, foods, bakeries and wine tasting rooms where quality Italian products are promoted and sold. It has been defined by Tardi (2007) as a "megastore" that "combines elements of a bustling European open market, a Whole-Foods-style supermarket, a high-end food court and a New Age learning center". After the inauguration, several shops have been launched worldwide, and currently there are nine in Italy (in Rome, Florence, Milan and other important cities), two in the United States (Chicago and New York), one in Japan, one in Turkey and one in Dubai (www.eataly.it). Supported by Slow Food and developed with a specific focus on educational and cultural values of food, this chain represents a flagship for the Italian food system and its agricultural sector.

Another exciting initiative is FICO, or Fabbrica Italiana Contadina. FICO covers an area of 2 hectares of open-air fields and stables where visitors can pursue an educational experience. FICO was also launched by Oscar Farinetti, and it is located in Bologna. In the area, there are typical restaurants, the availability of shows and exhibitions, educational tours even for children and families, a vast marketplace where EATALY products can be sold and a congress center. FICO's mission is described on the official website "We aim at telling the world about the excellence of Italian food and wines" (www.eatalyworld.it/en/who-we-are/who-we-are). From January to March 2018, FICO registered 1 million presences: 8% of the visitors are foreign and 52% come from outside Bologna, and the 52% of the tourists that choose to come to Bologna addressed as their primary motivation FICO.

The changing process of a food destination: is Italy still synonymous with virtuous food-related habits?

Despite the huge basin of traditions and the availability of excellent food and wine products, Italy and other Mediterranean countries are experiencing what can be called "the Mediterranean diet paradox". The places where the healthiest nutrition consumption model – the Mediterranean diet – was born are experiencing a profound crisis regarding food choice and health. In this section, we will outline some considerations upon the progressive abandoning of the Mediterranean diet paradigm in Italy.

Overweight and obesity of young generation

Recent data revealed that Italian children, as well as Spanish and Greek children, are suffering from health problems: 40% of them are affected by obesity, as reported by the *Guardian*. Romagnolo and Selmin (2017) have underlined that the Mediterranean diet fits with the dietary patterns outlined in the *2015–2020 Dietary Guidelines for Americans*. If on one side, the Mediterranean diet seems to be the most effective tool for a population that is strongly affected by nutritional problems, on the other, this dietary pattern shows weaknesses in its countries of origin. Researchers have investigated the reasons behind this problem, and it emerges that changes in consumption reflect the changes that are occurring in the society at various levels.

Global market versus local supply chain

In 2005 the United Nations underlined the risk of a loss of adherence to the Mediterranean diet paradigm, due to the growing presence on the market of imported consumption patterns UNEP/MAP (2016). In other words, as long as there is a linkage between local suppliers and consumers, the latter have the chance to buy local products and ingredients, and they are facilitated to follow the Mediterranean diet. Furthermore, Bach-Faig et al. (2011) underlined that the general Western-type economy and ongoing globalization are reshaping the Mediterranean diet paradigm; the representation of the Mediterranean diet (the Mediterranean diet pyramid) itself has evolved.

The Mediterranean diet is a model that integrates variations within each country (Romagnolo and Selmin, 2017). As outlined by Dernini and Berry (2015), the Mediterranean diet model is not a single one, but its principles adapt to a country's culture and heritage. The Mediterranean diet is the expression of many cultural lifestyles and has gone through a process of "nutritional transition" (Dernini and Berry, 2015).

The strong dependency with the local cultural and heritage system means that, once they change, even the Mediterranean diet paradigm changes. Italy, as well as Europe, is experiencing a profound change: the composition of the local population has changed over the last decades, and Italy is becoming a multi-cultural society in light of migration flows. Also, globalization is reshaping consumer consumption and retailing and distribution system, and it is revolutionizing the availability and accessibility of food.

Thus, the role played by the conservation of a heritage of food and culture is crucial for the preservation of the principles of the Mediterranean diet, based on a local supply system of inputs and seasonal foods. This fact, together with education of consumers on the importance of seasonality and healthy diets, are important assets to preserve an international reputation of Italy.

Economic crisis and societal changes

A combination of economic and social issues has slowly transformed the Italian population and its habits. The financial crisis started in 2007 gained the name of "the big recession" (Pozzolo, 2011). Given the difficult times, consumers have changed their buying and consumption behavior even for food. The typologies of food that Italians are buying has changed (Romano, 2011).

Furthermore, due to the social changes occurring among family system since the 1970s and the growing rate of female employment, Italians have changed their approach to lunches and dinners (Lombardi and Verneau, 2013). Even if in Italy, the share of female employment is still low if compared to UE28 (Istat, 2014), women are more involved in the workplace, and the traditional vision of women being responsible for housekeeping and food preparing (Casarico and Profeta, 2011) is changing as well. Changes in women's role have created changes in the way women approach lunch and dinner for their families (Sassatelli, 2015): some women tend to buy commodities or inputs that reduce the time needed for cooking; others cook when they have enough time for preparing meals.

Another element that has to be considered is the population age. According to Eurostat, the Italian population is getting older. This means that in the coming decades, new needs regarding food consumption models and trends will emerge.

The debate on the impact of age on food consumption and lifestyles, in general, is wide and complex: Healy (2014) has outlined how aging can influence eating habits. According to Euromonitor (2017), there is no doubt that as the population gets older, new needs will emerge. Generally speaking, older people tend to reduce the budget spent for eating out; they are involved in preparing food, and since they eat less, they would probably have a reduced budget for buying food. The growing share of the aging population is slowly reshaping the competitive scenario. Older adults also tend to choose food according to their personal and health needs. It is easy to understand the economic implication of the aging population for the food business.

Research objectives and methods

Italy and Italians are experiencing many changes: the picture of food habits and consumption of Italians today is entirely different from the one of the 1970s. A complex system of drivers have modified society and, as a consequence, the approach that Italians have to food. Although Italy is one of the countries of the Mediterranean diet, today Italians seem to adopt behaviors that diverge from the Mediterranean diet paradigm.

This research aims to explore factors related to how the Italian food consumption model has changed over the years. Why are Italians getting far from this savvy approach to food? Thus, in the next paragraphs, we provide an overview of the factors that inhibit or promote the implementation of the Mediterranean diet model among Italians.

We have collected both primary and secondary data. For what concerns desk research, we have collected information from market and company reports that contain data about food consumption forecasts, trends and statistics. The source database also includes magazines and specialized press in the food and beverage sector. A complete list of information sources is displayed in Table 9.1.

We have also collected primary data, and we have carried out an explorative research by adopting the key informant technique (Tremblay, 1957; Casini, Cavicchi and Corsi, 2008; Cavicchi et al. 2016): key informants have an in-depth knowledge of the examined issues and, given their active involvement in the context, they can provide useful and reliable insights on the topic under investigation (Montanari and Staniscia, 2009). Interviews (face to face and telephone) have been conducted from May to July 2015. The people interviewed are involved in all the phases of the food chain, from inputs production to services, media, research and policymaking.[5]

According to emerging insights from preliminary desk research, we have elaborated some questions. Questions aim to explore the trends in consumption and

Table 9.1 Sources of information (desk research)

Research and market reports

Title of the document	Company/Institution
Global Powers of Retailing	Deloitte (2015)
Global Powers of Consumer Products	Deloitte (2015)
Italian consumers in 2020 – A look into the future	Euromonitor International (2010)
Italian consumers in 2020 – A look into the future	Euromonitor International (2015)
Consumer Lifestyles in Italy	Euromonitor International (2014)
Gli Italiani e il cibo – Rapporto su un'eccellenza da condividere	Censis (2015)
La grande consommation: 1985–2015–2045	PriceWaterhouseCoopers (2015)
Cibo di Oggi, Cibo di Domani	Doxa-Coop (2015)

Specialized press

Magazine	Publishing Company
Food	Food srl
Mark-Up	New Business Media srl
GDO Week	New Business Media srl
Largo Consumo	Editoriale Largo Consumo srl
Bargiornale	New Business Media srl
Distribuzione Moderna	Edizioni DM srl
Food Magazine	Gruppo Comunicare Italia
Retail Food	Edifis spa

the drivers behind their changes (cultural issues, economic crisis, information sources and so forth).

Thus, interviews were based on informants' perception of changes in consumer behavior and the current cultural perception of food. The impact of the economic crisis that has affected Italy since 2008 is examined as well as the role of information sources. Furthermore, informants' perception of education and European policies are examined.

Results

The scenario of purchasing behavior and consumption is multifaceted and complex. On one side, the economic crisis has pushed Italians to choose retailers that offer promotional sales and discounted prices. On the other, we can see that food with specific claims on the label (functional, organic, biodynamic and so forth), are growing: according to Nielsen, the so-called "rich in" products grew by 8% in 2017 (+5.4% in 2016); the "free from" food grew by 8.4% in 2017, and organic and vegan product sales in retailing grew almost by 15% and 9.8%, respectively, between 2016 and 2017.

Thus, retailers are facing a new competitive scenario (Nielsen Italia, 2018, in foodweb.it[6]), and these contrasting trends are confirmed by field research. On one side, consumers seek for convenience and choose discounts; on the other, consumers look for specialty food and high-quality products.

New trends in food consumption have emerged, and they reflect the changes occurring in Italian society.

The contamination among cultures influences what people eat and consequently what they buy: there is a growing interest for ethnic food, and a considerable percentage of people that eat out prefer ethnic food (Nielsen, 2018). Therefore, through food, ethnic groups can affirm their presence in a specific area, and an ethnic presence that is witnessed by food is more tolerated by locals (Papotti, 2002).

The high accessibility of ethnic food has nurtured an interest for this cuisine: the diffusion of online food delivery service is progressively reshaping Italians' food consumption habits even at home (Nielsen Italia, 2018). E-commerce and web-based services have a meaningful impact on consumers' habits.

Besides e-commerce, Italy has seen a growth of alternative retailing channels: Italians have discovered the importance of collective food purchasing networks and more specifically of GAS (gruppi d'acquisto solidale), that stand for Solidarity Purchase Groups. GAS can be defined as

> small networks of family units that source food (but not only) according to sets of ideas surrounding solidarity. GAS are informal, non contractual and fluid groups of people that negotiate both amongst themselves and their suppliers, in order to choose and procure food and household objects according to different (and also changing) criteria: from locally sourced to organic food, to food and items produced without labour exploitation, and a combination of these and other requirements.
>
> (Hankins and Grasseni, 2014, p. 6)

GAS promote a sense of responsible purchasing, with the accessibility to health and seasonable food. The search for trustable and authentic food is confirmed by the growth of farmer markets and farmers' direct sales (Biobank, 2013).

After the crisis, consumers have adopted different behaviors: some people have tried to maximize their budget by seeking offers and promotions and by relying on retailers' private labels (Ancc-Coop, 2014), since a private label can have a price that is 30% lower than branded products (SymphonyIRI Group, 2012). Other consumers have decided to adopt responsible behaviors: they have decided to reduce food waste, to seek for alternative market channels and to cut the prices of healthy products by buying directly from producers.

We can say that Italians have adopted, in some cases, resilient behavior that follows the tradition: the food heritage in some areas is full of examples of recipes that are designed for saving food or for reducing waste. In other cases, by shortening the distance between producers and consumers and by seeking for direct marketing, Italians have created a breeding ground for rediscovering the seasonality of food and for appreciating local production.

We have seen that the competitive scenario is extremely complex. The key informants we have interviewed have outlined some useful insights for interpreting inner dynamics and trends in Italians food habits and consumption.

The first issue that emerges, from secondary data, is the value that food has for Italians: we have seen, even with regard to its interpretation as a mean for achieving an ethnic integration, that it has a high cultural component. Preparing a dish means having to deal with tradition, with local inputs, with a specific know-how that can become a cultural heritage of a specific area or population (Sassatelli and Scott, 2001; Meglio, 2012). Also, the act of sitting around a table and having lunch or dinner together is part of local culture. The preparation of a dish can represent a cultural value (Sassatelli and Davolio, 2015).

Media has contributed to creating awareness among Italians, even if, according to some interviewed (for instance, a Michelin star chef), this can create some problems with the management of information:

> society is evolving. People can have wide access to information, even if I think that TV culinary shows can create confusion: they have increased awareness towards cooking and typical cuisine, but most of the time they do not contribute to building a real food culture.

The importance of media and information for the nurturing of an awareness towards nutrition and food emerges also from other interviews.

The changes in consumption habits and the need for eating out due to working reasons, have also reshaped the type of services offered. New trends emerge: there is the *low love cost* type that includes pizzeria gourmet or restaurant-bistros that are opened by a famous chef, or the *fast and good* trend that is characterized by a Slow Food approach (Ristoranti & Imprese del gusto, 2013).

One of the interviewed (a journalist and director of a famous food-related magazine for professionals) has outlined that the competitive scenario seems very challenging: the polarization of the market drives to a very high-quality offer or to a standardized and industrial one. This trend partially reflect the economic situation in Italy.

The contraposition between McDonaldization (Ritzer and Liska, 1997) and tradition is emerging. The high quality of inputs and the importance of tradition can be, according to one of the interviewed – the president of the Ordine dei Tecnologi Alimentari – a key leverage for branding Italy.

Another interviewed, a professor in food economics whose research interests cover food marketing, has outlined that while a relative percentage of Italians are progressively adopting Northern American and Northern Europe consumption habits, there is still an interest for what is local, typical and for tradition. There is not a unique diffused consumption model in Italy, and this can also be motivated by the cultural differences that are diffused among the Italian society.

This finds some confirmation in the scenario depicted by Euromonitor in October 2014:

Potential threats to growth are, for burger fast food, the increasing popularity of artisanal burgers. Moreover, the growing trend towards healthy food will play an important role, as fast food menus are often perceived as unhealthy, and companies will have to initiate strategies in order to pull away from this image.

Fast food operators are expected to introduce local food, which is perceived by Italians to be higher quality and healthier. Companies such as McDonald's and Burger King are expected to introduce more Italian foods in order to give a Mediterranean twist. Indeed, as this experiment had good success for McDonald's during 2013, it is expected that it will continue with this strategy, and other companies will follow this trend.

(Euromonitor, 2014)

The Slow Food philosophy can be a successful leverage for facing the McDonaldization process (Meglio, 2012).

We have already underlined that the personal and economic situation influences consumer choices. The economic crisis has contributed to the emerging of differences among people who adopt different food consumption and choice habits (Meglio, 2012). Some food products are hardly accessible to those who have limited economic resources; Italians in many cases seek for a combination of ethical and economic motivations when they choose their food products (Sassatelli, 2015). Furthermore, a considerable segment of Italian population should evaluate food choice in light of some specific diseases. According to the latest report published by the Italian government, in Italy, the 1% of the population is affected by celyachia (Ministero della Salute, n.d.),[7] and the percentage has registered a constant growth over the last decade.

In light of the contrasting trends outlined here, it is useful to stress the importance of educational programs aimed at both promoting healthy lifestyles and safeguarding the reputation of Italy as a synonym of food quality and Mediterranean diet.

Discussion

Food and Gastronomic Cultured, Professionalism in the hospitality sector and the importance of food literacy program.

According to Stančová and Cavicchi (2019), in order to promote enduring knowledge and engagement in the food system, educational activities related to sustainability, nutrition, food preparation and community are needed. Such activities make communities aware of the impact that food choices have on health, environment, community public food procurers and urban households of disadvantaged segments/areas. Introducing food literacy as a means to avoid erosion of agro-biodiversity and allowing the establishment of successful food systems means to draw from locally available genetic resources, food variety and traditional food cultures.

A growing educational effort to promote sustainable practices in light of an increasing demand by consumers and citizens is demonstrated worldwide by Higher Education Institutions that are actively involved in the provision of Food Literacy programs.[8]

Conclusion

According to UNESCO (2013), the Mediterranean diet, as intangible cultural heritage, involves a set of skills, knowledge, rituals, symbols and traditions concerning crops, harvesting, fishing, animal husbandry, conservation, processing, cooking and, particularly, the sharing and consumption of food. Food is seen a medium to favor social exchange and communication, and thus, to share values of respect for diversity, intercultural dialogue and social cohesion. The deep linkage between food and culture emerges from desk and field research, and it finds a further confirmation in the positive trend of ethnic and specialty food. The motivations that drive consumers towards ethnic food are not only the high availability of ethnic food thanks to the diffusion of e-food delivery systems or the interest for something new. The recognized importance of cultural elements of food is a further reason that motivate consumers to choose a specific type of food: food is a means for establishing a dialogue among people and cultures. Therefore, food vehiculates local culture.

The importance of the deep linkage between food and culture characterizes Italian rural areas. These regions are often marginalized, they have a scarce per-capita GDP and they are more concerned with day-to-day business survival than with developing long-term sustainable development strategies (Cavicchi et al., 2013). Nevertheless, as it emerges from the research, consumers seek for quality food, and they are interested in local food products. Rural areas in Italy combine some strategic issues: a deep linkage with local resources and productions; the Mediterranean diet model and the relevance of the cultural feature of products. The amalgamation of the elements described here can be strategically employed for the planning of long-run development strategies for rural areas.

The combination of an international recognition and reputation of the Mediterranean diet as an essential asset for tourism motivation choice, and the presence of these characteristics in rural areas can represent an excellent opportunity for economic development and income redistribution.

Thus, it is necessary on one side to consider the evolution of eating habits of the Italian population (and consequently of social practices and conviviality) whose outlook, as evidenced earlier, suggests the setting up of food literacy programs. On the other side, the current context calls for training programs addressed to citizens in rural areas in order to increase their professionalism in tourism and hospitality. From the interviews and the collected data, it emerges that Italy is slowly abandoning the virtuous Mediterranean diet model. An interesting question arises about the role of the hospitality system when educating visitors and consumers: how can the hospitality system educate visitors and consumers? The dramatic scenario that appears from collected data suggests that there is the urgency of an educational activity that involves different stakeholders, including professionals that work in the tourism industry; the importance given to food literacy at various levels would create benefits not only for customers but also for professionals who operate in the tourism business and who would further differentiate their business through an image of healthiness inspired by the Mediterranean diet paradigm.

On the other side, from the interviews, it emerges the proactive role that media can have for nurturing an awareness towards food and local products. Media have stimulated consumers' interests towards Italian cuisine in Italy, and they could be strategically employed for disseminating reliable information about the Mediterranean diet and its virtuous paradigm.

The study of consumption and food practices in Italy represents a complex task ascribable to numerous variables and apparently contrasting trends. On the one hand, for example, there are health trends contrasted with worrying data about the growth of the obesity phenomenon in the younger segments of the population, or the recovery of the central role of the Mediterranean diet is contrasted with a contraction in the consumption of some types of foods typical of this diet. On the other hand, the renewed interest in organic contrasts with the choice of low-cost supply methods or budget management for food spending.

The growing diffusion of direct sales (GAS, farmers' markets and so on) can promote the creation of a reliable network of relationships between producers and consumers, and it can foster the consumption of seasonal food. We have seen that this could be helpful for promoting the Mediterranean diet.

It is certain that a cultural revolution is underway: the crisis has accelerated some negative behaviors (worsening of wrong eating habits, for example), but it has also promoted the recovery of traits of conviviality and cooperation that often provoke ethical reflection on consumption. Furthermore, the consumer begins to make effective use of the impressive amount of information to which he/she has easy access: the comparison of prices and brands is favored; word of mouth helps in choice; the relationship between food and well-being is also understood, and those who have a more solid cultural base can also understand the nutritional value of food, trying to adopt a complete and functional diet for the well-being of the body.

In this crisis, in our opinion, information can play a fundamental role. Information about promotions determines the purchase of branded products at the most convenient price and allows you to stock; information about how to prepare and store food offers the possibility of reducing waste and optimizing the use of fruit and vegetables; information about the origin and seasonality of products makes it more convenient to purchase; finally, information about alternative ways of buying to the GdO (GdO stands for Grande Distribuzione Organizzata and it indicates the retailing system), and the strengthening of relational networks between consumers is helping to change the way of making purchases.

This complex period, therefore, marks a crucial shift in food purchasing and consumption habits, which has strengthened the decision-making and organizational independence of consumers, who, faced with increasingly tight budgetary constraints, have had to reorganize their priorities differently. The prospects for food purchases and consumption are closely linked to economic trends, with the hope of a rapid recovery, but also to consumers' capacity for initiative and personal innovation, who, once new styles and models are established, may not be willing to return to pre-crisis behavior.

The future, therefore, seems to be even more complex, and more in-depth research on the motivations that guide consumption and the role of information is desirable, in order to put policy makers, actors in the supply chain and consumers in the best position to make informed choices.

Notes

1 We must emphasize that it is extremely difficult to find out official data about the number of the cities that are members of the previously mentioned networks. The aim of the provided data is to offer an idea of the extensive number of networks, activities and associations established among cities about the business of typical products.
2 www.unioncamere.gov.it/P43K1460O/turismo-eno-gastronomico.htm
3 www.lastampa.it/2018/01/23/societa/boom-del-turismo-enogastronomico-italiano-cresce-del-la-toscana-tra-le-mete-top-YwFVXe1wSaqPBSrzAMZSSP/pagina.html
4 www.istat.it/it/files//2017/10/movimento_2016_rettifica-1.pdf
5 In particular, we interviewed a Michelin star chef, two business professionals in the food and beverage business, an agrifood technician, three scholars involved in research on agrifood in research foundations and universities, a president of local association (pro-loco) and a food and wine journalist.
6 www.foodweb.it/2018/05/nielsen-come-cambia-il-carrello-della-spesa/
7 www.salute.gov.it/portale/salute/p1_5.jsp?lingua=italiano&id=131&area=Malattie_dell_apparato_digerente
8 E.g. the case of Harvard (www.dining.harvard.edu/food-literacy-project).

References

Agriturismo-Sicilia.it (2012). *Foodies 2012: Gambero Rosso and Negroni's guide to Italian foods*. Available at: www.agritourisme-sicile.com/blog.cfm?id=745
Ancc-Coop (2014). *Rapporto coop, 2013* "Indagini di customer satisfaction nei servizi pubblici", Giugno 2014.
Bach-Faig, A., Berry, E.M., Lairon, D., Reguant, J., Trichopoulou, A., Dernini, S., . . . Serra-Majem, L. (2011). Mediterranean diet pyramid today. Science and cultural updates. *Public Health Nutrition*, 14(12A), pp. 2274–2284.
Biobank (2013). *Rapporto Biobank 2013*, available from: https://www.biobank.it/?mh1=8&cs=8
Casarico A., Profeta P. (2011). Le disuguaglianze di genere, Università Commerciale L.Bocconi.
Casini, L., Cavicchi, A., & Corsi, A. M. (2008). Trends in the British wine market and consumer confusion. *British Food Journal*, 110(6), 545–558.
Cavicchi, A. (2014). Italy: A synonym of good food?, in Getz, D., Robinson, R., Andersson, T. and Vujicic, S. (eds) *Foodies and food tourism*. Oxford: Goodfellow Publishers.
Cavicchi, A., Frascarelli, A. and Porrini M. (2016). Consumi, socialità ed educazione alimentare, Fondazione per la Sussidiarietà. Milano.
Censis (2015). Gli Italiani e il cibo – Rapporto su un'eccellenza da condividere, available from: http://www.censis.it/Censis/browse/7?shadow_comunicato_stampa=121024
Deloitte (2015). Global Powers of Retailing, available from: https://www2.deloitte.com/content/dam/Deloitte/global/Documents/Consumer-Business/gx-cb-global-powers-of-retailing.pdf

Dernini, S. and Berry, E.M. (2015). Mediterranean diet: From a healthy diet to a sustainable dietary pattern. *Frontiers in Nutrition*, 2, 15.

Doxa-Coop (2015). Cibo di Oggi, Cibo di Domani, available from: http://www.territori. coop.it/cultura/%E2%80%9Ccibo-di-oggi-e-cibo-di-domani%E2%80%9D-viaggio-con-coop-nelle-filiere-del-futuro

Episteme (2013). L'agroalimentare Italiano: centralità valoriale, strategicità economica. *Presentation at Buying Tourism Online – 6th Edition, Florence (Italy)*, 4–6 December 2013.

Euromonitor. (2017). https://go.euromonitor.com/white-paper-survey-2017-lifestyles.html

Euromonitor International. (2010). Italian consumers in 2020 – A look into the future, available from: https://www.euromonitor.com/

Euromonitor International. (2014). Consumer Lifestyles in Italy, available from: https://www.euromonitor.com/

Euromonitor International. (2015). Italian consumers in 2020 – A look into the future, available from: https://www.euromonitor.com/

Gatti, S. and Incerti, F. (1998). The Wine Routes as an instrument for the valorisation of typical products and rural areas, typical and traditional products: Rural effects and agro-industrial problems. *52nd seminar of the European association of agricultural economists, Parma, Italy*. 19–21 June 1997.

Grasseni, C. and Hankins, J. (2014). Collective food purchasing networks in Italy as a case study of responsible innovation. *Glocalism: Journal of Culture, Politics and Innovation* (1–2).

Gray, L. (2018). *The Mediterranean diet is in retreat even in Italy. What now for the foodies' ideal?* Available at: www.theguardian.com/commentisfree/2018/may/26/mediterranean-diet-on-retreat-even-in-italy-what-now-for-foodies-ideal

Healy, A.E. (2014). Eating and ageing: A comparison over time of Italy, Ireland, the United Kingdom and France. *International Journal of Comparative Sociology*, 55(5), pp. 379–403.

Istat (2014). Il mercato del lavoro, available from: https://www.istat.it/it/files/2014/05/cap3.pdf

Lombardi P., and Verneau F. (2013). "Dinamiche di consumo ed evoluzione degli stili alimentari attraverso l'indagine Istat sui consumi delle famiglie", ECONOMIA AGRO-ALIMENTARE.

Mark-Up (2009). Foodies, esercito che avanza, 9 October 2009. Available at: www.mark-up.it/articoli/0,1254,41_ART_3646,00.html

Meglio L. (2012). "Sociologia del cibo e dell'alimentazione, un'introduzione", Franco Angeli editore, Milano 2012.

Montanari, A., and Staniscia, B. (2009). Culinary tourism as a tool for regional re-equilibrium. *European Planning Studies*, 17(10), 1463–1483.

Papotti, D. (2002). I paesaggi etnici dell'immigrazione straniera in Italia. In: M. Varott and M. e Zunica, eds. (a cura di), *Studi in ricordo di Giovanna Brunetta, Padova, Dipartimento di Geografia "Giuseppe Morandini"*. Padova: dell'Università degli studi di, pp. 151–166.

Pozzolo A. (2011). "Le prospettive dell'economia mondiale e le difficoltà dell'Italia", in: De Filippis F., (Eds), Crisi economica e manovra di stabilizzazione, Quaderni Gruppo 2013, Edizioni Tellus, Roma: 13–31.

Price Waterhouse Coopers (2015). La grande consommation: 1985–2015–2045, available from: https://www.pwc.fr/fr/publications/distribution-biens-de-consommation.html

Ristoranti & Imprese del gusto (2013). issue of December 2013, available from: https://www.bargiornale.it/riviste/ristoranti-imprese-del-gusto-dicembre-gennaio-2013/

Ritzer, G., & Liska, A. (1997). McDisneyization' and 'post-tourism': complementary perspectives on contemporary tourism. *Touring cultures: Transformations of travel and theory*, 96–109.

Romagnolo, D.F. and Selmin, O.I. (2017). Mediterranean diet and prevention of chronic diseases. *Nutrition Today*, 52(5), p. 208.

Romano D. (2011). "L'evoluzione strutturale dei consumi alimentari in Italia", Università degli Studi di Firenze Workshop–Roma.

Santini, C., Cavicchi, A. and Belletti, E. (2013). Preserving the authenticity of food and wine festivals: the case of Italy. Il Capitale Culturale. *Studies on the Value of Cultural Heritage* (8), pp. 251–271.

Santini, C., Cavicchi, A. and Canavari, M. (2011). The Risk™ strategic game of rural tourism: How sensory analysis can help in achieving a sustainable competitive advantage. In: *Food, Agri-Culture and Tourism*. Heidelberg, Berlin: Springer, pp. 161–179.

Sassatelli R. (2015). "Fronteggiare la crisi", Bologna, Il mulino.

Sassatelli R., Davolio F. (2015). "Dimmi come mangi e ti dirò chi sei. Ceto medio e alimentazione" in "Fronteggiare la crisi", Bologna, Il mulino.

Sassatelli, R., and Scott, A. (2001). Novel food, new markets and trust regimes: responses to the erosion of consumers' confidence in Austria, Italy and the UK. *European Societies*, 3(2), 213–244.

Stančová, K. C., and Cavicchi, A. (2019). Smart Specialisation and the Agri-food System. In Smart Specialisation and the Agri-food System (pp. 43–57). Palgrave Pivot, Cham.

SymphonyIri (2012). In foodweeb available from: https://www.foodweb.it/2013/01/symphonyiri-il-bilancio-della-pl-nel-2012/

Tardi, A. (2007). Spacious food bazaar in Turin plans Manhattan branch. *New York Times*, 24 October 2007. Available at: www.nytimes.com/2007/10/24/dining/24eata.html?pagewanted=print&_r=0 132 133

Tremblay, M. A. (1957). The key informant technique: A nonethnographic application. *American Anthropologist*, 59(4), 688–701.

UNEP/MAP (2016). Mediterranean Strategy for Sustainable Development 2016–2025. Valbonne: Plan Bleu, Regional Activity Centre.

Unesco (2013). Mediterranean diet, available from: https://ich.unesco.org/en/RL/mediterranean-diet-00884

Unioncamere (2017). Press Release, available at: www.unioncamere.gov.it/P43K14600/turismo-eno-gastronomico.htm

World Tourism Organization (2012). *Global report on food tourism*. Madrid: UNWTO.

Websites

www.italia.it/en/travel-ideas/gastronomy.html
www.italiaatavola.net, www.eataly.it

10 Promoting the Slow City concept as a sustainability strategy

The Seferihisar case

Gonca Güzel Şahin

Introduction

The characteristics such as fast and competitive life, standardized holiday habits, food and beverage types, styles of clothing and the like which are among the most important impacts of globalization direct the societies to destroy their unique values. For the purpose of making this new world order more humane, social movements have started to emerge as a reaction to this situation. One such movement that emerged through the end of the 20th century is the "Slow City" movement. This social movement has put forward the planning approaches focused on local products and maintaining their sustainability by bringing a different perspective to urbanization policies. Some of the gourmands in Italy have vitalized "Slow Food" as a reaction to this uniformity especially in foods and beverages. In the transformation of Slow Food into a fast-emerging movement in the world, the masses have become influential that do not just consume to fill their stomachs and have the consciousness of the food and beverage culture and its uniqueness. The Slow City movement, which is the continuation of the Slow Food movement, is a developmental model that relies on local characteristics with a similar way of thinking. The disadvantaged groups generally live in the rural areas, and problems such as migration, unemployment, socioeconomic problems and irregular urbanization have emerged in the big cities. Many European countries like Italy have found the solution to the problem in turning towards the rural areas, and the Slow City concept has been adopted as a sustainable rural developmental model.

Sustainable rural development is the formation of the processes that would provide the development of the production, income and welfare levels of the people living in the rural areas in a way that would change their structures in socioeconomic and cultural aspects, eliminate inequalities and provide better evaluation of the agricultural products. When we implement the three dimensions of sustainability (economic, environmental and social-political) to the Slow City concept, the Slow City movement means sustainable urbanization, sustainable tourism and sustainable development that protect the economic resources which are social and sensitive towards the environment (Ergüven, 2011; Nistoreanu, 2011; Yurtseven and Kaya, 2011; Semmens and Freeman, 2012). A city which is a Slow City protects its unique characteristics while fulfilling the international requirements of becoming a part of the network.

The Slow City concept (Cittaslow), which started in Italy in 1999 and has become gradually more widespread around the world, is an important movement within the framework of protection of the local culture and the cultural heritage, improvement of the local values and quality of life and sustainability in Turkey. While Pink describes slow cities as "settlements that use the ideas that include protection of environment, sustainable development alongside with the improvement of urban life and that use the natural and environmentally friendly techniques in food production" (Pink, 2008), Mayer and Knox describe slow cities as "places where the local people and the administrators care about the local history and benefit from different local resources to achieve better and sustainable development" with a similar expression (Mayer and Knox, 2006). The Slow City movement aims to provide an alternative for the city life and design where the contemporary fast and consumption-based living philosophy is dominant. Towards the direction of this purpose, differentiation of many cities of the modern world, developing strategies in the name of protecting their local characteristics, protecting and owning local values are perceived as the biggest necessity (Sırım, 2012).

According to Cittaslow International (n.d.), currently there are 235 Slow Cities in 30 countries, where Turkey also takes part. It is seen that among the 30 countries, Turkey ranks fourth in accordance to the list of Slow Cities. Italy, Spain and Poland take place on the top.

Sustainable tourism concept

Ercoşkun (2007) defined sustainability as

> the limitation of the contemporary generation of the use of the unrenewable resources and the keeping of the negative impacts of the humanity on the ecosystem in a way that those impacts do not exceed the system's bearing capacity for the purpose of transferring all the variety in the ecosystem and the unrenewable resources to the future generations.

Sustainability expresses a kind of the correct usage formula in the name of allowing the use of the resources by future generations in an order within the bearing capacity by preserving the balance of the nature and all of the living creatures within the ecosystem (Keskin, 2012). As an extension of the capitalist order, a life focusing on excessive consumption has started, and it has started to present continuity by purchasing more than the needs and consuming fast and purchasing again. Due to the unconscious consumption behavior of people, which is difficult to prevent, the harming of the environment and of nature has started to show a tendency to reach up to extinction, primarily with the bearing capacity, air pollution, water pollution and noise pollution (Kuter and Ünal, 2009). Fast depletion of the already-existing resources takes place as an outcome of excessive consumption in the capitalist order. As an extension of producing more than the need, consumption more than the need takes place. People keep spending more as their consumption increases, and in order to replace what they have spent, they keep working faster as their consumption increases. As a result of this, everything that is performed to live speeds up (Petrini and Padovani, 2012). The sustainable rural development concept is described as "development that is able to meet the contemporary needs without compromising the possibility of the future generations to meet their own needs" in the report published by the World Commission on Environment and Development, WCED (1987).

UNWTO embraces sustainable tourism, and the principle of sustainable development in tourism, by observing the protection and development of future opportunities and by supplying the needs of the contemporary tourists and of the host regions. Thus, the management of all resources and the continuity of the cultural unity, mandatory ecological processes and biological diversity and life support systems are maintained, and they are prioritized in a way that the economic, social and aesthetic necessities are met. As Gössling describes, sustainable tourism may be possible only by providing the environmental and the related ecological balance. Here, an environmentalist administration and planning understanding are the bases (Gössling, 1999). With the development of sustainable tourism, attention towards local resources has increased, the local people are provided with obtaining income and new employment opportunities are created. The accumulative impact created as the result of the damages caused by tourism demands that are intense and accumulated around certain regions on the environment and the ecological balance did not just negatively affect the tourism movements, but also affected the vital factors in terms of people. The diminishing of revenues obtained from the traditional rural sectors such as agriculture and forestry as the result of experienced fast industrialization, change of the agricultural technologies and globalization have caused the need for economic diversification and to seek alternative economic revenues in the rural areas. After the narrowing down of the traditional rural economy, tourism has become evaluated as a source of alternative income, and it has come to the public's agenda as a solution to the socio-economic problems of the rural areas (Ertuna and Kırbaş, 2012). One of the ways of increasing tourism revenues in a destination is related to increasing the availability of local agricultural products. Increasing revenues is related to three areas that support sustainability: sustainable agriculture, sustainable cuisine and a sustainable tourism sector. In order to develop sustainable cuisine, it is necessary to develop the "from the field to the restaurant" concept, and it needs to be supported by sustainable agriculture and local products (Berno, 2006). The concept of ecotourism has emerged for the purposes of protection and providing consciousness partially due to this reason. Especially in the beginning of the 1990s, through the increase and change of the dimensions of environmental problems, it would be correct to say that it has become an alternative type of tourism that is brought to the public's agenda fast which is developed as an alternative action plan (Kuter and Ünal, 2009).

Slow City promotes the protection, sustainability and development of historical textures and local resources. Slow City, which is a movement focused on humanitarian values, aims to make the life of the city more meaningful by knowing the values of the city where people live and by protecting those values. Additionally, the living culture, especially the culture of cuisine in the city, forms the basic elements of the Slow City (Pajo and Uğurlu, 2015). The basic purposes of the Slow City, which overlap with the purposes of sustainability, are the following (Yurtseven and Kaya, 2010):

- By using technology, providing the quality and inhabitability of urban life.
- Providing sustainable development with the values that are intrinsic to the region.
- Providing equality of income by providing contribution to the local economic life.
- Protecting the natural environment and historical values

Slow Food movement

According to Slowfood (n.d.), the Slow Food movement is a movement that has become official with the manifesto that was published under the leadership of Carlo Petrini in 1989. The main topic indicated in the manifesto is the speeding up of food activities and feeding habits in connection with the speeding up of life. The manifesto also focused on local production, clean food and traditional delicacies that fade into oblivion. According to the manifesto, the Slow Food movement aims at offering a lifestyle of better quality. The starting point of the movement is known as the reaction that emerged against McDonald's, one of the leading fast food chains that attempted to be established on the Spanish Stairs in Rome (Petrini and Padovani, 2012). Honore (2008) described the Slow Food movement as representing "everything that McDonald's failed to do: fresh local seasonal products, recipes that pass through generations, prudent farming, and local shop products, having enjoyable meals with family and friends".

Slow Food, before anything else, substantially has the characteristics of a human rights movement. The founder and leader Carlo Petrini defends that not just getting full, but also enjoying the food is a human right. He emphasizes that protection of the rights of the producers and betterment of their living standards are part of gastronomy. In this context, every plate on the table is directly about the problems of the world. Contrary to what is believed, a plate of food is related to the scientific and social area a lot more. Primarily agriculture, the sciences of physics, chemistry, biology, botanic, zoology, genetics, medicine, ecology and environment, are about our every bite. History, sociology and anthropology, as well as politics, economy and geopolitics, guide what we put on our plates (Yalçın and Yalçın, 2013).

The philosophy of the organization had focused on consuming "good, clean and fair" food. The three principles of food and consuming food in the Slow Food philosophy may be characterized as follows:

- Good: good food is a fresh and delicious seasonal diet satisfying the senses and part of the local culture.
- Clean: clean food is characterized as food production and consumption that does not harm the environment, human and animal wealth or health.

- Fair: fair food represents affordable prices for the consumers and for the fair conditions and making payments for the small scale producers.

At the same time, this perspective also supports the local and small-scale producers. As an extension of this, philosophy is enriched with the lateral views such as consumption of the local products locally. Good and clean foods correspond to the existence of natural agriculture applications and protection of the producer in the transfer of the foods from production to delivery (Özkan, 2011).

Slow Food, which is also an area of activity nested with local production and organic nutrition, closely supports the healthy and additive-free nutritional movements for human life to be sustainable (Yurtseven and Kaya, 2011). According to Petrini and Padovani, it is not just sufficient for the eaten foods to be good, delicious and quality; they need to be fair in addition to those. Fairness of the food adds a new dimension to gastronomy and emphasizes the significance of questioning of the food consumed by each individual (Petrini and Padovani, 2012). The significance of traditional delicacies mean substantially not just for clean and healthy nutrition, but also for the protection of cultural values (Savaş, 2014). The Slow Food movement provides the local cultural values and the registration and makes the geographical indication of the local foods for their protection. As the products that receive a geographical indication have a brand value, they may be used in the regional promotion and marketing.

According to Slowfood (n.d.), the snail that was chosen as the logo and symbol of the Slow Food movement has a philosophical meaning. The snail is an animal which moves at a slow pace, may travel a distance of only 110 meters per hour, consumes food continuously but in small amounts, has difficulties with living in environments where there is no water and carries its own home on its back. By assuming that it can represent the movement with its creational characteristics, the snail has become the symbol of both the Slow Food and the Slow City philosophies.

Slow City

Slow City is a union of the towns and cities that do not want to become homogenous places created by globalization, that want to take part in the world stage by protecting their local identities and characteristics, because the local dynamics are more sustainable and long-lasting in terms of economic, cultural and social aspects (Mayer and Knox, 2006). According to Cittaslow (n.d.), Slow City is the movement which targets the sustainable development by protecting what is local through purification from the negative impact of the global life over people and spaces. The movement which has emerged as a reaction to fast life embraces a more tranquil living philosophy. According to Cittaslow Türkiye (n.d.), Slow City includes 72 criteria under seven main headings. Those criteria are as follows:

Environmental and energy policies

It is the documentation of air and water cleanliness within the parameters indicated by the laws, comparison of tap water consumption with the national averages, taking energy consumption of the public energy use and energy use in the residences under control and the public sector's production of energy from renewable energy sources, collection of urban waste by separating them and creation of wastewater treatment facilities for urban sewage waste and protection of biodiversity.

Infrastructural policies

It is the removal of the architectural obstacles in regards to the disabled people, making of transportation plans alternative to the use of private vehicles, creation of bicycle parking spots at public transportation transfer centers to disseminate transportation with the bicycle, and improvement of the bicycle roads by comparing the existing bicycle roads with the vehicle roads in terms of kilometers, sparing special parking spots in the city centers and hospitals for pregnant women.

Urban quality of life policies

It is the making of public building arrangements for the resistance and betterment of the urban values of the city, formation of green areas to increase urban inhabitability, making the investments that would make it easier to access to the information and communication technologies and Internet network of the interactive service development for the urban residents and visitors, forming the areas where the local products may be commercialized, protection and increasing the value of the already-existing production workshops to serve for this purpose, encouragement of the personal sustainable urban planning and public sustainable urban plans and forming incentives that would support the social infrastructure.

Policies regarding agriculture, tourism, tradesmen and artisans

It is the promotion of development of agro ecology (certifying local products), protection of traditional working techniques and artisanship, handicrafts and labeled or branded tradesman/artisan products by supporting them, increasing added value of the rural areas by providing the rural inhabitants with access to services, prohibition of the use of genetically modified organisms in agricultural production and promotion of the use of organic products in the restaurants that belong to the public, protection of the local and traditional cultures, providing taste education in the culinary sector and promotion of the use of organic local products, taking the developed regions under re-planning that had been previously used as agricultural areas.

For hospitality, awareness and education

It is the arrangement of activities that would provide the visibility and recognition of the Cittaslow Organization as well as regular and permanent training regarding the Cittaslow philosophy to the residents of the city, creating NGO structures that would carry out the studies between the local governments and the Cittaslow Organization, adoption and implementation of the bottom-up participation in regards to the important administrative decisions about the city, creation of slow routes and organization of local good welcoming through those routes.

Social compliance

It is the tolerant treatment of minorities and not having any discrimination, adopting a stance against discrimination based on ethnic background and embracing homogenous distribution in residential places, fighting poverty and supporting youth employment, providing the adaptation of disabled individuals, realizing cultural harmony between cultures and providing participation into politics.

Partnerships

It is the formation and supporting of Slow Food organizations and campaigns, support of natural and local foods by the Slow Food and other institutional organizations, forming matching projects and cooperation in the developing countries for the purpose of expanding and development of Cittaslow and the Slow Food philosophy.

Importance of sustainable tourism for Turkey

Due to the strong relationship between sustainability and competition in tourism, it is necessary to develop tourism policy within the axis of sustainability for the purpose of placing Turkey at the top in the competitiveness index and supporting the developing tourism sector with long-term plans. The common point of the precautions that had been taken to develop the tourism sector in the world is the providing of the sustainability of tourism activities for the duration of 12 months by evaluating the already-existing resources that protect the environmental and cultural values in a complementary way. Restructuring that takes place in the world's tourism sector has made it mandatory to plan the tourism investments in Turkey again. Within this scope, in the basis of the planning approach of the Ministry of Culture and Tourism in the planning of tourism investments in Turkey, the principles of protecting and using natural resources take place through the ecological and economic efficiency within the sustainable tourism strategy. The sustainable tourism policies that start a new period in tourism also fall within the legal regulations. The Turkey 2023 Tourism Strategy and 2013 Action Plan aim at using the natural, cultural, historical and geographical values of Turkey within the protection-use balance and increasing the share that it would get from tourism by developing its tourism alternatives. The Slow City movement is one of the alternative approaches in dealing with tourism resources in such a way that they form tourism regions, tourism cities and ecotourism regions.

Sustainable rural development has a strategic significance in the removal of imbalances between the regions and cities for developing countries, especially as in Turkey. When statistics are examined, it is seen that the rural population has been decreasing while the share of agriculture in the GDP and employment has been decreasing. Concepts such as the demand of the people to have access to more and correct information regarding the products that people consume – natural, fresh, organic and traditional products – increase the interest of consumers in the local and small-scale production. Gastronomy and local cuisine alongside with the Slow Food movement have been influential in selection of tourists' destinations, and it provides a serious contribution to the economy of the region with the added value and employment that it creates. Additionally, protection of the culinary culture with sustainable restaurants, biological diversity and traditional production develop the agricultural activities in the locality and will realize the sustainable rural development targets by protecting them.

Slow City Seferihisar

According to İzmir Kultur Turizm (n.d.a), Seferihisar is located in the southern part of İzmir, with its surface area of 386 square kilometers located on the coast of the Aegean Sea within the borders of İzmir province. Seferihisar, which has an advantageous location in terms of its proximity to the city center of İzmir and the İzmir airport, is a touristic destination that grabs attention with its geothermal water resources and cultural values. The population of Seferihisar is 37,697 according to the 2016 census. It is seen that Seferihisar has become an attention-grabbing attraction as it was included into the Slow City network in 2009. As it is known that the history of Teos, which is known as the oldest settlement of the sub-province of Seferihisar, goes back to 2000 BC, it has been proven that it is a city that was established by the Cretans and that belonged to the Carians. Many remains have been found within the boundaries of the Seferihisar sub-province that belong to the Persian, Ionian, Aka and Caria civilizations alongside the Byzantium, Seljuki and Ottoman periods. The richness of the archeological sites located in Seferihisar is the biggest obstacle against the irregular urbanization that has formed in recent years along the Aegean coasts.

According to Seferi Pazar (n.d.), agricultural products form the main source of means of living in Seferihisar. The olive gardens, artichoke fields, citrus gardens and foliage plant greenhouses and animal breeding have recently become an important source of means of living for the people. While fishing continues to become a source of means of living in the sub-province, the roadmap in tourism sector has been notably formed by being included into the Slow City network, and nowadays tourism has become the most important sector that generates revenues for the sub-province.

Seferihisar and the Slow City movement

As mentioned earlier, Seferihisar, which has the title of first Slow City in Turkey, joined the Slow City network in 2009. It was the first Slow City whose application had been accepted without a regional inspection as a result of the application file that the Seferihisar Municipality submitted at the Slow City International Coordination committee meeting in Italy in 2009. According to İzmir Kultur Turizm (n.d.a), the Teos antique city excavations have been initiated by the Ministry of Culture and Tourism with the attempts of the Seferihisar Municipality in 2010, and after the first five-year work plan, the biggest Dionysus Temple in the world, an antique theatre, agora, Odeon, remnants of the port and the city walls have been unearthed.

The Seferihisar Municipality has been organizing "Seed Exchange Festivals" every year for the purpose of distributing thousands of different seeds produced at the Can Yücel Seed Center that it had established in 2011 by realizing a project that would provide the transfer and sustainability of local seeds that are under threat to future generations. Another project that was done within the scope of supporting local production targeted to improve Seferihisar Fishing Cooperation in regards to sustainable fishing within the scope of an EU project. In accordance with the Slow City membership criteria, Seferihisar maintained studies to protect the local foods and to provide the sustainability of the food culture, and under the light of the collected information, the book titled *Slow Foods of Seferihisar* was prepared. Within the scope of protection of local produces and production, another project that was realized in 2013 was the "Tangerine Producers' Union" (Akman, Akman and Karakuş, 2018). According to Seferihisar Belediyesi (n.d.a), another union established after the Tangerine Producers' Union in 2013 was the "Olive Producers' Union". The primary target of this project was to unite the olive producers under one roof and to create an organizational unity, offer technical and occupational training possibilities and provide branding by increasing the quality of production. For the purpose of providing the sustainability of local production, with the "Good Agriculture Project from the Field to the Table" which was initiated by the leadership of the Seferihisar Development Cooperative in 2013, it was planned to "spread the good agriculture applications, to develop organic agriculture, to increase the revenues of the producers and to create opportunities for the consumers to have access to safe food" in Seferihisar. For the purpose of raising new generations who are focused on production and are sensitive to the environment in Seferihisar, vegetable gardens had been established at schools, a producer identity was developed among the students at a young age and the students were allowed to earn their own pocket money through the sale of the grown vegetables. It has been seen that Seferihisar has implemented all of the works that it has carried out from 2009 until now regarding production and development, becoming a sustainable city and protecting cultural heritage by taking sustainability principles into account.

In addition to these, Seferihisar has carried out some improvements after becoming a Slow City. These are as follows (Tunçer and Olgun, 2017):

- Gardens have been created so that children learn natural production.
- A "Village Market" was established for the purpose of complying with the criteria regarding the establishment of commercial centers to support local production.
- The project of making of the bicycle roads in Seferihisar is still going on. Various attempts have been made to revitalize the buggy tradition in the city.
- Renovations continue in the streets with visual pollution.
- Works such as painting the facades of the houses and placing of geranium plants outside of the houses have been performed.
- Seferihisar, which has 300 sunny days per year, also has rich thermal energy sources and a powerful wind corridor. In this regard, it is targeted that primarily geothermal energy is to be used in the heating of the city. Additionally, in the illumination of the city, solar and wind energy are used.
- The process of creating local restaurants was sped up. In this regard, training of the restaurant owners continues with the support taken from the universities in İzmir.
- Efforts have been placed for maturing a project where boutique hotels that are appropriate to the natural and historical architectural texture and that are respectful of guest houses and the environment are prioritized instead of all-inclusive systems in the tourism sector. In this regard, it has been targeted to make the whole city a touristic center for the purpose of spreading ecotourism.
- For the purpose of supporting the producers, the "Seferi-market", serving in the interactive setting, was established by the women of Seferihisar, allowing the producers and consumers to meet without any intermediary.
- For the protection of the olive, which is one of the most valuable produces of Seferihisar, the inventory of the 1,000-year old monumental olive trees are made by determining those trees in the sub-province.

According to EDEN (n.d.), Seferihisar has rich touristic attractions with its geographical location, historical richness, customs and traditions. While the tourism activities had been maintained until 2009 at the coastal region extending for 49 kilometers, Sığacık Fort and Ürkmez regions, the city's inclusion into the Slow City network in Turkey has prevented the problems of fast consumption of natural and cultural assets, which are among the biggest problems faced by many other touristic destinations. While maintaining the characteristics to become a touristic destination, the local and cultural assets are protected, and the city moved towards protecting the character to be a sustainable destination.

As Seferihisar is a coastal city, tourism developed heavily as domestic tourism until 2009. The thing that revived foreign tourism and the most important development on behalf of Seferihisar was that the city became a Slow City. Seferihisar has become the first city of Turkey to join the International Union of Municipalities and achieved the title of "Turkey's Slow City Capital". There are other types of tourism and other attractions of the sub-province other than sea tourism to be made in Seferihisar. Wind surfing, thermal tourism and rural tourism rank among the activities that may increase Seferihisar's share in tourism. With its number of blue flagged beaches, Seferihisar ranks as the first in İzmir. Besides, Seferihisar has a rich potential that would allow opportunities to develop health tourism with its sun, wind, beaches, sea water and thermal water characteristics. Seferihisar has a strong potential to become a global Bio thermal and Thalasso Center. Seferihisar is also a sub-province having important attractions in terms of rural tourism (Soykan and Emekli, 2004). Another type of significant tourism that may be done in Seferihisar is gastronomy tourism. One of the important matters whose significance has increased in the recent years is local cuisine. Along the way village restaurants and diners have been opened in Seferihisar as it is close to İzmir. Additionally, facilities providing foods and drinks in the coastal towns have proliferated. The Seferihisar cuisine is undoubtedly a sample of the Aegean cuisine, and it is dominated by vegetables, fruits, olive oil, herbs and seafood.

According to Seferihisar Belediyesi (n.d.b), Sığacık is one of the most visited districts of Seferihisar with its proximity to the center of the sub-province, the Teos Antic City, fish restaurants, fishing boats lined up in its port, its unique architecture and the Sığacık Fort. The Sığacık Fort which was built with the order of the Ottoman king Kanuni Sultan Süleyman in 1521–1522 was made for the purpose of preliminary preparation for the Rhodes expedition. In the construction of the fort, which was used as a naval base, stones brought from the Teos Antic City were used. The streets currently named as Kaleiçi region alongside with the Sığacık Fort have gained a new view. In the Sığacık Kaleiçi, which includes 284 residences, 27 property owners have received certificates by successfully completing the Guesthouse Training, which was initiated with the cooperation of the Seferihisar Municipality and Yaşar University, and their residences were converted into guesthouses. Those guesthouses are run by the property owners and a contribution is made to the Seferihisar tourism, and the guests who come from outside of the city or the country have the chance to live life in the city, accommodate there and get to know the local culture because of the guesthouses.

Sığacık has a significant tourism potential in regards to its natural assets. Additionally, the city's historical and cultural values have significantly increased the tourism potential of the city. Those values that are influential for the city to become a Slow City have been protected at a certain level from the intense pressures of tourism with the impact of the natural sites in the area. With Seferihisar's Slow City status and, within this scope, the impact of the projects that have been carried out in the city, tourism movements proceed under control. It may not be said that Sığacık is subjected to an intense mass tourism when it is compared with other tourism centers located on the western coast of Turkey (such as Kuşadası, Bodrum, Marmaris and the like). The basic purpose of the city in obtaining Slow City status by being committed to the criteria of the Slow Cities Union is partially to protect the city from the pressure of rentier-based tourism.

According to Seferi Pazar (n.d.), "Agricultural Development Cooperative" was established in 2009 within the scope of the criteria of "protection of local produces" and "supporting local producers" that are among the membership criteria. The purpose of establishing the cooperative is to provide the improvement and strengthening of women in the economic and social areas who live in Seferihisar and are unable to participate into the social life in the city. Owning the values that belong to Seferihisar, protection of local products, encouragement of women to produce, providing the sustainability of local foods and culinary cultures and providing of the female producers a contribution to their domestic economies are targeted.

Conclusion

Nowadays, people seek a more humane and sustainable life in the cities where they reside. Thus, the Slow City movement was initiated for the purposes of "achieving a more humane and better quality living environment whose architecture, nature and cultural values are protected that envisages a sustainable local production". It is thought that the Slow City model significantly contributes to the local development at the same time as a good example of ecotourism. In recent years, it has been seen that the consumer choices in the tourism sector are in the tendency to protect the traditional values and consume the local products. The cities that join the Slow City movement, which emerged in Italy and is currently spreading around the world, reach the targets of sustainable tourism by prioritizing their unique local differences besides becoming a member of an international network.

The spread of the Slow City movement in such a short amount of time to different countries around the world and its adoption by the local people in this level in the cities where the movement has been actualized originate from the movement's improvement of the people's quality of life in an economic, social and cultural sense. Seferihisar's achievement of the title of Turkey's first Slow City has become possible by the administrators of the local governments who have a vision, taking the necessary steps in this direction and raising the consciousness of the people in regards to the topic and by the public providing all kinds of support.

Within the Slow City concept, the purpose of sustainable tourism in Seferihisar is to develop tourism without harming the environment, society, historical, natural and cultural assets in a way to continuously contribute to the local economy and social life. Prioritizing the local people in the touristic arrangements, spreading tourism into 12 months, prioritizing public transportation, providing social participation, protection of social and cultural identity and having tourism investments that are long term and open to development may be counted as the general principles of sustainable tourism. To become a Slow City, criteria such as environmental policies, infrastructure, and protection of the texture of the city, supporting the local production and products and hospitality are required. The principles of sustainable tourism and the principles of Slow City overlap exactly. The sustainable development activities of the Slow City Seferihisar will be followed up through an international inspection. Thus, the city may follow its sustainable tourism strategy.

Seferihisar has realized activities and organizations that would increase its level of welfare by joining the Slow City network, by initiating the local potentials, natural and cultural values that it has and by taking important steps that would provide its socio-economic and cultural development. Nowadays, the sustainable tourism and Slow City applications have been gaining significance as a local development strategy. In Turkey, every passing year, many small cities and towns having rich natural, historical and cultural assets join the Slow City movement for the purpose of providing their local development in recent years.

The criteria that the Slow City (Cittaslow) approach – which is a different model regarding development of sustainable tourism – wants to realize in the cities have parallels with the principles and indicators of sustainable tourism. The sustainability indicators which may be brought together under economic, ecological and sociocultural values, such as the use of renewable energy sources, water and air quality, biodiversity and improvement of the quality of life, are also the criteria of the Slow City. When it is considered that the condition of having a population of less than 50,000 of the cities that have been introduced for membership, the Slow City is an alternative sustainable tourism model that is developed for many small cities in Turkey. It may be seen as an opportunity for Anatolian cities that have a significant potential in terms of especially natural, historical and cultural assets. Those cities may turn into an attraction and a global brand both for the residents and the tourists with the criteria within the framework of the Slow City.

References

Akman, E., Akman, Ç. and Karakuş, M. (2018). Yavaş Şehir Kriterleri Üzerinden Seferihisar Belediyesinin Faaliyetlerinden Vatandaş Memnuniyetinin Analizi, *Afyon Kocatepe University Journal of Social Sciences*, 20(2), pp. 65–84.

Berno, T. (2006). Bridging sustainable agriculture and sustainable tourism to enhance sustainability. In: G.M. Mudacumura, D. Mebratu, and M. Shamsul Haque, eds., *Sustainable development policy and administration*. New York: Taylor & Francis, pp. 207–231.

Cittaslow International (n.d.). *Association*. Available at: http://cittaslow.org [Accessed 28 Sep. 2017].

Cittaslow Türkiye (n.d.). *Şehirler*. Available at: www.Cittaslowturkiye.org [Accessed 17 Feb. 2018].

EDEN Türkiye (n.d.). *İzmir Seferihisar*. Available at: http://eden.kulturturizm.gov.tr/TR-127874/izmirseferihisar.html [Accessed 26 Nov. 2017].

Ercoşkun Yalçıner, Ö. (2007). *Sürdürülebilir Kent için Ekolojik-Teknolojik (EKO- TEK) Tasarım: Ankara – Güdül Örneği*. Ankara: Doktora Tezi, Gazi Üniversitesi, Fen Bilimleri Enstitüsü, Şehir Ve Bölge Planlama Anabilim Dalı.

Ergüven, M.H. (2011). Cittaslow – Yaşamaya Değer Şehirlerin Uluslararası Birliği: Vize Örneği. *Kırklareli Üniversitesi Turizm Fakültesi Organizasyon ve Yönetim Bilimleri Dergisi*, 3, pp. 206–207.

Ertuna, B. and Kırbaş, G. (2012). Local community involvement in rural tourism development: The case of Kastamonu. *Pasos*, 10, pp. 17–24.

Felsen Savaş, E. (2014). Adil Yemek. *Lezzet Dergisi*, 210, pp. 18–22.

Gössling, S. (1999). Ecotourism: A means to safeguard biodiversity and ecosystem function?. *Ecological Economics*, 29, pp. 303–320.

Honore, C. (2008). *Yavaş, Hız Çılgınlığında Baş Kaldıran Yavaşlık Hareketi.* İstanbul: Alfa Yayınları.

İzmir İl Kültür ve Turizm Müdürlüğü. (n.d.a). *Üç Bin Yıllık Tarih Ortaya Çıkıyor.* Available at: www.izmirkulturturizm.gov.tr/TR-76616/3-bin-yillik-tarih-ortaya-cikiyor.html [Accessed 15 Jan. 2018].

Keskin, E.B. (2012). Sürdürülebilir Kent Kavramına Farklı Bir Bakış: Yavaş Şehirler Cittaslow. *Paradoks Ekonomi, Sosyoloji ve Politika Dergisi*, 8, pp. 81–99.

Kuter, N. and Ünal, H.E. (2009). Sürdürülebilirlik Kapsamında Ekoturizmin Çevresel, Ekonomik ve Sosyo-Kültürel Etkileri. *Kastamonu University Journal of Forestry Faculty*, 9, pp. 146–156.

Mayer, H. and Knox, L.P. (2006). Slow cities: Sustainable places in a fast world. *Journal of Urban Affairs*, 28, pp. 323–333.

Nistoreanu, P. (2011). Strategic directions in sustainable tourism development through rural tourism activities. *International Society of Commodity Science and Technology*, 1, pp. 116–123.

Özkan, C.H. (2011). *Bir Sürdürülebilir Kent Modeli: Yavaş Şehir Hareketi.* İstanbul: Yıldız Teknik Üniversitesi, Mimarlık Anabilim Dalı, Bina Araştırma ve Planlama Programı, Yüksek Lisans Tezi.

Pajo, A. and Uğurlu, K. (2015). Cittaslow Kentleri İçin Slow Food Çalışmalarının Önemi. *Electronic Journal of Vocational Colleges*, 5, pp. 65–73.

Petrini, C. and Padovani, G. (2012). *Slow food devrimi.* İstanbul: Sinek Sekiz.

Pink, S. (2008). Sense and sustainability: The case of the slow city movement. *Local Environment*, 13, pp. 95–106.

Seferi Pazar (n.d.). *Seferi Pazar.* Available at: https://seferipazar.com/ [Accessed 10 Jul. 2018].

Seferihisar Belediyesi (n.d.a). *Seferihisar Hakkında.* Available at: http://seferihisar.bel.tr/ seferihisar-hakkinda/ [Accessed 10 Oct. 2017].

Seferihisar Belediyesi (n.d.b). *500 yıllık kale dünyanın en eski, en sakin, en gerçek tatil köyüne dönüşüyor.* Available at: http://seferihisar.bel.tr/500-y-ll-k-kale-duenyan-n-en-eski-en-sakin-en-gercek-tatil-koeyuene-doenuesueyor/ [Accessed 17 Aug. 2018].

Semmens, J. and Freeman, C. (2012). The value of cittaslow as an approach to local sustainable development: A New Zealand perspective. *International Planning Studies*, 17, pp. 353–375.

Sırım, V. (2012). Çevreyle Bütünleşmiş Bir Yerel Yönetim Örneği Olarak "Sakin Şehir" Hareketi ve Türkiye'nin Potansiyeli. *Tarih Kültür ve Sanat Araştırmaları Dergisi*, 1, pp. 119–131.

Slowfood (n.d.). *Slow Food.* Available at: www.slowfood.it [Accessed 23 Jun. 2018].

Soykan, F. and Emekli, G. (2004). *Tüm Yönleriyle Seferihisar.* İzmir: Seferihisar Kaymakamlığı.

Tunçer, M. and Olgun, A. (2017). A review of Cittaslow practices on the economic and fiscal structure of Seferihisar. *International Journal of Economics and Innovation*, 3(1), pp. 47–72.

WCED, 1987. Our Common Future. World Commissionon Environment and Development. Oxford University Press, Oxford.

Yalçın, A. and Yalçın, S. (2013). Sürdürülebilir Yerel Kalkınma için Cittaslow Hareketi Bir Model Olabilir mi?. *Sosyal ve Beşeri Bilimler Dergisi*, 5, pp. 31–41.

Yurtseven, R. and Kaya, O. (2010). Topluluk Girişimciliği ve Geleneksel Meslekler. *Girişimcilik ve Kalkınma Dergisi*, 5, pp. 21–28.

Yurtseven, R. and Kaya, O. (2011). Slow tourists: A comparative research based on Cittaslow principles. *American International Journal of Contemporary Research*, 1, pp. 91–98.

11 Health tourism in the Mediterranean

Melanie Smith

Introduction

Health tourism is often seen as being the "umbrella" term for wellness tourism and medical tourism, and is based on forms of tourism where tourists proactively seek health-enhancing destinations and activities. Whereas medical tourism is often based on curative approaches to health and tends to involve surgery, wellness tourism is more preventative and includes leisure and beauty spas as well as holistic retreats. Two "gray" areas are cosmetic surgery, as this combines both medical and wellness approaches (i.e. surgery may be used for beauty enhancement), and medical thermal waters or balneotherapy, because such water-based treatments are not included or accepted in all healthcare systems worldwide (Smith and Puczkó, 2017).

The links between health and sustainability are becoming increasingly significant, as outlined by Bushell (2017) in her chapter about "healthy tourism", where she argues that a healthy form of tourism should benefit local people and places as much as it does visitors. This chapter is concerned more with health tourism, but there is a recognition that there is a need to manage Mediterranean destinations differently from how they were managed in past decades. The traditional reliance on mass beach tourism is diversifying into different forms of tourism (e.g. cultural tourism, ecotourism, health tourism) using a more sustainable approach to development. Although many Mediterranean coastal destinations are already at the stagnation or decline stage of Butler's (1980) TALC model, the Mediterranean Balkan region includes countries that attract fewer tourists than Spain, Italy or Portugal (with the exception, perhaps, of Greece). Reasons for this include 50 years of state socialism until 1989 and the Yugoslavian War from 1991 to 2001.

This chapter provides an overview of the Mediterranean Balkan region, including Albania, Bosnia and Herzegovina, Croatia, Greece, Montenegro, Slovenia and Turkey. Almost all of the Balkan countries have thermal and mineral waters which have been used for healing in the past and are often still used as the basis for health tourism. However, in some of the countries, a very small percentage of the available waters are actually used for health tourism, and many facilities that do are in need of urgent regeneration. In order to be economically sustainable, facilities and services may need to be upgraded in order to attract an international market to this relatively undiscovered region. Other potential developments may include thalassotherapy (seaside-based therapies), wellness spas and stronger connections to natural landscape (e.g. forest therapy). In these cases, sustainable approaches will be needed to landscape and water management.

An overview of health tourism resources in the Mediterranean Balkan countries

The Balkan region has a long history of health tourism, in many cases going back to Roman times. Vitic and Ringer (2008, p. 128) stated that "Health-oriented tourists and spa visitors are . . . considered a potentially lucrative market, given the therapeutic role that sanitariums and allegoric treatments have long played in eastern Europe, Russia, and the Balkans." For many decades there was a major focus on balneology. Stăncioiu, Botos and Pargaru (2013) state that the Balkan Peninsula is dominated by the existence of balneotherapy resources in an overwhelming proportion in comparison with other countries of Europe. Balneotherapy includes the treatment of diseases through the methodic use of thermal or mineral water and muds. Balkan traditional medicine may also be included, such as treatments involving medicinal plants. Karagülle (2013) suggests that a "traditional Balkan spa" offers a combination between elements of balneology, climatology and environment. Stăncioiu, Botos and Pargaru (2013) define balneotherapy resorts as those where specific diseases are treated using therapeutic use of mineral waters, hydrotherapy, application of therapeutic mud and gases, kinetotherapy, occupational and massage therapy, electrotherapy and respiratory therapy. The study by Horwath (2013) analyzes the situation of spas in Bosnia and Herzegovina (as well as Serbia) where the term health tourism is also associated with the use of curative thermal and mineral springs, gas and therapeutic muds primarily for rehabilitation and mainly for domestic visitors.

Stăncioiu, Botos and Pargaru (2013) state that plants are of great importance in health recovery or disease prevention in the Balkan countries, not only in balneotherapy destinations but also throughout the entire region. Natural treatments are integrated into traditional medicine. They give the examples of the curative effects of local natural herbal teas such as the sedative actions of chamomile, the digestive actions of hyssop (pertaining to all Balkan countries), tonic effects of sage (Albania) and anti-depressive effects of cedar (originally from Turkey). Since ancient times, the majority of herbal drugs in the Balkans have being used for the treatment of respiratory illnesses, gastrointestinal disorders, skin conditions, urinary system infections, insomnia, nervous tension and stress (Redzic, 2010).

Another dimension of health and well-being which seems to be growing in importance is Balkan cuisine. Stăncioiu, Botos and Pargaru (2013) suggest that an additional element for the future Balkan balneotherapy product could be gastronomy, especially the ingredients which are specific to the region. Of course, the regional cuisine varies considerably in terms of its healthiness. Those cuisines which are strongly influenced by the Mediterranean tend to be considered the healthiest. The life expectancy in Greece and Slovenia is quite high, and despite other human development problems, it is also high in Albania. This could be related to the Mediterranean diet (Ginter and Simko, 2011). Šimundić (1997) suggests that healthy Croatian food could be the main driving force for health tourism, and Renko (2010) adds that the domestic food offer in Croatia is based on nature, such as aromatic spices, wild growing plants, vegetables and seafood. Stăncioiu, Botos and Pargaru (2013) mention bee products such as Croatian chestnut honey which can be used to regulate blood flow, or the disinfecting power of Greek thyme or pine honey. Nedelcheva (2013) states that many of the traditional foods have strong healing or strengthening qualities and are used for medicinal purposes and included in a prevention or healing diet.

Finally, Stăncioiu, Botos and Pargaru (2013, p. 13) mention the importance of religion in the everyday life of people in the Balkans, even though they do not all share a common religion. They state that an important part of health tourism is "aiming at the 'health' of the spirit, by completing bodily health with the feeling of peace and purification of the soul".

The country case studies in this chapter contain more specific details of health tourism in the different countries as derived from secondary data sources. However, the common points are the following:

- Almost all of the Balkan countries have thermal and mineral waters which have been used for healing in the past and often are still used as the basis for health or wellness tourism. However, it is often the case that a very small percentage of the available waters are actually used for health tourism. Some countries also have therapeutic mud or gas as well as a healing climate in places.
- Some of the countries have traditionally focused on rehabilitation for residents or domestic tourists, which takes place in sanatoria or thermal baths with medical facilities (e.g. Bosnia, Croatia, Slovenia). The move towards wellness is relatively recent and is more developed in some countries than others (e.g. Slovenia, Greece).
- Although there is potential for the development of international spa or wellness tourism, there is a need to improve the overall infrastructure of thermal bath or spa centers, including accommodation, facilities, services and treatments. The decline has mainly been the result of public or state funding ending and privatization not yet taking place.
- (Surgical) medical tourism is a relatively recent development in the region as a whole. It is offered only in certain destinations, and it currently represents the smallest segment of health tourists.
- There is a growing number of hotels with spa and wellness facilities, many of them in seaside locations or in cities.
- Although most of the Balkan countries promote health tourism, it is usually only on a sub-page of their online communication, and health tourism represents a relatively small percentage of tourists overall (sometimes as little as 1%).

Health tourism in the Mediterranean Balkan countries: case studies

The following section provides an overview of the health tourism development in the Mediterranean Balkan countries, including existing resources and potential for development.

A brief overview of health tourism in Albania

The tourism supply of Albania has been more focused on history, archaeology and other cultural attractions, as well as natural resources (e.g. mountains, national parks and seaside) (Marku, 2014). The tourism strategy of the country focuses on these features, but health tourism is not a current focus for the National Tourism Office. However, according to the *Tirana Times* (2013), a rising number of tourists, although still negligible, visit Albania for health tourism purposes. This includes medical tourism such as dentistry, plastic surgery and orthopedics (ATMA, 2014).

Gambarov and Gjinika (2017) discuss the potential for Albania's thermal waters, which are available in most of the country. However, they emphasize the need to improve infrastructure and facilities in order to meet customers' needs. Albania also has quite a strong tradition of herbal remedies (for example, using sage as a tonic or acacia honey for combatting metabolic and nutritional disease (Stăncioiu, Botos and Pargaru, 2013). TripAdvisor also lists several spa and wellness hotels and resorts.

A brief overview of health tourism in Bosnia and Herzegovina

Health tourism has been identified as one of the major opportunities for the development of the Bosnian economy (Felic, 2013). Bosnia and Herzegovina have hyper-thermal, thermo-mineral, calcic and sodic waters (Stăncioiu, 2013). The term "banja" is used for areas with natural therapeutic factors (thermal and mineral water, gas and therapeutic mud), whose medicinal properties have been scientifically researched and proven. Spas or "banja" accounted for only 5% of the total overnights in Bosnia and Herzegovina in 2012, of which 14% were domestic visitors. The average length of stay in spas was 4.8 days in 2012. All of these numbers represent an increase compared to the year before (Horwath, 2013).

Horwath (2013, p. 37) states that

> we can conclude that the development of health tourism in Bosnia and Herzegovina and in Serbia is still at early stages in terms of the foreign market and it is completely functional at the national level due to the existing healthcare system that limits the private sector access.

The majority of spas have not yet gone through the process of privatization and conceptual restructuring in regard to modern market trends. Consequently, the majority of spas are still mainly treatment and rehabilitation centers for domestic visitors. Felic (2013) suggests that most of the users of health tourism services are local, although the number of foreign tourists is growing. However, there is a need to improve the overall infrastructure of spa centers, including accommodation, facilities, treatment and recreation opportunities. In 2014, six health spas (three in Bosnia) were renovated using EU funding in the cross-border area between Bosnia and Hercegovina and Serbia (Andrews, 2015), and Bosnian authorities have been actively investing in modernizing the spa facilities based on thermal waters which are available in at least 15 locations (My Bosnia, 2017).

A brief overview of health tourism in Croatia

Euromonitor International (2014a) suggested that health and wellness tourism in Croatia continued with a positive trend throughout 2013. This is especially true of medical tourism, but it is confined to certain destinations or regions only. Spa-oriented hotels which offer a wide range of services are growing, and along with the well-known coastal destinations, it is thought that the spa tradition in the northern mainland could be of interest to future investors. Although several coastal destinations offer spa and wellness hotels or resorts, most of the thermal spas are in northern and eastern Croatia.

According to a study by Kesar and Rimac (2011), four segments of Croatian health tourism can be differentiated:

1   Medical tourists: These tourists arrive for rehabilitation, mainly in one of the five biggest, famous sanatoria based on thermal and mineral springs.
2   Spa-thermal tourists and thalasso tourists: These tourists visit the thermal-water based facilities and hospitals used by the locals and tourists.
3   Wellness tourists: The main target segments visit wellness centers and resorts and mainly have stress-management and relaxing treatments.
4   Clinical tourists: These tourists use healthcare services. This type of tourism is less developed than the others.

Renko (2010) emphasized the importance of local food and regional cuisine for adding value to service offered to tourists in Croatia and for supporting the overall tourist experience. Food is important for sustainable ecotourism and cultural heritage tourism as well as health tourism (e.g. healthy Mediterranean cuisine). Šimundić (1997) had suggested earlier that healthy Croatian food could be the driving force for health tourism.

Bradbury (2017) noted that Croatian medical tourism is growing slowly but surely, especially in Zagreb. IMTJ (2016) suggested that health and especially medical tourism should be promoted better in Croatia, arguing that there are 1,100 actual potential providers of health and medical tourism who could provide for foreign markets, predominantly coming from Italy, Slovenia and Bosnia. IMTJ (2016) also described how the Croatian government and health tourism bodies were planning 2017 projects, which include benchmarking for spas and specialist and tourism promotion for spas and wellness hotels.

A brief overview of health tourism in Greece

Despite devoting a sub-page of its online communication to health tourism, Constantinides (2013) describes how Greece has, until recently, been one of the laggards in the health tourism sector. For example, GTP (2010) suggested that Greek spa resorts lacked highly trained professionals like spa managers and directors, aestheticians and therapists. Although the Greek Medical Tourism Council started to promote medical tourism, due to the political and economic situation in Greece, major cuts to the healthcare system and poor infrastructure means that the growth of medical tourism may be temporarily hindered. Euromonitor International (2014b) showed that health and wellness tourism actually declined in current value terms in 2013. In contrast, the spa sector is set to continue growing, reaching 370 outlets, including growth in value sales, by the end of the forecast period. Visit Greece (2014) declares that Greece is one of the richest countries in the world in terms of natural spas. Thermal and mineral springs appear at 850 different geographical locations. Many of these have therapeutic properties which have been known about since ancient times. The forms of hydrotherapy treatment applied in Greece are spa or mud therapy and drinking or inhalation therapy. However, Health Tourism Greece (HTG, 2017) stated that Greece has only about 82 thermal springs, which are activated, and only 38 are officially recognized for therapeutic indications. Considerable potential was also proposed for thalassotherapy, as well as medical tourism and especially dentistry. It was suggested that "Health tourism will be one of the most important pillars of the Greek economy for the coming decade" (ibid.)

A brief overview of health tourism in Montenegro

The Ministry of Tourism in Montenegro is focusing partially on health tourism, although the online communication is limited in comparison to the promotion of the seaside and natural resources. However, Riggins (2014) suggests that health tourism in Montenegro has increased by 20% in the past five years, mainly because of the medical tourism industry (e.g. dentistry, rheumatics, cardiac rehabilitation programs). The Montenegro Tourism Development Strategy 2020 (Montenegro Ministry of Tourism and Environment, 2008) mainly focuses on Montenegro as a destination offering healthy outdoor activities such as hiking and cycling in natural landscapes, as does Greenhome (2012). Spas and coastal wellness centers are starting to integrate experiences of the surrounding landscape (e.g. views, sunsets). The Strategy also suggests several approaches to introducing wellness programs and products, which include using olive oil and derivative products, medicinal herbs and curative mud from Igalo (Ariwa and Syvertsen, 2010). The Chamber of Economy Montenegro (2015) suggested that health tourism could be promoted in the future, especially wellness and spas and dental tourism.

A brief overview of health tourism in Slovenia

Rančić, Pavić and Miljatov (2014) discuss how Slovenia, although a small country, has many natural resources including healing thermal waters and good climatic conditions. Health tourism is promoted in online communication in addition to seaside, mountains, lakes and gastronomy, including healthy local food. There are 15 spas and thermal baths which are represented by the Slovenian Spas Association. Lebe (2013) describes how 80% of spa guests were referred by insurance companies until 1990, but after that the spas had to find most of their business on the free market. This meant operating more like entrepreneurs, establishing marketing departments and attracting visitors. Between 1995 and 2010, all Slovenian spas renewed their swimming pools, upgraded and sometimes enlarged their accommodation facilities and added wellness programs to their offer. However, there was recognition that the health/medical service and wellness markets were not necessarily compatible

Pak and Altbauer (2014) estimate that 32% of overnights in Slovenia in 2013 were taken in spa resorts, 22% of total international overnights and 47% of total domestic overnights. The top five markets for spas come from Austria, Italy, Russia, Germany and Croatia. The average length of stay is about 3.98 days. Euromonitor International (2014d) suggested that health and wellness tourism declined by 4% in 2013 in terms of current value sales, mainly because fewer foreign visitors went to health and wellness centers. On the other hand, the number of local visitors marginally grew. Unfortunately, medical tourism also dropped by 5%. This could perhaps be attributed to the lower number of Russian tourists traveling to Europe at present. On the other hand, health and wellness tourism is one of the most promising areas in Slovenia despite the competition from Austria, Hungary and Germany. The IMTJ (2017) describes how Slovenia was celebrating the "Year of Healthy Waters" in 2017, which includes the abundance of natural thermal and mineral water springs with proven healing properties. In 2017, the Republic of Slovenia Statistical Office estimated that 23% of tourist overnight stays were in health spa resorts, a 9% increase from 2016.

A brief overview of health tourism in Turkey

Under the Ministry of Health, a Department of Health Tourism was established in 2011, and health tourism was one of the priority areas identified in the 2023 Draft Report of Tourism Strategy of Turkey. The Ministry of Health considers health tourism under three main titles (Barca, Akdeve and Gedik Balay, 2012):

- Medical (medicine) tourism
- Thermal tourism
- Elderly and disabled tourism

Turkey is one of the seven main countries in the world in terms of thermal source richness with almost 1,300 thermal springs throughout Anatolia. However, only a small percentage of these are used (GoTurkeyTourism, 2015).

Turkey has a relatively strong reputation in the field of medical tourism, including a large number of internationally accredited hospitals. It is supported by government and the Turkish Healthcare Council. According to Korkmaz et al. (2014), IVF and ophthalmology are the most popular areas of medical tourism. More than 100,000 international tourists use healthcare services yearly, stay for four to five days, and spend five times more than holiday tourists.

Euromonitor International (2014c) describe how in the previous two years the Turkish government introduced incentives to encourage growth in health and wellness tourism. These included issuing licenses to a higher number of natural spas which attracted a high number of local and foreign tourists. The number of hotel/resort spa outlets increased by 17%, to 106 in 2013.

In 2017, it was estimated that health tourists spend ten times more than vacationers and could be divided into three subgroups, namely, "medical tourism", "tourism for the senior and handicapped" and "thermal tourism". Hair transplants are now a well-known specialty, as well as eye surgery (Daily Sabah, 2017).

Health tourism development opportunities and challenges: a Delphi study

A Delphi study with expert researchers and practitioners working within the region was undertaken to gain their opinions of the main resources, attractions and products which exist in health tourism, as well as some of the challenges and opportunities for development, including image. Hsu and Sandford (2007, p. 1) describe a Delphi technique or study as "a group communication process that aims at conducting detailed examinations and discussions of a specific issue". In this case, the Delphi aimed to identify which resources and products exist in the Balkan region and how they might be developed for health tourism. A Delphi study offers an alternative to traditional face-to-face consensus-seeking research approaches, such as focus groups, group interviews and think-tank committees (Gordon, 1994). The use of the Delphi technique for solving complex tourism problems has been recognized for many years (Green, Hunter and Moore, 1990; Garrod and Fyall, 2005). It can also help to inform policy development/enhancement process (Donohoe and Needham, 2009). Delphi studies have also been used successfully in other health and wellness tourism contexts, e.g. the establishment of the Nordic Wellbeing network (Hjalager et al., 2011) and a Baltic Health Tourism Cluster (Smith, 2015), as well as for hot springs-based tourism in Taiwan (Lee and King, 2009).

Best practice has been established for Delphi studies, including anonymity of experts and no information flow between them (Gordon, 1994). Most studies use panels of 15 to 35 individuals (Gordon, 1994; Miller, 2001), and Pan et al. (1995) recommended a Delphi study with not more than two rounds. This study included 33 participants and two rounds. In tourism research, attrition rates (i.e. drop-out rate in the second and subsequent rounds) are usually between 20% and 25% but can be as high as 45% to 50% (Miller, 2001). Here, the second round generated 22 responses in a period of four weeks, which represented around 67% of the original sample.

Expert participants were recruited using the researchers' contacts from a Hungarian government-funded project about well-being in the Balkan countries (2012–2014) as well as snowball sampling with the assistance of existing participants. An online questionnaire was sent by email consisting of 10 open questions in the first round and 12 in the second. It was estimated that the questionnaire should take no more than 20 minutes. The researchers allowed four to five weeks for the first round. The second ("convergence") round consisted of an online questionnaire accompanied by the results of the first round in information-graphic format (e.g. word clouds, tables, diagrams). The questions were directly related to the data and results and aimed to elicit either correction, critical comment or identification of omissions. The first round of the Delphi generated some detailed responses which were then analyzed and returned to the second round participants for comments. The findings represent the cumulative responses from the first and second rounds. The main focus is on the respondents' views about challenges to development and suggested opportunities for overcoming these.

Delphi study findings

Respondents were given a number of statements and asked whether they agree or disagree with them. The results appear in Table 11.1.

The majority of respondents thought that the potential for health and wellness tourism is quite considerable even if there has been a longer tradition of thermal medical and rehabilitation spas for domestic visitors. Some respondents thought that there were good opportunities for spa and wellness tourism in some countries, but not in all. It was noted that if government funding ends, then it will be necessary to consider other options like wellness spas; Slovenia already started this process of development (as discussed by Lebe, 2013). This is seen as a major challenge, as the region is still mainly known as being for medical or rehabilitation spas for local and domestic visitors rather than wellness spas for international tourists.

Table 11.1 How far do you agree with the following statements about health tourism in the Balkans?

Statement	Agree	Disagree	Undecided
The Balkans provide mainly sun, sea and sand tourism. There is not much potential for health and wellness tourism development.	2	20	
The Balkans mainly offer good opportunities for spa and wellness tourism for leisure tourists.	15	2	3
The Balkans mainly specialize in thermal medical spas and rehabilitation for social tourists (e.g. government-funded).	12	4	5
The Balkans has good potential for health, wellness and spa tourism but the infrastructure and services need some development and improvements.	27		2

The potential for health tourism is seen as considerable, but the product needs to be developed further. Respondents agreed that the region needs some improvements to infrastructure (especially accessibility and transport) as well as services. It was thought that service could be friendlier and of higher quality. It was suggested that a network of training centers for spa and wellness staff could help to improve this aspect. On the other hand, the medical staff are considered to be very well trained (it should be noted that the former socialist countries often followed the Soviet model of insisting on spa or thermal bath staff being medically trained). It was suggested that the development of public-private partnerships can be challenging in this region because private companies work faster and with greater flexibility and innovation than governments. However, it is crucial for the two to work together.

In the first round of the Delphi, respondents were asked to state what they thought were the unique selling propositions for the Balkan region, especially for well-being and health tourism. From a list of 12 main elements, the second-round respondents were asked to identify their top 6. These results are found in Figure 11.1.

It was interesting and somewhat unexpected that food and wine were at the top of the list, but given the global reputation of Mediterranean cuisine as being one of the healthiest (if not *the* healthiest) in the world, this is perhaps not that surprising.

Delphi respondents were also asked to comment on some of the main problems and challenges of developing health tourism, some of which have already been discussed in the short country case studies. Their responses are found in Figure 11.2.

More detailed comments were also given by respondents in the second round. They believe that the history of instability, conflict and mistrust in the Balkans hinders development in many countries in the region. Lack of funding is also a major issue but is needed for renovation and upgrading as well as new developments. Respondents suggested that some education and training is needed to bring

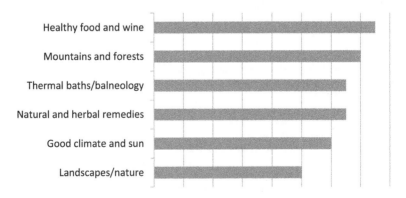

Figure 11.1 Top six identified unique selling propositions

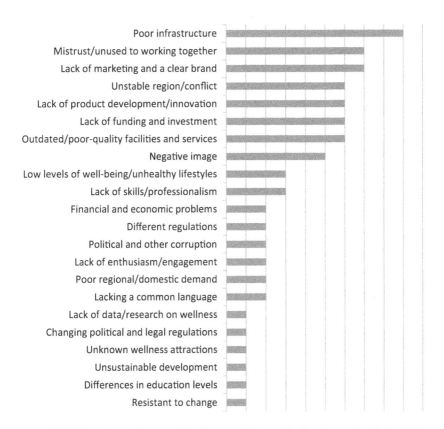

Figure 11.2 The main problems and challenges of developing health tourism in the Balkan region

employees up to a similar standard across the whole region. Although the Balkan people are thought to be hospitable, they are not yet very service-oriented and can be resistant to change. The relatively low levels of well-being and health, including life expectancy, mean that the region is not entirely conducive to developing health tourism. Even the persistence of unrestricted smoking in public places in some countries is perceived by a few respondents to be a problem. Salaries and disposable income in the region are generally very low, so although there is still domestic demand for government-funded health or rehabilitation spa tourism, most people would not be able to afford wellness and spa holidays.

Respondents suggested that more knowledge is needed about how to develop and manage tourism in a sustainable way to create maximum benefits for the Balkan countries and their economies. More research and data are needed on health and wellness tourism markets, as well as more up-to-date evidence-based research about the health benefits of thermal waters, for example (outside the region, the healing benefits of thermal waters are not always recognized or accepted).

Wellness facilities and services were seen to be lacking in sophistication, and infrastructure also needs considerable improvement. Lack of marketing was also seen to be a major problem, but the point was also made that it is hard to engage in effective marketing without a good-quality, attractive product supported by a strong infrastructure and high-level services.

The respondents were asked to make some suggestions for health tourism product development in the Balkan region. Figure 11.3 summarizes their responses.

The concept of ecovillages may not be widespread in tourism, but there is a Global Ecovillage Network (2015) which describes ecovillages as "an intentional or traditional community using local participatory processes to holistically integrate ecological, economic, social, and cultural dimensions of sustainability in order to regenerate social and natural environments". One of the main aims is to create areas where people can once more live in communities that are connected to the earth and live in a way that ensures well-being for people and environment alike. There is also a Balkan branch of the network called the Balkan Ecovillage Network, which lists ecovillages in Croatia and Slovenia. National Geographic (2015) also describes ecovillages in Montenegro and Bosnia and Herzegovina as part of so-called "geotourism".

The outdoor recreation potential of the Balkans should clearly be developed further according to some respondents. It is certainly true that although the seaside areas have sometimes been overdeveloped, the inland and hinterland areas such as mountains and villages are relatively under-visited. One respondent stated that "unfortunately the Balkans have limited themselves to this pattern of tourism,

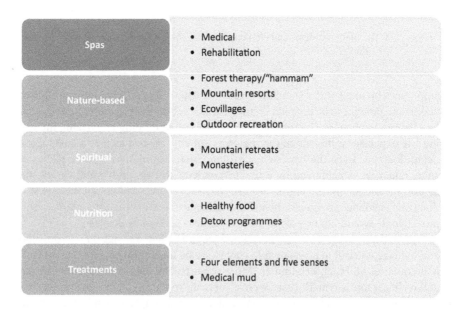

Figure 11.3 Suggested ideas for health tourism development in the Balkans

Table 11.2 A SWOT analysis of health tourism in the Balkans

Strengths	Weaknesses
• Long history of health tourism in the form of balneology and rehabilitation spas • Strong traditions in herbal and plant medicine • Favorable climate • Beautiful and often pristine natural environment • Tasty and healthy gastronomy and wines • Accessible region from many countries • Competitive and sometimes cheap prices for international tourists	• Relatively poor infrastructure • Lack of service quality • Low level of education, training and skills • Negative or unknown image for some countries • Mistrust and inability to work together

Opportunities	Threats
• Renovation of spas and balneological facilities • Promoting natural healing resources and landscape-based well-being • Including herbal and plant medicines and therapies in health and spa treatments • Developing health tourism clusters or collaborations	• Ongoing conflicts and instability • Outmigration of talented employees because of low salaries • Lack of government funding for domestic health tourism in the future • Political and other corruption

when the inland is actually the more authentic and real experience, with beautiful unspoiled nature and hospitable people". The emphasis on ecovillages by respondents shows the growing significance of environmentally and socially sustainable tourism development in this region.

Although the Delphi study required respondents to comment on the Balkan region rather than individual countries, it is difficult to generalize, as some countries are more advanced than others and they have developed in different directions depending on their resources (e.g. some for sun-sea-sand tourism like Greece, Turkey and Croatia; others for balneology and thermal spa tourism like Bosnia or Slovenia). Clearly, there are still many challenges to developing health tourism in the region, but there is considerable potential to do so. Table 11.2 presents a SWOT analysis including the challenges and opportunities of developing health tourism in the Balkan region as discussed so far.

Conclusion

This research has demonstrated that although there are a number of significant challenges to developing health tourism in the Balkan region, there is considerable potential to do so. The area is rich in natural resources such as thermal waters, sea coasts, mountains, forests and an abundance of herbs and plants which can be used for both cuisine and healing. However, so far the development of health tourism has often been based on government-supported domestic rehabilitation spa and balneology-based tourism. Given the lack of funding for many development activities in the region, especially for non-EU countries, it is debatable how long the Balkan countries can continue to rely on government funding for health tourism. Because of the high levels of poverty and low salaries in many countries in this region, it is unlikely that the existing domestic tourists would be able to afford alternative forms of health tourism such as wellness hotels or leisure spas. New developments of this kind therefore depend on the interest that can be generated among international foreign visitors, for whom the region is still relatively cheap and somehow "exotic". It may be possible to attract those visitors who are already familiar with the existing traditions of rehabilitation spas and balneology, such as Russian-speaking tourists. Indeed, many destinations in the region already accommodate large numbers of Russian or Russian-speaking visitors. Attracting those tourists, for whom the region is unknown or has a negative image, might be more challenging. However, countries like Slovenia and Croatia have already proved that it is possible to become highly successful tourism destinations. Greece and Turkey are already well known for their beach tourism, but in the future, health tourism may provide a niche alternative to sun, sea and sand. Albania, Bosnia and Herzegovina and Montenegro are not yet as well known, especially in terms of health tourism, but the potential is there to be developed. It may therefore be only a matter of time before the countries of the Mediterranean Balkan region manage to improve their offer, promote new products and place themselves firmly on the map of European or even global health tourism.

References

Andrews, H. (2015). EU-financed spa tourism project between Bosnia-Herzegovina and Serbia hailed a success. *spabusiness.com*, 20 January, Available at: www.spabusiness.com/detail.cfm?pagetype=detail&subject=news&codeID=313558 [Accessed 4 Dec. 2017].

Ariwa, E. and Syvertsen, C.M. (2010). Informatization of economic growth in the health-tourism industry in Montenegro using insights from regionalization. *Journal of Internet Banking and Commerce*, 15(1). Available at: www.arraydev.com/commerce/JIBC/2010-04/Ezendu%20and%20Carston%20Paper%20for%20Informatization%20and%20HealthcareUpdate.pdf [Accessed 16 Sep. 2015].

ATMA (2014). *Albanian medical tourism agency*. Available at: www.medicaltourismalbania.com [Accessed 20 Sep. 2015]

Barca, M., Akdeve, E. and Gedik Balay, I. (2012). *Evaluation report on medical tourism in Turkey 2012*. Turkey: Ministry of Health.

Bradbury, P. (2017). Health tourism is coming home: Why Zagreb is the next big medical tourism destination. *Total Croatia News*, 19 September 2017, Available at: www.mybosnia.net/index.php/tourism/spa-and-health [Accessed 4 Dec. 2017].

Bushell, R. (2017). Healthy tourism. In: M.K. Smith and L. Puczko, eds., *The Routledge handbook of health tourism*. London: Routledge, pp. 91–102.

Butler, R.W. (1980). The concept of a tourism area cycle of evolution: Implications for management resources. *The Canadian Geographer*, 24(1), pp. 5–16.

Chamber of Economy Montenegro (2015). *Potentials of health tourism*, 16 April. Available at: www.privrednakomora.me/en/saopstenja/potentials-health-tourism

Constantinides, C. (2013). Times are changing as Greece tries to become a major destinations, 29 November, *IMTJ*. Available at: www.imtj.com/articles/times-are-changing-greece-tries-become-major-destination [Accessed 15 Sep. 2015].

Daily Sabah (2017). Health tourists spend 10 times more in Turkey than vacationers, 15 August. Available at: www.dailysabah.com/tourism/2017/08/16/health-tourists-spend-10-times-more-in-turkey-than-vacationers-1502822698 [Accessed 4 December 2017].

Donohoe, H.M. and Needham, R.D. (2009). Moving best practice forward: Delphi characteristics, advantages, potential problems, and solutions. *International Journal of Tourism Research*, 11(5), pp. 415–437.

Euromonitor International (2014a). *Health and wellness tourism in Croatia*. Available at: www.euromonitor.com/health-and-wellness-tourism-in-croatia/report [Accessed 30 Aug. 2015].

Euromonitor International (2014b). *Health and wellness tourism in Greece*. Available at: www.euromonitor.com/health-and-wellness-in-greece/report [Accessed 17 Sep. 2015].

Euromonitor International (2014c). *Health and wellness tourism in Slovenia*. Available at: www.euromonitor.com/health-and-wellness-tourism-in-slovenia/report [Accessed 17 Sep. 2015].

Euromonitor International (2014d). *Health and wellness tourism in Turkey*. Available at: www.euromonitor.com/health-and-wellness-in-turkey/report [Accessed 17 Sep. 2015].

Felic, E. (2013). Health tourism opportunity for BiH. *Balkan Insight*, 30 July. Available at: www.balkaninside.com/health-tourism-opportunity-for-bih [Accessed 17 Sep. 2015].

Gambarov, V. and Gjinika, H. (2017). Thermal spring health tourism in Albania: Challenges and perspectives. In: V. Katsoni, A. Upadhya and A. Stratigea, eds., *Tourism, culture and heritage in a smart economy*, pp. 455–465.

Garrod, B. and Fyall, A. (2005). Revisiting Delphi: The Delphi technique as a method of tourism research. In: B.W. Ritchie, P. Burns and C. Palmer, eds., *Tourism research methods: Integrating theory with practice*. Wallingford: CABI, pp. 85–98.

Ginter, E. and Simko, V. (2011). *Balkan: New data on health, life expectancy and mortality, internal medicine, no. 3*. Available at: www.medicina-interna.ro/articol.php?articol=659andlang=ro [Accessed 9 Oct. 2014].

Global Ecovillage Network (2015). Available at: http://sites.ecovillage.org/en/global-ecovillage-network [Accessed 21 Sep. 2015].

Gordon, T.J. (1994). *The Delphi method: Futures research methodology*. Available at: www.gerenciamento.ufba.br/Downloads/delphi%20(1).pdf [Accessed 21 Oct. 2015].

GoTurkeyTourism (2015). *Thermal springs in Turkey*. Available at: www.allabouturkey.com/spa.htm [Accessed 17 Sep. 2015].

Green, H., Hunter, C. and Moore, B. (1990). The application of the Delphi technique in tourism. *Annals of Tourism Research*, 17, pp. 270–279.

Greenhome (2012). The study on the potential of health tourism in Montenegro. In: *Adriatic health and vitality network*. Podgorica.

GTP (2010). *Greek spa industry lacks trained professionals*. 1 March. Available at: http://news.gtp.gr/2010/03/01/greek-spa-industry-lacks-trained-professionals [Accessed 15 Sep. 2015].

Health Tourism Greece (HTG) (2017). *Health tourism meets its Ithaca – Conference conclusions*, 31 May. Available at: https://healthtourismgreece.com/index.php/news/22-health-tourism-meets-its-ithaca-conference-conclusions

Hjalager, A., Konu, H., Huijbens, E.H., Björk, P., Flagestad, A., Nordin, S. and Tuohino, A. (2011). *Innovating and re-branding Nordic wellbeing tourism*. Available at: www.nordicinnovation.org/Global/_Publications/Reports/2011/2011_NordicWellbeingTourism_report.pdf [Accessed 10 Mar. 2016].

Horwath (2013). *CrossSpa study on joint potential of health and wellness tourism development in the cross-border area (Sarajevo macro region and tourism region of Western Serbia)*. Belgrade: Horwath, Belgrade.

Hsu, C. and Sandford, B.A. (2007). The Delphi technique: Making sense of consensus. *Practical Assessment, Research & Evaluation*, 12(10), pp. 1–8.

IMTJ (2016). Medical Tourism to Croatia has great potential. Available at: www.imtj.com/news/medical-tourism-croatia-has-great-potential [Accessed 4 Dec. 2017].

IMTJ (2017). Slovenia promotes spas and resorts in 30 December 2017. Available at: www.imtj.com/news/slovenia-promotes-spas-and-resorts-2017

Karagülle, M.Z. (2013). *Wellness at traditional Balkan spas; Innovation or authenticity?*. Serbia: 3rd Balkan Spa Summit.

Kesar, O. and Rimac, K. (2011). Medical tourism development in Croatia. *Zagreb International Review of Economics & Business*, 14(2), pp. 107–134. Available at: http://hrcak.srce.hr/78762 [Accessed 11 Feb. 2015].

Korkmaz, M., Aytaç, A., Yücel, A., Kiliç, S., Toke, B.F. and Gümüş, S. (2014). Health tourism in Turkey and practical example of its economic dimensions. *IIB International Refereed Academic Social Sciences Journal*, 15(5), pp. 229–246.

Lebe, S.S. (2013). Wellness tourism development in Slovenia in the last two decades. In: M.K. Smith and L. Puczkó, eds., *Health, tourism and hospitality: Spas, wellness and medical travel*. London: Routledge, pp. 315–319.

Lee, C. and King, B.E. (2009). Using the Delphi method to assess the potential of Taiwan's hot springs tourism sector. *International Journal of Tourism Research*, 11, pp. 415–437.

Marku MA, A. (2014). Tourism strategy of Albania. *European Scientific Journal*, February (2), pp. 57–66.

Miller, G. (2001). The development of indicators for sustainable tourism: Results of a Delphi survey of tourism researchers. *Tourism Management*, 22, pp. 351–362.

Montenegro Ministry of Tourism and Environment (2008). *The Montenegro tourism development strategy 2020*, Podgorica.

My Bosnia (2017). *Spa and health*. Available at: www.mybosnia.net/index.php/tourism/spa-and-health [Accessed 4 Dec. 2017].

National Geographic (2015). Available at: www.balkansgeotourism.travel [Accessed 22 Sep. 2015].

Nedelcheva, A. (2013). An ethnobotanical study of wild edible plants in Bulgaria. *EurAsian Journal of BioSciences*, 7, pp. 77–94.

Pak, M. and Altbauer, I. (2014). Strategy for development and marketing of Slovenian Spas. *SPACE*, 24 October. Available at: https://docplayer.net/24311100-Strategy-for-development-and-marketing-of-slovenian-spas-maja-pak-iztok-altbauer.html [Accessed 10 Dec. 2017].

Pan, M.S.Q., Vella, A.J., Archer, B.H. and Parlett, G. (1995). A mini-Delphi approach: An improvement on single round techniques. *Progress in Tourism and Hospitality Research*, 2, pp. 27–39.

Rančić, M., Pavić, L. and Miljatov, M. (2014). Wellness centers in Slovenia: Tourists' profiles and motivational factors, *TURIZAM*, 18(2), pp. 72–83.

Redzic, S. (2010). Wild medicinal plants and their usage in traditional human therapy (Southern Bosnia and Herzegovina. *W. Balkan, Journal of Medicinal Plants Research*, 4 June, 11, pp. 1003–1027.

Renko, S. (2010). Food in the function of rural development in the context of tourism industry. *Book of extended abstracts of 5th international conference economic development perspectives of SEE region in the global recession context*, pp. 179–180.

Republic of Slovenia Statistical Office (2017). *Tourism arrivals and overnight stays*, 31 July. Available at: www.stat.si/StatWeb/en/News/Index/6846 [Accessed 4 Dec. 2017].

Riggins, N. (2014). Montenegro's tourism industry turns a corner. *Business Destinations*, 17 September. Available at: www.businessdestinations.com/acte/montenegros-tourism-industry-turns-a-corner [Accessed 16 Sep. 2015].

Smith, M.K. (2015). Baltic health tourism: Uniqueness and commonalities. *Scandinavian Journal of Tourism and Hospitality*, 15(4), pp. 357–379.

Šimundić, B. (1997). Healthy food as the basic for health tourism. *Proceedings of the 4th international conference: The promotion of health tourism*, Opatija, pp. 167–178.

Smith, M.K. and Puczkó, L. (2013). *Health, tourism and hospitality: Spas, wellness and medical travel*. London: Routledge.

Smith, M.K. and Puczkó, L. (2017). Balneology and health tourism. In: M.K. Smith and L. Puczkó, eds., *Health, tourism and hospitality: Spas, wellness and medical travel*. London: Routledge, pp. 271–281.

Stăncioiu, A., Botos, A. and Pargaru, I. (2013). The Balkan balneotherapy product – An approach from the destination marketing perspective. *Theoretical and applied economics*, XX,10(587), pp. 5–22.

Tirana Times (2013). *More visiting Albania on health tourism purposes*, 19 April. Available at: www.tiranatimes.com/?p=115057 www.tiranatimes.com/?p=115057 [Accessed 15 Sep. 2015].

Visit Greece (2014). Health and wellness spa. Available at: www.visitgreece.gr/en/leisure/wellness [Accessed 15 Sep. 2015].

Vitic, A. and Ringer, G. (2008). Branding post conflict destinations. *Journal of Travel and Tourism Marketing*, 23(2–4), pp. 127–137.

Index

Note: Page numbers in *italic* indicate a figure and page numbers in **bold** indicate a table on the corresponding page.